Alascattalo Tales

This book is dedicated
to my parents,
who taught me that
life is too funny
to be taken seriously

Alascattalo Tales

A TREASURY OF ALASKAN HUMOR

by
Steven C. Levi

McFarland & Company, Inc., Publishers
Jefferson, North Carolina, and London

British Library Cataloguing-in-Publication data are available

Library of Congress Cataloguing-in-Publication Data

Levi, Steven C.
    Alascattalo tales : a treasury of Alaskan humor /by Steven C.
Levi.
      p. cm.
    Includes bibliographical references (p.) and index. ∞
    ISBN 0-89950-864-2 (sewn softcover : 50# alk. paper)
    1. Alaska — Social life and customs — Humor. 2. American wit and
humor — Alaska. I. Title.
F904.6.L48   1993
979.8 — dc20   92-56660
                                                     CIP

Manufactured in the United States of America

McFarland & Company, Inc., Publishers
  Box 6ll, Jefferson, North Carolina 28640

TABLE OF CONTENTS

INTRODUCTION

There are many kinds of laughter. There is the quick, sharp shriek of surprise, as well as the low, malevolent "ho ho" when a dirty secret is revealed. Then there is the deep belly-laugh and the intellectual chuckle, the chortle when an off-color joke is told or the short "humph" to indicate that the humor has been acknowledged — though not necessarily appreciated.

This is a book of Alaskan humor, a heretofore unknown specimen in the taxonomy of American folklore. In the following pages there is something for everyone: ghosts and scoundrels, lawyers and drunks, mistakes and practical jokes. This work was specifically written to display the concept of "funny" in every shade of that emotion. It is also a book designed to illustrate the robust flavor of Alaskan humor, and particularly Alaska's rich and unique heritage of absurding.

It is important to note, however, that this book is not a work of folklore or folk humor. This is a work of history. To the best of the author's knowledge, every incident in this book is true or was told to the author as true. Some of the incidents collected were from books, others were passed along as personal reminiscence. No names have been changed to protect the innocent or those seeking reelection, and the bulk of the material can be found through sources listed in the bibliography.

No one can put a book like this together without quite a bit of help. I would like to acknowledge the assistance of the dedicated staff of the Z.J. Loussac Library, particularly Bruce Merrell and Dan Fleming, as well as the other librarians in the Alaska Room who put up with my outrageous requests; Dianne Brenner at the Anchorage Museum of History and Art, who keeps a sharp eye out for unique Alaskana; and India Spartz at the State Library in Juneau, who long ago became accustomed to my strange phone calls. Other people who were indispensable in the creation of this book include Joan Antonson, Dennis Walle, Bob DeArmond, David Powers, Beth Burgos, Tina Hanson, Joanne Townsend, Heinz "Der Kraut" Noonan, Terry "The Petersburg Flash" Otness, Mills & Sanderson, Ann Chandonnet, George Guthridge, Jean Oldham, Priscilla

Wilson, Kathy Hunter, Jeanine Greene, Ruben Gaines, the Alaska Legislature, the late Commander John Hale, Fred Goodwin, Danny Daniels, the folks at KPXR and a host of others who threatened my life if I revealed their names.

Steven C. Levi

1
TO LIE LIKE AN ALASKAN

When it comes to tall tales, Alaskans are king. No one can tell a whopper like an Alaskan. In fact, telling fabricated tales of the Northland and being an Alaskan go hand-in-hand. This is not to say that all Alaskans tell lies — most of them do, though not all of them — but so many Alaskans have grown accustomed to telling wild tales about the northland that the only person with less credibility than an Alaskan with a bear story is a politician proposing a tax cut three days before a primary election.

And Alaskans have such easy marks! For the most part, Outsiders, i.e., people from the Lower 48, are amazingly ignorant when it comes to Alaska. Though Alaska is a state of the United States, many Americans continue to believe that it is a different country, uses another form of currency and requires a visa for travel. These same people, many of them with college educations, also fervently believe that Alaska is a land of ice and snow where the residents live in igloos and breed penguins. In fact, in downtown Anchorage it is not uncommon to hear tourists ask which restaurants serve blubber stew, the location of the nearest igloo or where the Northern Lights go when the sun is up for twenty hours a day.

During the summer, it takes Alaskans all of about two weeks to get tired of setting the record straight for Outsiders. It is just too time-consuming for Alaskans to be truthful because of the number of visitors that flood the state during the summer months. Anchorage, Alaska's largest city, only has 265,000 residents, but it hosts more than one million travelers during the 90 days of summer. That's quite a few people to set straight. After about the 15th of June, tired of constantly telling tourists that there are no igloos in Alaska or that penguins are only indigenous to Antarctica, Alaskans begin to fudge on the truth. They aren't really lying; it's an Alaskan folk art form kindly known as "absurding."

More precisely, absurding is a technique similar to the tall tale. But it is different from the tall tale because it is the art of deliberately confirming whatever bizarre fantasy a tourist believes of Alaska, regardless of how incredible that might be, and then expanding the absurdity even further. For example, if a tourist were to ask where he or she might see a penguin nest, an Alaskan intent on absurding might respond, "Well, it's been a lean year for penguins because the alligators keep forcing them out of the beaver lodges. That's where they spend the summer, you know, in beaver lodges."

While this may sound like a bizarre answer, it is not. Astoundingly, tourists will believe just about any tale about Alaska, and the more fantastic the lie, the more believable it will appear to be. From giant, maneating crabs in the Kuskokwim River to a genetic cross between a moose and a walrus (called an "alascattalo"), tourists are constantly being absurded by Alaskans who weave the most ludicrous of stories from the threads of the tourist's imagination.

What makes this task easy for Alaskans is the incredible diversity of the state. Since Alaska is so large, there are few statements that are true from Ketchikan to Barrow. Take the myth of Alaska's seasons. In the far north at Barrow, on the shore of the Arctic Ocean, the sun is aloft for months at a time during the summer. It does not "set," as people in the Lower 48 know the word, for 84 days. The sun simply circles the horizon. Time of day is indicated not by when the sun sets, but at what point of the compass it happens to be.

Then there is the flipside to this good news. During the winter there are 67 days when the sun does not "hop" above the horizon at all. In other words, on November 18, the sun "sets" and does not "rise" until January 24.

But in Anchorage and Fairbanks there are sunsets during the summer and sunrises during the winter, just as there are in Seattle, Denver, Chicago and New York. Yet, over the years, textbooks have mistakenly stated that Alaska, the Land of the Midnight Sun, has six months of darkness and six months of light, leading many college-educated Americans to believe that Alaska has six months of pitch darkness followed instantaneously by six months of unbroken sunshine.

Living in Alaska also requires an adjustment in one's vocabulary. While most Alaskans speak English, there are many terms which Alaskans use daily that are not even in uncommon usage in the rest of America. "Sitka slippers," for instance, are plastic boots with felt liners which are the preferred footwear in cities like Sitka, obviously, where the only time it isn't raining is when the storm clouds are gathering. A "cache" is a place to store food, and "hooch" is a cheap form of alcoholic beverage.

Alaskans, to the distress of *Cheechakos*, frequently use such terms as *taku, kuspik, chinook, williwaw, Orca, muktuk,* blue ticket, Lower 48, pingo, berm, breakup, scrimshaw, square tires and termination dust. While each of these has a specific, Alaskan meaning, sometimes the use of these terms can lead to humorous confusion.

One evening a news reporter called a public relations representative for a large oil company only to be told by the man's wife that he was "outside." "Outside," to an Alaskan, means the Lower 48 or, to *Cheechakos,* the contiguous 48 states.

"Will he be gone long?" the reporter asked, assuming that he was in Seattle.

"I hope not," his wife replied. "He's only taking out the garbage."

Alaskans also thrive on the differences between their state and the rest of the union. Beards and bear stories are in; yuppies are out. Functional dress is expected; a three-piece suit is reserved for IBM salesmen and Xerox repair personnel. Backpacks are as accepted at business meetings as briefcases.

Alaskan humor is different as well. Take Alaskan holidays. Every February, Cordova, on the shores of Prince William Sound, sponsors an Ice Worm Festival to commemorate the beastie of Robert Service invention. Though there really are ice worms which live near the surface of glaciers, the one Robert Service created was a piece of spaghetti with inked-in eyes that was dropped into a shotglass of whiskey to bamboozle a *Cheechako.* Honoring the ice worm, and Alaskan humor, each year the citizens of Cordova conclude their Ice Worm Festival with a parade highlighted by the appearance of a 150 foot "iceworm" that weaves its way along the parade route.

Farther north, Talkeetna sponsors a Moose Dropping Festival with contests involving another item of Alaskan humor: moose "nuggets." In Anchorage, each November there is the Alascattalo Day Parade. Taken from a story in Warren Sitka's *Sourdough Journalist,* the alascattalo is a genetic cross between a moose and a walrus. Billed as the longest running, shortest parade in American history, the Alascattalo Day Parade is one block long down an alley. It is held the first Sunday after the third Saturday in November and begins at precisely 12:03. "If you want to march in the parade," Warren Sitka advises, "you'd better be on time. If you're 30 seconds late, the parade's half over."

Alaskan humor is different because Alaska is different. While many regions of America can point with pride to their own homespun humorists, Alaska is not so fortunate. Mark Twain captured the spirit of Western humor while Uncle Remus did the same in the South. In the

East there is Washington Irving. Alaska, however, is a land without a written heritage of humor.

But Alaskans, one by one, and each in his or her own small way, are changing that. One winter during the Anchorage Fur Rendezvous, for example, a bearded Alaskan was pawing through a pile of imported kangaroo pelts on the floor of a fur shop. Looking for just the right color combination to make himself a floppy winter hat, he was dividing the pelts into piles of possibilities. Just as he was finishing, a tourist, fresh from the thrill of her first open-air fur auction, stepped into the shop and spotted this bearded character, clearly one of those grizzled sourdoughs of which she had read so much, with piles of pelts on the floor. Pulling out her camera and adjusting the focus, she asked what kind of pelts he was handling.

"Kangaroo," he said without looking up.

"Oh," she replied. "Are they Alaskan?"

An evil gleam flashed in his eye for a split second. "Yeah," he grumbled without looking up, "from up 'round Bethel."

And right now, somewhere in upstate New York, there is a woman swearing to her friends that there really are kangaroos in Alaska.

2

ALASKA'S CLOWN PRINCE

"Ya hear that noise? Christ, that ain't static; that's a bear! Yeah,
I gotta bear in the plane with me, and he's broke loose! He's
climbin' right up here beside me, growlin' an' showin' his
teeth—big sharp teeth! Oh Jeezus, he's tryin' ta eat up the
fuselage! There's two of us up here now, but it looks like purty
soon there's only gonna be one 'n' it ain' gonna be me! Stand
by, I'll call ya every other minute!"—Archie Ferguson giving
his blow-by-blow description of the baby polar bear which became loose in his plane while he was aloft.

"The best landing that Archie Ferguson ever made."—anonymous bush pilot when he was told that a baby polar bear had
been at the controls when Archie's plane landed.

He was Alaska's Clown Prince, one of the Territory's most infamous
bush pilots. It wasn't that he was a great flyer; rather, he had a personality
that you could absorb through your skin. He was, quite literally, a laugh
a minute. Who was this colorful man of the North? He was Archie
Ferguson from Kotzebue, the Flying Clown, and he had a string of zany
achievements to his name that would have made the Marx Brothers
proud—but there were four of them.

Ferguson came to the Territory of Alaska in 1917 when his family
opened a trading post in the Kotzebue area. Thin as a young man, he
was described later in life as gnarled, dumpy and "built like a potato." In
his heyday, the 1950s, Archie resembled one of the seven dwarfs more
than a bush pilot in the swashbuckling mold of Harold Gillam or Bob
Reeve.

And Archie was a prankster. Always looking for a laugh, when he got
one he joined in—except that his laugh was unique, a cackle like Donald
Duck would make. Always talking, always laughing, another bush pilot
remarked that Archie would "fly three hundred miles, ask three hundred
questions, answer them all himself and fly three hundred miles back."

Other descriptions were both earthy and accurate. "Maybe he's a pilot," a lot of flyers lamented of Archie, "but he shouldn't be."

Claiming to have had more crack-ups than any other pilot in Alaska—quite possibly an accurate claim—Archie ran the farthest north flying service under the United States flag. His company was Ferguson Airways, and his motto was "Anywhere, Anytime." He meant it too. He loved to fly. Even on those days when it was impossible for him to make a trip, he would clamber aboard his plane and fly in circles around Kotzebue. Asked why, Ferguson would often reply, "I dunno, somehow in a plane I feel differ'nt. I'd go nuts if I couldn't fly."

Archie's first trip in an airplane was with another legendary Alaskan bush pilot, Noel Wien, in 1926. Once aloft, Wien proceeded to scare the living daylights out of Archie by doing barrel rolls and loops, watching in amusement while the frightened Ferguson gripped the sidewalls of the plane in terror. But instead of convincing him to stay on solid ground, the flight sharpened Archie's desire to fly. Deciding to buy his own plane, he spent $4,000 in 1931 for a Great Lakes Trainer and spent another thousand to get it to Kotzebue. Then he hired a trainer, Chet Brown, whose advertisement he had seen in a flying magazine. He paid for Chet's flight north, to what the trainer probably believed was the end of the earth.

After sixty hours of training, *seven* times longer than was normally required of a student pilot, Archie was still not ready to fly solo. But *Archie was* ready to fly solo. Archie wanted to fly solo, and by *&% he was going to fly solo. Finally Brown relented and let Archie go up by himself. But, taking the lead from Archie's book of ongoing practical jokes, Brown slipped an alarm clock under the pilot's seat. It was set to go off ten minutes after Archie left the ground.

"Go right up over town," advised Brown with a pleasant smile on his lips and an evil one in his heart. "Climb to a thousand feet and circle around, and be sure to take your time."

All went well for nine minutes and 59 seconds, with Archie flying steadily. Then the alarm went off and the plane began wallowing across the sky, as if a wild man was in the cockpit—which one was. "Gosh I was scairt," Ferguson said later. "I thought it was some kind of a signal!" Archie managed to land safely, but he brought the plane down on a sandbar in the Kotzebue lagoon rather than on the landing strip.

Archie's record with both cargo and passengers was replete with unique incidents and humorous anecdotes. He was also infamous for monopolizing the air waves—even during the war years when radio silence was the established rule. Once a radio operator in Nome who was not familiar with Archie and his antics tried to get him to stay off the air.

Ferguson began the conversation in his own inimitable style: "Nome Radio, Nome Radio. This is Cessna Two Zero Seven Six Six. Gosh it's startin' to rain up here! Looks like some awful dirty stuff ahead! Gimme yer weather in the clear!"

Mindful that the only authorized chatter on the radio was for an emergency, the operator asked innocently: "Cessna Two Zero Seven Six Six, do you declare this an emergency?"

"Yer darn right," snapped Archie into his microphone. "Any time I'm in the air it's an emergency!"

In addition to being a pilot, Ferguson was also a successful entrepreneur. He and his brother built a sawmill and operated a handful of trading posts in the vicinity of Kotzebue. They also started and operated a mink farm, built and operated the first movie house in the Arctic, brought the first automobile (an International pickup) above the Circle and imported the first cow and motorcycle.

Archie's parents, incidentally, were scared to death of Archie in a plane, and every time he approached their home in Shungnak they would look up in trepidation. Passengers also had their moments of terror. One winter Archie's plane broke through the ice at Shungnak, and several inches of the wooden propellor were sheared off before Ferguson could get the plane onto solid ice. Hefting an axe, Archie sheared off a few inches of the undamaged end of the propellor while the passengers watched with incredulity.

"I'll fix this baby," Ferguson said jovially. "We're really going to fly today!"

It took the plane more than three miles of skipping along the ice, "rattling like a sawmill," before the aircraft finally lifted into the air.

Another time he was transporting a baby polar bear from Point Hope. The two had been aloft for about ten minutes when Archie became aware that the cub had gnawed through its bonds and was roaming around the back of his plane. Not familiar with an airplane, the cub would take bites out of the pilot's seat and claw at the fuselage. Finally the bear settled down. As long as the flying was smooth there was no problem, but whenever there was turbulence, the bear became rambunctious.

Archie did make it down, and the polar bear cub, which grew rather large, became a fixture in Kotzebue for years. During the winter it would stay under the Wien Hotel; but throughout the tourist season, the bear would lounge around in the sun and attract the attention of Outsiders. The bear was also adept at frightening tourists. Often it would lie on its belly hiding the chain with its body. Whenever a tourist to whom the bear took a particular dislike approached, the animal would explode off the

ground and charge to the very end of its chain. The shocked tourist
would usually stumble backwards, often ending up seated in a muddy
pool of water. If the bear could have laughed, it probably would have.

A list of Ferguson's antics could go on and on. One time he reported
seeing a Japanese submarine moving north along the Arctic coast.
Another time he took out ten yards of telephone line and flew into Nome
with the wire wrapped around his prop. On another occasion, while
hunting wolves from his airplane, he became so excited he actually shot
his own propeller off.

But of all his escapades, Ferguson is probably best known for what
is called the "Arctic Bump." For Archie, there was no such thing as a trip
without excitement, even if he had to create that excitement himself.
Flying between Kotzebue and Nome he had to cross the Arctic Circle.
When Ferguson crossed over that theoretical line, he would sometimes
cut the gas to the engine.

"We're cummin' ta the Arctic Circle!" he would shout excitedly as he
secretly reached for the gas line switch. "Ya can't see it but you'll sure
know when we hit it. The engine'll quit! There's no air in that darn circle
for eight hundred feet!"

Then he'd cut the gas line, and the plane would go into a steep nose
dive. Passengers would shriek and cry in terror as the plane plunged hundreds of feet. When he'd had enough fun, Archie would reopen the gas
line and restart the prop.

The man who popularized the Arctic Bump commercially was Fred
Goodwin. Although he never turned his engine off to frighten his
passengers, while flying for Wien he would "push it over and give the
tourist the same sensation as when they went over the top of a roller
coaster." But he flashed the seat belt sign first to make sure everyone was
strapped in.

Ferguson retired in 1949. He turned his flying business over to his
adopted sons and maintained the family businesses in Kotzebue. Never
one to pay taxes, the IRS eventually caught up with him in the early 1960s.
The IRS froze his assets and forced him to make his living as a miner.
With his second wife, he left Alaska for Mexico, where he intended to
start a barge operation in Guadalajara. He died in Mexico in 1967.

Though Archie Ferguson is dead, he is not forgotten. Part of the
humorous heritage of the northland, pioneered by Archie, is the "Arctic
Bump." As the story is now told, when pilots first flew across the Arctic
Circle they discovered an air pressure differential. The air above the Arctic Circle, most likely because of its proximity to the polar ice cap, was
colder and thus thicker than the air on the southern side of the Circle.

Where the thick air mass from above the Circle collided with the thinner, warm air from the Alaskan Interior, there was a convection current. This mixing, interestingly, was in a clockwise direction because of the Coriolis Effect.

At the actual point where the two air masses meet, on the Arctic Circle, flying conditions change. If a small plane is flying north over the Arctic Circle, it will rise suddenly when it encounters the colder, thicker air from the polar ice cap. Conversely, a small plane heading south will lose altitude rapidly when it passes out of the thicker air and into thinner air blankets. Larger planes have much less difficulty because of their size. But even on the modern jets, a slight bump, strong enough to spill coffee, can often be felt when the Arctic Circle is crossed. This is known as the "Arctic Bump."

Today, Alaska's pilots play this bit of absurding to the hilt. When crossing the Arctic Circle, Alaska Airlines pilots still "bump" their planes. Their home office keeps this legend alive as well. When reached for comment, Lou Cancelmi, Assistant Vice President of Communications for Alaska Airlines, noted with a straight face that the rarified air above the Arctic Circle actually made flying smoother. "Because of the thicker air currents above the Circle," Cancelmi noted, "pilots are able to make more fluid, banking motions when landing. These are known as 'Arctic turns.' When properly used," Cancelmi stated, "these turns can save on fuel consumption."

Note: The bulk of this came from "Archie Ferguson" in Jean Potter's The Flying North, *a gem of Alaskana as well as of American nonfiction. Under her married name, Jean Potter Chelnov also wrote* Flying Frontiersmen. *Almost all of the quotes came from Potter. The rest of the material came from personal interviews with Fred Goodwin, Lou Cancelmi and Sam Shafsky, among others.*

3
THE KAGUYAK TELEPHONE

It started as a joke, a publicity stunt. It ended as a gold nugget of Alaskan humor.

In the late 1950s, John Cushing, one of the owners of Sitka Telephone, was convinced that telephone exchanges in small Alaskan communities could be made into a paying proposition. Everyone else in the telecommunications business in Alaska thought John was a bit daffy. After all, added together the Territory of Alaska had fewer than 10,000 phones, and almost every one of those was in the "big" cities of Anchorage, Fairbanks, Juneau and Ketchikan. How could anyone make money by providing service to Eskimos? But Cushing was convinced that it was possible to make a bush telephone network that was a viable economic endeavor—to Eskimos, Tlingits, Aleuts and Athabascans, as well as the non–Natives that lived in the Alaskan bush.

Flaunting convention had always been a hallmark of Cushing's character. Whenever someone told him something *couldn't* be done, he would work all the harder to prove that it could. So, when the harshest criticism of a bush telephone network was voiced—that Natives would be "confused by the numbers" on the phone—John created a telephone that had no numbers. Taking a red rotary dial phone, Cushing glued ivory figures over the numbers. Concentrating on animals with which Natives in Southeast Alaska would be familiar, he used a goose, seal, whale, caribou, crab, bull walrus, salmon, fox, bear and duck.

Then his sister-in-law, Virginia, created a phone book with people's names and phone "numbers" that were actually a sequence of animals. Operator, for instance, was "goose, goose." Complaints could be aired by dialing "crab, crab, crab," and the telephone manager's office could be reached by dialing "bull, bull, bull."

At the next convention of the fledgling Alaska Telephone Association, Cushing presented the phone as a humorous retort to those who said that Natives would be confused by the numbers. The phone was an

10

The Kaguyak phone. (Courtesy Danny Daniels.)

instant hit, as was the phone book that included the names of many of the people at the convention. It was such a hit that it was written up in the local papers, and the story, in turn, was picked up by several national telephone magazines and eventually by *Reader's Digest.*

The story of a telephone with Alaskan animal sequences for numbers was so believable, even to Alaskans, that what started out as a practical joke became part of Alaska's heritage. Today the Telephone Utilities of Alaska sponsors the annual *Cushing Kaguyak Telephone Award,* which is presented to the Alaska telecommunications person of the year. The award, needless to say, is a telephone with ivory animals glued over the numbers.

While it is easy to assume that the Kaguyak telephone is a reasonable assessment of the ability of bush people to operate a telephone, the fact of the matter is quite different. Far ahead of the rest of the country, Alaska has already stepped into the 21st century. Today, while many remote communities in the Lower 48 are struggling with ancient telephone lines and service that is only as good as the weather, in Alaska medical computers in Unalakleet communicate with hospitals in Anchorage and San Francisco. Residents of St. Mary's can be interviewed by radio stations on the East Coast, FAX machines can be found in even the most remote of villages, and live feeds of the Iditarod sled dog race are beamed to Japanese and German television stations where they will be taped for rebroadcast later in the day, an ironic twist of history since for years Alaskans had to tape news programs that would be rebroadcast later in the day.

But far more impressive is the crystal clear day-to-day telephone contact between people. Right now, out in Hooper Bay, a mother is singing "Happy Birthday" to her daughter in college in California, and the daughter can hear every note—clearly.

4

THE CITY IN THE MIST

Richard G. Willoughby
and Alaska's *Fata Morgana*

Richard G. Willoughby was hardly what many residents of Juneau called a model citizen—even at the turn of the century. What he did was absolutely reprehensible—unless, of course, you happened to have an exquisite sense of humor. Or were an Alaskan. While today he is remembered only as the namesake of a street in Juneau, in his day he was known as the creator and shameless promoter of Alaska's best known *Fata Morgana*. Cursed by some and revered by others, there are few who would dispute that Richard G. Willoughby added to the charm and folklore of Alaska.

Though the meaning has changed over the centuries, a *Fata Morgana* is the mirage of a city where a city is not. That is to say, it is the mirage of a city that may appear over a body of water or in the clouds above a mountain peak. Sometimes it is an unknown city, and other times it is a city that is recognizable, a city thousands of miles away made visible by an atmospheric condition which cannot be explained by conventional science. The first recorded *Fata Morgana* was in 1773 and appeared on the Straits of Messina in the Mediterranean. Described by a Dominican friar, Antonio Minasi, this *Fata Morgana* was so detailed that armies of men on foot and on horseback could be seen in the foreground. Arches and castles were visible in the distance, and on the distant hills, flocks of sheep could be seen placidly grazing. Though Minasi claimed to have seen the mirage on three separate occasions, history does not record a corroborating witness.

Interestingly, the term *Fata Morgana* comes from King Arthur's enchantress sister, Morgan Le Fey. Among her many powers was the ability to make cities "appear" on rocky shores wherever she willed it, and it was

Richard Willoughby. (Courtesy Alaska State Library, Winter and Pond Collection, 87-2367.)

said that many a sailor was lured to a watery grave by the promise of a safe haven on the rocky shore of the sea.

True *Fata Morganas* are very rare. They are so rare that many in the scientific community believe them to be frauds. But, from a historical perspective, there have been enough sightings that the phenomenon has been written up in source books. One such book, *Handbook of Unusual Natural Phenomena*, even lists Richard Willoughby's phantom city.

Willoughby called his *Fata Morgana* "The Silent City of the Muir Glacier." It was quite a sight! There, hovering above the Muir Glacier, was the mirage of an entire city, complete with flat-topped houses made of brick and stone, ships, tall elm trees, and churches with onion-like domes. Willoughby claimed he had first seen the mirage on the morning

Richard Willoughby's "City in the Mist." (Courtesy Alaska State Library, Winter and Pond Collection, 87-2738.)

of June 21, 1885, while prospecting for gold—alone—in the Glacier Bay area. The phantom vision had lasted for about a half an hour, he later stated to bemused residents of Juneau, and was so clear that a photo could have been taken of the apparition. Everyone in Juneau had a good laugh at the story, but no one believed him.

Over the next few years Willoughby claimed that he saw the city a number of times. Since he was always alone, though, there was no one to corroborate his tale. Then, as Willoughby aged, he began to see that money could be made with this "Silent City in the Mist." Changing his vocation from miner to shill, he moved into Juneau and began a career of greeting tourists on the Juneau docks and signing them up for a tour of Glacier Bay. Not only would they see a mighty glacier, he said, but they just might see one of the most amazing sights in the entire world: a city hovering in midair.

Once in Glacier Bay, the tourists weren't going to see any "puny, pusillanimous gobs [of ice] that Europe advertises as a glacier." No, he assured them, they would see glaciers calving into the sea along a two-mile front, and "if you arrive there at the right time, you may see suspended in the sky above the glacier the mirage of a great unknown city—steepled churches, business blocks, trees waving into walled parks." (Those who claimed to have seen the mirage were given a certificate by Willoughby—which "costs but a drink of whiskey" witnesses related.)

His tours were quite successful. A well-educated man who was described by his contemporaries as both elegant and sophisticated, Willoughby made his living selling an image of Alaska as a land where *anything* was possible. His tours were usually packed, and he went along as "Professor" Willoughby and billed his talks as "scientific lectures." Though not very many tourists ever saw the Silent City, its fame, along with that of Willoughby, spread far and wide and fast.

Then Willoughby developed an even more ingenious way to fleece the tourists. He claimed to have purchased a camera and a number of highly sensitized plates from San Francisco and announced plans to photograph this mysterious city of the mist. He set out for the glacier to wait for the conditions to be just right. On June 21, 1888, according to Willoughby, he spotted the city again, hovering above the Muir Glacier. Taking his time, he took a photograph of this elusive *Fata Morgana*. When the plates were developed, they revealed a ghostly city, just as Willoughby had predicted.

The photograph was an instant hit. It was also a financial gold mine. During the tourist season the photos sold out frequently, with many people standing in line to buy copies. Many tourists bought them by the dozen for friends and relatives in the lower states. As more and more photos sold, the fame of the Silent City grew so fast that it was often said in Juneau—and was probably true—that the Silent City of the Muir Glacier was the most well-known Alaskan town in the rest of the world.

At first the residents of Juneau scoffed at the photograph. No one could possibly believe that there really was a city in the sky, they thought. But they thought wrong. The City in the Mist attracted people from around the world. Finally, as more and more tourists flooded into Juneau, many of them bent on seeing this phantom city, the merchants began to realize that a profit could be made on the travelers. Here was a gold mine that had required no mules or tunnels. Juneau's tourism industry was booming. Clothing stores, general stores, grocery stores and hardware stores expanded to supply the expeditions to Muir Glacier. Boat traffic north to the Muir Glacier was heavy. Not to be left out of the rush he had engendered, Willoughby enhanced his own fortune by selling copies of his photograph for 50 cents apiece.

As expected, the scientific community eventually felt compelled to examine the photograph. One photographic expert, Dr. Charles H. Gilbert, who happened to be in Juneau, took it upon himself to look over the evidence. He examined Willoughby's plates and found them to be "ordinary." He reported that when Willoughby was asked about his photo developing techniques, Willoughby was vague and evasive. The exposure for the city had to be very long, Willoughby claimed, so there had to be a corresponding adjustment in the developing process. Once the plates were exposed they had to be soaked for at least three months in a "secret compound." Interesting, this exposure process was done in sunlight rather than a darkroom.

Gilbert was later paraphrased in the *Popular Science Monthly* (1896) that Willoughby's lack of understanding of the function of a darkroom led him to conclude that the photograph was a fake. When he examined the original negative, Gilbert found it to be a "very old, stained, and faded plate, apparently a negative which had been discarded because [it was] underexposed."

As the photographs were distributed to ever larger numbers of people, the authenticity of its subject matter was tested as well. Sooner or later someone was going to recognize the city. That's exactly what happened. Dr. William H. Hudson of Stanford University looked at the photograph and instantly recognized the Silent City as Bristol, England. Also paraphrased in *Popular Science Monthly* (1896), he was even able to identify the spot from which the photograph was taken, Brandon Hill, above the town. Noting the scaffolding around the towers in the foreground, he was even able to state conclusively that the photo had to have been at least 20 years old.

But these revelations did nothing to stem the interest in the Silent City. If anything, the identification of the city seemed to enhance the mirage's reputation. Neither the tourist traffic nor the sale of photographs diminished.

Eventually the truth was revealed. After years of watching tourists buy photos, a disgruntled Juneau-ite — and one who was probably not partaking of the profits of the miraculous city venture — leaked the story that Willoughby had once paid a stranded English photographer ten dollars for the wanderer's camera and photographic plates. The photograph of the "Silent City in the Mist" was actually a photograph of Bristol that had been overexposed and thrown away by the original photographer. Willoughby, this man claimed, had simply used the photo.

Instantly the citizens of Juneau divided into three groups. There were those who felt that the Silent City was truly in the mist and that Willoughby had been able to photograph Bristol courtesy of some bizarre atmospheric aberration. Then there were those who felt it was a fraud cooked up by Willoughby to feather his own nest. There were also a number of Juneau-ites who felt that the culprit in this case was the wayward English photographer who had left the exposed plates in the camera to fool Willoughby into believing he had photographed the city. The arguing was fierce and bitter.

But the arguing did not seem to affect Willoughby in the slightest. It did not seem to affect the tourist trade either. This final revelation, like those before, did nothing to stem the tide of interest in the Silent City. Travelers still came from around the world to Juneau. The tours to the Muir Glacier continued, and Willoughby had no difficulties drawing large crowds — and selling great numbers of his photograph at the now-inflated price of 75 cents a copy. Interest in the *Fata Morgana* did not abate until Willoughby sold the negative of the Silent City to a "well known San Francisco photographer, I.W. Taber," for $500 in about 1900.

Thus another piece of Alaskan folklore passed from the pages of history. While Willoughby was possibly only interested in making money, what he probably did not know was that his Silent City scam became one of the first tidbits of Alaska's heritage of absurding. Since tourists coming north wanted to believe the most outlandish tales about Alaska, some Alaskans have not been above creating improbable myths and legends to satisfy the most fertile of imaginations. The concept of a city in the mist was so unbelievable that it could *only* be found in Alaska. That's what the tourists wanted to believe, and Richard G. Willoughby provided them with that myth. As the tourists stared into the mist above Muir Glacier, Willoughby laughed all the way to the bank.

After Willoughby sold his celebrated negative, he left Juneau and went back to prospecting. He died in 1902 and took to his grave the true story of Alaska's only *Fata Morgana*.

Note: The best source for Willoughby is Barrett Willoughby, no relation, whose article "The Silent City" appears in Alaska Sportsman, *June 1959. There is also an article in* Popular Science Monthly *in 1896. Juneau historian Bob De Armond has also written a number of articles on Willoughby.*

5

"IT MUST BE TRUE.
I READ IT IN THE PAPER"

The Rev. Sheldon Jackson also has his place in Alaskan absurding. The *Alaska Searchlight*, February 12, 1898, credits him with finding not just one woolly mammoth but many of them. Jackson alleged to have come to a dead glacier and there found "legs embedded in the ice; they were there by the hundreds and, I may truly say, by the thousands and were attached to huge animals, the mastodons or elephants of the Arctic, still perfect in form, some standing, other sitting on their haunches, with large trunks hanging between massive ivory tusks. They were caught in the embrace of the deadly foe, which preserved them as freshly as though they had only been imprisoned but yesterday. Taking a knife from my belt, I slashed a piece of the flesh and gave it to the dogs, and they ate it ravenously as though sliced from a fresh quarter of a moose."

In December of 1989, flamboyant Anchorage defense attorney Edgar Paul Boyko complained that a prosecution witness, a policeman, was being allowed to wear his service revolver on the witness stand. Replied Judge James Hanson, "If he shoots you, I'll find him in contempt" (Anchorage *Daily News*, December 9, 1989).

In 1906 it was revealed that E.T. Barnette, the founder of Fairbanks, had been convicted of larceny in Oregon. His reputation was muddied again in 1911 when his bank failed, leaving hundreds of Alaskans broke. Taken to trial in Valdez, he was convicted and fined $1,000 in what the *Fairbanks Daily News Miner* called the "rottenest judicial farce the North has ever witnessed." Barnette fled Alaska, but for years the Fairbanks paper used the term "Barnette" as the verb "to rob."

On May 22, 1987, in Soldotna, someone put out a fire that had started in his catalytic converter with a six pack of Coca-Cola. Total damages: $200 "and about three bucks for the six-pack."

According to the *Nome Nugget* of May 10, 1905, a three-headed lamb was born at the stables of Carstens Bros. & Dashley. The lamb, according to witnesses, was "lively, and the possession of the two extra heads [did] not interfere with its comfort in any way."

On April 22, 1987, according to the *Kodiak Daily Mirror*, Travis Murphy was standing on a boat in St. Paul when a 2,400-pound sea lion lunged seven feet out of the water, grabbed him by his buttocks and dragged him under the sea. Murphy fought for his life and came away from the struggle with a "large laceration and bruise on his backside."

As seen in the *Nome Chronicle*, August 11, 1900:

> You can tell a camp's development by the price of drinks. Four bits means recent occupation, unsettled conditions and the presence of ½ barrel which has just come over the trail. Two bits means a regulation boom is on, that the tenderfeet are plenty and that regular communication with the outside is established. Next drop is for one and a half. Not a sign of slump but shows first excitement is passed — the town is getting down to business basis. Fifteen cents means the business basis reached, court and school are going, claim-jumping has become bad form, plug hats are tolerated and faro banks have moved upstairs. Any further decline, however, is a danger sign. Two for a quart whiskey is a sure sign of deterioration and 5 [cent] beer mean[s] the stampede has started for the next digging.

During the 1987 Iditarod, several mushers claimed to have seen a UFO. According to the March 25 *Palmer Frontiersman*, Joe Runyan saw it as "biblical-star type stuff . . . a greenish orb with a bright center and a fantail light." Sue Firman said it was "huge and fiery colored." Dewey Halverson said he recognized that description, "I saw the same dang thing this morning when I woke up on the floor of the Bering Sea Saloon."

When Charles Lestor was arrested for sedition in Nenana in July, 1917, United States Marshal Erwin of Fairbanks noted that Nenana was clearly full of men like Lestor who should also be arrested. It was his intention, Erwin said in the *Seward Gateway*, July 23, 1917, to arrest every guilty person in Nenana. "I'll fill this jail so full of them," he snapped, "that their feet will stick out the windows."

On April 1, 1987, an Alaska Airlines Boeing 737 had a mid-air collision with a fish. According to the *Anchorage Daily News*, an eagle with a fish in its talons was flying at an angle across the Juneau airport runway as the airplane was taking off. Just before the two flight paths intersected, the eagle dropped the fish. The fish and the airplane collided in midair. The eagle escaped, but the "fish, species unknown, was presumed dead." The fact that the incident occurred on April Fool's Day led some to believe that the story had been faked. It had not.

The article also revealed that there had been a collision between a moose and an airplane in Cordova a decade earlier. "The moose collision" was different, as the newspaper clearly stated, for it "occurred on the ground."

On the night of November 17, 1986, veteran JAL pilot Kenju Teruchi saw a flying saucer following his plane as he was approaching Anchorage. The alien spacecraft followed him for about 50 minutes and then disappeared. The strange craft was also picked up on radar, but later "radar experts" stated that the sighting was a "radar echo." An artist's rendition of the alien spacecraft appeared on the front page of the *Anchorage Daily News* on January 15, 1987.

According to the *Nome Daily News*, November 28, 1900, two
travelers, Fred Welty and Ernest Johns, found themselves trapped in a
blizzard outside the community of Mary's Igloo. The storm raged for
three days, during which time neither the men nor their horses had
anything to eat. Finally, in desperation, the horses ate the tent which was
covering the two men causing them to come close to freezing to death.

According to the October, 1986, *Chugach Outlet*, the Chugach Electric Cooperative newsletter, the "Offalot" is an animal that goes around
to elementary schools teaching children about energy conservation.

On March 11, 1988, the *Bristol Bay Times* ran a story on the new local
leash law. To get the reaction of the public, the paper interviewed dogs.
Bowser Livermeal stated, "[The new leash law] really makes my tail twitch
every time I think about it." Said another dog, Dodo Alpo, "I just had puppies. They're all attached to the doghouse with pink and blue ropes. I'm
asking you, is this any way for a bitch to raise her puppies?"

Other dogs were interviewed as well. Wolf Junkyard said that his
days of chasing away rabid foxes and escorting pick-up trucks through
town were over and, since he was leashed, he wouldn't be dragging any
caribou carcasses off either. Bingo Flea was a bit snippy. "When was the
last time they arrested a dog for driving while intoxicated, huh?" Prince
Wag wanted to know what humans were going to be doing about cats.
It was also reported that "some militant dogs had formed a protest group
under the motto BITE THE HAND THAT FEEDS YOU."

The only human quotes in the article came from a King Salmon dog
owner. When asked if he was complying with the leash law, the owner
replied, sure, "my dog's on a leash. She drags it behind her" everywhere
she goes.

On August 31, 1966, the *Alaska Independent Shopper* ran an article
by Paul Harvey in which he revealed how "an Eskimo kills a wolf."

According to Paul Harvey, the Eskimo buries a knife handle deep in
the snow and coats the blade heavily with blood. The wolf is drawn to
the blood and begins licking the knife blade. In the process, the wolf cuts

its tongue. But "in the arctic night, so great becomes his craving for blood that he does not notice the razor-sharp sting of the naked blade on his own tongue." The more the wolf licks, the more he bleeds, until "dawn finds him dead in the snow."

In the mid–1960s, the *Ketchikan News* did a review of Rand Mc-Nally's latest book, which included some rather startling information about Alaska. The most interesting tidbit appeared on page 78 and stated that, "thanks to the greater range of their firearms, the Eskimos have become hunters and have changed from the kayak to the horse-drawn sledge. But horses have to be fed with meat, and this unfortunately has to be supplied by the walrus."

Two fishermen in Fairbanks, the *Anchorage Times* reported on December 8, 1986, took a home movie camera with them on a fishing trip. The camera jammed during the trip, and they had to take it to a repair shop when they returned home. The video repairman was able to fix the camera but, in viewing the home movies, saw the men snagging salmon. He informed the Fish and Wildlife Protection Division and the two fishermen were arrested.

Legendary Alaskan and Klondike humorist Stroller White got his due, or so reported the *Skagway Daily Alaskan* on December 13, 1907. White's wife was out of town and the comic was baching it. Making the best of a bad situation, he bought a selection of T-bone steaks, turkey and sausage for his kitchen. As he left for work he accidentally left the back door of his home open.

Two hours later, the "charwoman" entered the premises and found two very satisfied dogs sleeping before the fire. "The carcass of the turkey was found in the vacant lot back of the barn. Of the sausages there was left no trace, and of the pig's feet only the mockery of bones picked clean." The woman cleaned up as best she could and then informed Stroller of the loss. Enraged, the comic went to the owner of the dogs. The man being out, Stroller placed a bill for $15 on his desk.

The next day, the owner of the dogs appeared in Stroller's office and apologized profusely for the loss. Stroller accepted the $15 and, being in a better mood, asked the man to stay for a piece of pie, an item the dogs had not devoured. It was cooking, and the aroma filled the room. The neighbor agreed to stay and held up his plate for the piece of pie. Stroller "drove down a bold spoon into the very heart [of the pie] and brought up a tangled mess of red flannel, scraps from the uniform of the NWMP" (North West Mounted Police).

Residents of Kenai were furious in late January of 1990, the *Anchorage Daily News* reported on February 1. It appeared that a band of vandals was going through the parking lot of the Central Peninsula General Hospital stealing windshield wipers. After a handful of incidents, Dr. James Zirul caught the culprits in the act.

Unfortunately there was nothing he could do about it, as the transgressors were ravens.

According to naturalist Boyd Shaffer, ravens love "things that'll flop when they pull 'em." Ravens will also steal shiny objects, Shaffer noted. A few years previously there had been a raven that was stealing gas caps when people took them off to fill their tank.

Shaffer did have a suggestion to stop the thieving: hide in the car and frighten the ravens when they come to steal the blades. Other than that, he lamented, there was not a lot anyone could do.

According to the *Kodiak Daily Mirror*, a Costa Hummingbird that wound up in Alaska got a free ride home — as carry-on baggage with a U.S. Fish & Wildlife agent. The 3-inch bird had been feeding off the fuchsias in an Anchorage backyard all summer.

"We kept waiting for him to pack his bags and go home," said Pat Bergt, but with the advance of winter it was clear the bird would not leave. So, according to the October 9, 1989, edition of the paper, the Bergts called the U.S. Fish & Wildlife.

As it turned out, the Costa was a bird that normally only travels as far north as Sacramento and heads for Mexico during the winter. How did the hummingbird get to Alaska? That's a good question. It is guessed that the bird was an unexpected part of someone's move north or "while in its cyclical quiet state, was on a plant that got packed for a journey to Alaska."

On March 20, 1974, according to the *Fairbanks Daily News Miner*, Alyeska Pipeline Service Company was going to bid on 3.4 million cubic yards of gravel along the pipeline route north of the Yukon River. The minimum bid was $.10 per cubic yard and the Bureau of Land Management did not expect any other bidders. After all, who was going to pay $1,000 for the right to bid on a resource that only Alyeska needed?

However, when the bidding began, David Wtipol of Indian topped Alyeska's bid by a cent. Alyeska then overbid and Wtipol overbid again. Cent by cent the price of the gravel rose and, with each cent, the cost of the gravel jumped by $34,000. After two hours of bidding, Wtipol had pushed the bid price up to 63 cents a cubic yard. When Alyeska went one penny more, Wtipol dropped out. What should have cost Alyeska $340,000 ended up costing a $2.1 million.

It was suspected, the *Daily News Miner* stated, that Wtipol was a speculator who intended to buy the gravel and then sell to Alyeska at a profit. No one could ask him, however, for just after Alyeska went to 64 cents, Wtipol disappeared.

Beavers, as some troops in Alaska learned, can be very frightening. On April 22, 1942, the *Kodiak Bear* reported that two privates on guard duty were startled when a male beaver "started rapid-fire thwacking his broad tail, simulating gunfire."

In May of 1953, the *Alaskan Reporter* stated that a woman in Mt. View shot a moose in her back yard. Her husband was furious, even though he was not home at the time. He was hunting for moose in the Chugach Range and came home without one.

In January of 1990, Richard Best was driving toward Fairbanks on the Richardson Highway when he hit a 500-pound moose. He got out of his truck, but he couldn't find the carcass. When he did, he was surprised. It was in the back of his pickup. He had been hunting moose for six years, and this was the first one he had ever bagged. But it cost him $1,500 in damages.

On March 19, 1974, according to the *Fairbanks Daily News Miner*, a skier at Girdwood had a cold run. In 30 degree temperatures a skier "streaked" the slope. "He was a good skier; at least he didn't fall down," a spectator noted. "By the time he hit the bottom he was yelling and screaming he was so cold."

————————

On February 16, 1960, according to the *Fairbanks Daily News Miner*, a 17-year-old boy was jailed in Anchorage for killing his father. The youth's classmates collected his books and passed them to federal jail authorities for their classmate. Also included was a tape recorder so he could tape his assignments in speech and "a personalized Bible with his name on it."

————————

On October 29, 1970, the *Kodiak Daily Mirror* reprinted an article from the *Wrangell Sentinel,* which claimed that Mr. and Mrs. Manne Landstrom had seen a "30 foot long serpent-like creature which lives in the depths of [Big Lake near Mt. McKinley]."

The couple claimed to have seen the creature twice but were unable to take a photo either time. According to the couple, it had a "flattened head like that of a crocodile, two eyes and a rounded, blunt nose and a long body about 12 inches in diameter. We could plainly see two curves in its back and two flippers or feet behind the head." Mr. Landstrom feels that the creature might be "the answer to numerous reports of lost fishing tackle" on the lake.

————————

According to the *New York Times* of October 11, 1887, a living mastodon was spotted in Alaska. Quoting from an Alaskan paper, the *Juneau Free Press*, local Indians found mastodon tracks and followed them until they were full of animal.

"[The Indian] described [the mastodon] as being larger than Post Trader Harper's store with great shining yellowish tusks and a mouth large enough to swallow him in a single gulp."

————————

According to Gene Joiner's *Mukluk Telegraph* of March 17, 1951, since Marshal Neily stated that he "was incompetent" in dealing with people who steal emergency equipment from bush planes, the pilots of the Arctic had decided to take matters into their own hands. According to the report,

> The local pilots recently agreed to work together and chop the fingers off anyone caught stealing emergency equipment from any of their airplanes. One pilot has been putting poison in some of his emergency food in an effort to kill off the thieves but to date has met with no success.

On January 19, 1960, the *Anchorage Daily News* reported that Mountain View had voted to remain dry by a margin of more than 2 to 1. The vote was 228 against and 162 in favor for a total of 390 "unspoiled ballots."

On October 23, 1971, according to the *Anchorage Daily News*, Del Lavon Thomas was the first person to skyjack an airplane in Alaska. Thomas hyjacked a Wien Consolidated Airlines jet on its way to Bethel.

According to the *Ketchikan Daily News*, March 3, 1947, a "confused alley cat named Ditto" had been teamed on a sled with "two mongrels who had never been harnessed before." The sled, incidentally, "was an improvised pushtype used in place of baby carriages." The unlikely team was entered in an Anchorage sled dog race. There is no mention of any awards garnered by this team.

According to the *Ketchikan Daily News*, March 12, 1947, bush pilot Don Emmons left Central, Alaska with two passengers and arrived with three. A baby boy was delivered 20 minutes before the plane landed in Fairbanks.

In a front page center editorial on March 5, 1947, the *Ketchikan Daily News* deplored the state of affairs in the city. "If we begin to allow honky-tonks all over the city," the editorial preached, "we soon shall have a 'wide-open' town for vice, gambling, drunkenness and even major crimes. One leads to the other. It won't be safe to walk on the streets at night."

On the same page was a story of the unsuccessful prosecution of one of the honky-tonks which resulted in a dismissal of all charges. The trial had all the trappings of a comedy. In testimony, the Chief of Police noted that the Lucky Sport "permitted dancing in the establishment" and "got more attention in red light calls than any three houses in town." There had been a handful of complaints but, when the police raided the restaurant, they only found a single bottle of liquor "in the bottom drawer of [the defendant's] wife's dresser."

———————————

On Easter Day, 1991, the ravens in Juneau poached about 600 eggs from the annual Easter Egg hunt. Doing a last minute check just before the children were to be released, the organizers of the hunt were horrified to discover that half of their eggs had been stolen — including some hard plastic ones. While the children hunted for those that were left, ravens were seen gorging on their stolen repast and "popping open plastic eggs that contained candy."

———————————

"If you recent high school graduates can measure up to the high standards for enlistment," an advertisement for the United States Army proclaimed in the August 1, 1947, edition of *Jessen's Weekly*, "you'll be better off than a civilian making $3,000 a year!" Pay, you ask? "In addition to a private's starting pay of $75 a month, you get food, clothing, housing, medical care, low cost insurance, all of which would cost a civilian $1,500 annually."

———————————

On September 12, 1947, according to *Jessen's Weekly*, Ann Joyce "of Honolulu and Australia" returned to the Nordale in Fairbanks. Since she was unable to get accommodations, "she was spending most of her time in the hotel lobby hopefully waiting for someone to give up a room."

———————————

In June of 1966, according to the *Ketchikan Daily News,* the Beatles made a stop in Anchorage. Since it was rumored that they were spending the night in the city, Beatles fans were calling every hotel in town to find the Fab Four. But it was unfortunately a sad turn of events for one traveler from Juneau who was staying at the Roosevelt Hotel at the time. His name was Homer R. Beedle and his room was deluged with calls for hours.

According the *Jessen's Weekly,* September 12, 1947, a manager of a touring company, unaware of conditions in Alaska, wired the proprietor of a theater where his troupe was to perform. "Would like to hold rehearsal next Monday afternoon at three o'clock," his wire read. "Have your stage manager, carpenter, property man, electrician and all stage hands present at that time."

Four hours later he received a reply from the theater manager, "All right. I'll be there."

On February 2, 1911, the *Anchorage Daily Times* reported an article by a New York lawyer concerning the quality of women in Alaska. Of Alaska's women he wrote:

> The white women are less numerous than the men. They are smaller and more wiry. Since most of them live a distance of several days from a physician and physically they are inferior to squaws, they usually practice race suicide. But they make devoted wives. Many who at their father's homes were accustomed to be waited upon in steam-heated apartments, live here cheerfully in log cabins, cooking, washing and making fires, without servants. They are rewarded by devotion and admiration. Old maids are unknown in Alaska. Most women have two or even three husbands, and a line waiting for any vacancy that might occur. In one respect they have reached an advanced state of civilization. A woman who has sinned in the past, if her life is now respectable, is respected by others.

Reprinting a story from the *Juneau Empire,* the *Anchorage Daily Times,* November 14, 1916, reported that the only witness for the defense, H.H. Rice, fell asleep in court. He began mumbling and the judge quieted the court to find the source of the disturbance. As soon as the court became still, much to the defendant's dismay, Rice was heard to state audibly, "Oh, they'll get him anyway. It's only a matter of time."

As the paper stated, "The incident amused the attorneys for [the defendant] and especially appealed to Assistant District Attorney John Reagan who had just completed his address to the jury."

The *Anchorage Daily Times,* November 13, 1916, reports "Clyde E. Kenyon, formerly an attorney of Spokane, was accidentally shot and killed while hunting alone in Alaska."

Slim Hopaway, quoted in the *Alaska Reporter* in June of 1953, stated that Alaskans could profit by cross breeding a cow and a bear to make a "bru-cow."

On June 2, 1990, most papers in Alaska carried the story of a Russian by the name of Anatoyla Bukreuv, who ran to the top of Mt. McKinley in a single day. He made the round trip from the 11,000 foot level in 10½ hours, a trip that takes most climbers five or six days.

There was great news for egg lovers on Wednesday, February 21, 1917, according to the *Anchorage Daily Times.* W.A. Ford, 77, was leaving Seattle to return to his homestead in Anchorage to "engage in chicken raising."

"There isn't a better place in the world to raise chickens," Ford proclaimed.

According to the *Anchorage Times,* on Christmas Day, 1989, these were some selected temperature highs and lows across Alaska.

	High	Low
Anchorage	32	25
Fairbanks	15	5
Kodiak	30	15
Kenai	32	25
Talkeetna	35	25
Nome	5	0
Juneau	48	40

Here is a selection of highs and lows across the United States on the same day:

	High	Low
Albany, N.Y.	11	−15
Atlanta	22	6
Atlantic City	24	6
Birmingham	19	4
Columbia, S.C.	23	19
Houston	28	11
Jackson, Miss.	19	7
Little Rock, Ark.	18	8
Louisville	13	−6
Memphis	14	4
Nashville	14	−1
New Orleans	24	15
Orlando	42	22
Raleigh	20	16
Tampa	42	24

By the evening, CNN reported that the low for Miami Beach (29) was lower than that of Anchorage (31).

According to the *Ketchikan Mining Journal* on February 1, 1916, a lineman for the Yukon Telegraph was subject to a strange occurrence. While he was checking the telegraph line "near Nahlin, south of Atlin," a huge meteor struck the earth killing his dogs and stunning him so badly that he remained unconscious for several hours. The lineman, Andy Johnson, was traveling about 50 feet behind his sled when the meteor struck. Reports stated that the meteor left a crater 50 feet in diameter.

According to the October 18, 1915, *Nome Nugget,* two insane men were brought to town. One of them, a white man, had "walked naked through the streets of Nome in broad daylight. The only covering on him was a cloth around the neck and a string around the waist but hanking [sic] to the string was an alarm clock."

According to the July 12, 1915, *Nome Nugget,* Bob Sheldon reopened his "automobile stage line over the big trail from Fairbanks to Chitina in the dead of winter." To negotiate the tight trails and utilize the track made by dogsleds, Sheldon had "cut down the axles of his Ford machine, narrowing them to a 44 inch tread."

On December 12, 1989, Fish and Wildlife Trooper Sgt. Richard Graham had a close encounter with a "very, very, very large bull moose." According to the *Palmer Frontiersman,* Graham tried to urge a moose off the highway by parking next to the disoriented animal and turning on his flashing lights and siren.

This did not work. The moose "reared up and began pounding metal" and proceeded to do "a tap dance" on the Trooper's brand-new automobile hood. When the dance was over, Graham's windshield was shattered and his hood full of dents. Asked how he felt about the encounter, Graham replied that he had done his job. After all, he noted, "I got the moose to move on."

On March 30, 1901, the *Ketchikan Mining Journal* reported that there had been a minor coal rush in Nome. It was reported that some miners cut a hole in the ice of the shore of the Bering Sea and discovered coal. This "caused a rush to the recorder's office, and the discoverer was obliged to adopt the shotgun policy to hold possession of his claim."

The coal rush did not subside in enthusiasm until it was learned that the coal from this supposed submarine mine was retrieved already sacked and thus had probably come from the "barge *Skookum* which stranded on that shore last fall."

Speaking of a character reference, on July 6, 1901, the *Ketchikan Mining Journal* noted:

> Ed C. Russell, but for the idiotic expression his not altogether otherwise unattractive countenance habitually wears, would be considered a good looking man. He is in the prime of his life, vigorous in everything except intellect, rejoices in a disposition as crossed as that of a sawhorse, stands five foot ten and a half inches in his stockings and never washed his feet. He is a self-made man, what there is of him, which accounts for the fact that he is better fitted to wrestle with the manure of a cow stable than for any other occupation on earth, unless it be that of scavenger pure and simple.

On April 9, 1904, the *Ketchikan Mining Journal* reported that an article had appeared in *Popular Science Notes* which described the men of King Island as being over six feet tall with brown beards. The women, the article claimed, were just as tall as the men, but stronger. Supporting this claim, the author alleged to have seen a woman who "carried off in her birch-bark canoe a stone weighing eight hundred pounds, which two strong men could not lift, and of another female who carried on her head a box containing two hundred and eighty pounds of lead."

In response, the *Mining Journal* noted that the author of the article "must have been an extraordinarily keen observer to discover birch-bark canoes" on King Island, as there are no trees on the island.

The *Iditarod Pioneer,* February 10, 1917, reported that Fairbanks had imposed a tax of $200 "on the personal property of all single men who [were] not paying taxes on other property in the town of Fairbanks."

According to the *Alaskan Reporter,* April 1953, a fur trader by the name of Schmitz found himself marooned when the ferry on which he was riding broke down between Dawson and the Alaska border in 1900.

With another trader, Schmitz hired a Native to take him down the river to Fort Yukon. Before they arrived, Schmitz became very concerned when he saw the trader and the Native exchanging weapons and talking excitedly. Since he had $20,000 on him, Schmitz decided not to take a chance. He told the two to take him ashore. There he waited for the ferry to pick him up as it came down the Yukon.

Twenty years later Schmitz came back to Alaska and, as fate would have it, came back to the same dock where the ferry had broken down two decades earlier. Walking into a general store, he was instantly recognized by an Indian. The Indian grabbed him by the arm and urged him across town. The Indian was very large and Schmitz small, so he went along. The Indian finally came to a cabin. Inside, Schmitz saw an old man in bed and recognized him as the trader with whom he had been in the canoe 20 years earlier. Though he was terribly ill, the trader was wild with joy.

After Schmitz had left the canoe, the trader had struck it rich. But for twenty years, everyone in the community had assumed that the trader had killed Schmitz for his money.

According to the *Iditarod Pioneer,* April 21, 1917, the University of Washington had received a giant Alaska spider crab which had been "captured by shrimp fishermen off the coast of Alaska at Ketchikan." Not only was it the largest crab of any kind ever brought to the University, it also belonged "to a species [of crab] which can run faster than a man."

On June 18, 1992, the *Anchorage Daily News* reported that the Fairbanks Correctional Center had been rated Number One in the nation by *Playboy* magazine. Pointing to such amenities as single cells, cable television and coed religious services, *Playboy's* three former inmate consultants placed the Fairbanks "Pen" ahead of jails which offered such amenities as order-out pizza, unlimited free local phone calls, smoke-free environment, "tradition of great cooking established by Sheriff's wife" and the right to place off track bets from the jail cell.

Referred to locally as "The Hotel," the Fairbanks Correctional Center offered such scrumptious prison food as Alaska king crab, prime rib, shrimp and fried scallops. A prisoner who spent too much time in the Fairbanks slammer, the *Daily News* reported, "could expect to gain about 20 pounds." Those days were gone by 1992, but the Fairbanks hoosegow's food was still rated "varied and plentiful."

How did the Fairbanks Correctional Center show its appreciation as being rated the plushest penal penthouse in America? The day the honor was announced, a dozen jail guards taped handmade paper badges on the reverse of their regular badges which read "We're Number One" under the *Playboy* bunny logo.

How did the inmates receive the news of the honor? "I feel fortunate to have done my crime in Alaska," stated Bill Arthur, awaiting sentencing for selling cocaine.

As it appeared in the *Fairbanks Daily News Miner* on August 10, 1953.

> Despite the fact that Alaska has no snakes roaming anywhere in its vast territory, a woman was treated at St. Joseph's Hospital during the early hours Sunday morning for a snake bite on her hand.
>
> The precedent-shattering injury occurred when Kay Starr, an entertainer at the Club Flamingo on South Cushman Street, was bitten by a 140-pound boa constrictor she uses in her night club act.

6

THE GREAT TANANA
RAFT CLASSIC

It was one of the most bizarre events in Alaska's maritime history. Actually there were four of them, one a year from 1968 to 1971. That's the number of times the Great Tanana Raft Classic took place. One of the zaniest races ever to take place on the water in Alaska — or any place, for that matter — the Classic is firmly entrenched in the northland's heritage of absurding.

The Great Tanana Raft Classic was born in Fairbanks, legend has it, when "two spirited, good-natured fools were boasting to one another of their fine abilities in just about any endeavor," and "one of the tipplers proceeded to [state] that he could float down the winding Tanana River on a homemade raft, faster than anyone else." The second person at the bar took up the challenge, and thereafter the Great Tanana Raft Classic was born.

Both contestants immediately set out to build rafts of whatever material they could find. Wood, tires, and empty oil drums were plentiful, and these were thus the stuff from which the race formed. Word quickly filtered through the community that something unusual was going to happen on the Tanana River, and before long, three or four more people began to think about building a raft of their own. But that was about as far as they got.

The first classic was sparsely attended. It began with all participants imbibing heavily before, during and after the Classic. This was, of course, in keeping with the tradition of the birth of the Classic — drinking, that is, as well as participating in strange and unusual events which would shock the sensibilities of those from the Lower 48.

"The raft race was named *great*," noted the self-dubbed Admiral of the Classic, Merritt Helfferich of Fairbanks. "It was the only [such race], and thus it had to be great as far as we were concerned and a *classic* because, for no reason we could discern, it seemed that any Alaskan event of substance was called a classic." Helfferich was, not surprisingly, one of the two tipplers who originated the Classic.

By the second year, the course was officially established as being roughly 80 miles in length, extending down the Tanana River from Pike's Landing to Nenana. A minimum of four, 55-gallon drums per raft was required, and all participants had to wear a Coast Guard approved life jacket. Furthermore, no raft was allowed to have more than 995 barrels, a limit with which no contestant had difficulty avoiding. All the rafts had to be homemade—which was not saying much, as there were very few commercial manufacturers of rafts that used 55-gallon drums for flotation.

To call the floats, er, rafts, strange would have been a compliment. Every configuration of barrels, wood, cardboard, pipe, bicycles, plastic and whatever-else-is-cheap-and-sort-of-water-resistant imaginable appeared on the river. These were not hastily put-together rafts either. In many cases, participants had been stealing, er, collecting 55-gallon drums and wood for weeks prior to the Classic. Paddle wheels, oars, long poles and just about every other means of naval locomotion were used.

Many of the floats were cleverly designed. In 1969, for instance, there was a fire-breathing dragon—which was not a description of Admiral Helfferich. Using a propane tank and a reasonable facsimile of a dragon's head, the raft seemed destined for the record books. Alas, the dragon only made it about 10 feet from the start before it went down to Davy Jones' Locker.

Other rafts were built for comfort. The Trans-Arctic Airlines float in 1970 had an onboard barbecue grill for the six pounds of hamburgers and three pounds of hot dogs that had been stowed on board—which, in this case, really was a board. It was a beam actually, which is a description of the wood, not of a part of the raft. Additionally, with the condiments and gallons of chocolate milk were six cases of beer—a Great Tanana Raft Classic necessity.

The zaniness of the Classic grew so quickly that by the fourth year there were more than 365 rafts, including entries by Howard Pollock, Alaska's lone Congressman, Senator Ted Stevens and then–Governor Bill Egan. A crowd of more than 2,000 well-wishers lined the start at Pike's Landing. After the race started, the crowd drove down to Nenana where they proceeded to party and wait for the first raft to arrive.

The award for winning the race, it should be added, was well worth the effort. First place in 1970, the fourth and final year of the race, was "an old, used bowling trophy plus one case of *very cheap* champagne." But there was more to the race than winning, because the first raft to make it across the finish line was always disqualified for "trying too hard." True Great Tanana Raft Classic participants, it was said with pride, were only interested in a finish above 150th place.

Once the race started it was absolute pandemonium on the waterway. Since no one was in any hurry to win and the race could last as long as 18 hours, there was no burning desire to move rapidly. So no one did. Bumping into one another, the rafts slowly moved out into the main current where they lazily made their way downriver. Tying onto another raft for conversation and beer was expected, and such hospitalities were frequently extended.

Some of the hospitalities, alas, included pulling luckless rafters from the drink. It was not unusual for a dozen or more rafts to capsize along the way. Others were beached — intentionally or otherwise — leaving the participants to make their way inland to the highway and the assistance of a friendly motorist.

Nenana, usually a sleepy community of barely over 500, turned into a boomtown over the weekend of the Great Tanana Raft Classic. Awash in people, beer and soggy clothes, the two taverns in town filled to capacity, and the beaches were littered with sleeping bags and fire pits. Celebration of the event lasted through the weekend, depending on each individual's personal constitution. By Sunday night, Nenana was back to the sleepy community it had been before the onslaught of the crowd.

Though the Classic is history today, there are many old-timers in Fairbanks who remember with a smile the days when they braved the waters of the Tanana River, and the bars of Nenana, in the name of the Great Tanana Raft Classic.

Note: The bulk of this information was provided by Admiral Merritt R. Helfferich. Steve Burseth did a write-up for the Anchorage Daily News *on May 29th, 1970. There is another article out on the Classic (May 1970), by Dave Webster, for a magazine that no longer exists,* Accent Anchorage.

7

THE HAINES PEACE ROCK

Every once in a while, an event occurs that is so strange it is hard to describe. You hear of it, and even though it has been explained in detail, you are not sure you believe it. Worse, you may not want to search for corroborating testimony because people might think you were a few bricks shy of a load just for believing such a preposterous idea in the first place. Such is the case of the Haines Peace Rock.

The saga of the Haines Peace Rock, also known as the Deer Rock (Guwakgan Teiyee), began long before the white man came to the Northland. The Tlingts of the Haines region established the rock as a sacrosanct area where peace talks could be conducted. When warring factions wanted to end the hostilities, the ceremonies were held at the Deer Rock.

The Rock served as a cultural landmark for the Tlingts until the mid-1950s, when the Federal Bureau of Public Roads made plans to widen the road to Chilkoot Lake along the Chilkoot River. But this was in an era before the EPA, OSHA, ASHA, and the alphabet soup of federal agencies. In the 1950s, when the Federal Bureau of Roads—also known as the "Bureau of Parallel Ruts"—came upon a boulder in the path of a proposed highway, a stick of dynamite solved the problem nicely.

Time moved on, and in the early 1980s, thirty years after the rock had been blown apart, a group of Natives from Haines went to their legislator, Representative Peter Goll, and said that the Rock, which had been so callously blown apart, had been a valuable piece of their cultural heritage and demanded its restoration.

A legislator is elected to serve his constituents, and when those constituents speak, a legislator is obligated to listen and respond—even if it is thirty years after the fact. Representative Goll responded and asked the State of Alaska's Department of Transportation and Public Facilities (DOT/PF) to restore what is now known as the Haines Peace Rock.

From DOT/PF's point of view, the assignment was, to say the least, unusual. While it was certainly a tragedy that the Rock had been destroyed

The Haines Peace Rock. (Courtesy Roy Lawrence.)

in the first place, there was really not much that DOT/PF could do to
restore it. After all, the boulder had been destroyed, and parts of it had
rolled into the river, while other pieces had been crushed and used in the
construction of the highway.

Further, it was bordering on the ludicrous to think of restructuring
a boulder that was not there. There were no pictures of the original
boulder and no historical descriptions available. There were several large
pieces which were tentatively identified by the Tlingit elders as having
been part of the original boulder, but the rest was missing.

To adhere to the legislative request, DOT/PF set about to reconstruct the boulder. A group of Tlingit elders created a line drawing based
on their collective memories of the Peace Rock, and this drawing was for-
warded to DOT/PF. Thus, over a three-day period, state construction
personnel took a crew to the site of the Rock and began stacking rocks
into a pile that approximated the line drawing in their possession.

The fact that the newly-created Haines Peace Rock was not the original did not deter the Tlingts from celebrating its recreation. On August
17, 1983, the rock was dedicated, and "colorful traditional Tlingit
clothing, traditional Tlingit foods, and the Tlingit language mingled with
contemporary non–Tlingit garb, standard picnic foods and American
English speech," reported the Haines newspaper.

When the news leaked to the press at the Capitol, very few reporters believed what they were hearing. After all, there are some things that reporters just won't believe. Right on top of that list was the State of Alaska sending men and equipment to reconstruct a rock that did not exist. One legislator's aide, however, did call DOT/PF to verify the rumor.

The DOT/PF spokesperson was, understandably, not enthusiastic about explaining the project.

"Did you have a work plan?" the aide asked.

"Nope," replied the DOT/PF spokesperson, "we had a line drawing some Natives had given us."

"Was it accurate?"

"How the &%$# should I know?"

"Were there any pieces of the original rock to use?"

"I don't know," replied the DOT/PF representative. "We just used the rocks in the vicinity."

"So there's no way of knowing if even one of the rocks you picked were part of the original Peace Rock?"

"We used the rocks that we were told were part of the original. That's all I know."

At this point, the validity of the Haines Peace Rock is hard to assess. If there has been an uproar, the community of Haines has not heard it. That could be because most Alaskans have never heard of the Haines Peace Rock. Those Alaskans who have heard of the Rock probably feel that someone down there in Haines has an exquisite sense of humor.

Further, when doubting Alaskans are convinced that such an artifact exists, they quickly divide into two camps: those who feel that the project was a legitimate, state-funded, cultural restoration, and those who feel that the project is so ludicrous that the only people who would consider it would be state legislators with the collective intelligence of a bed of clams who happen to live in an oil-rich state gushing with cash.

Former representative Peter Goll, understandably, takes a dim view of those who feel that the Haines Peace Rock is a laughing matter. When contacted, he noted:

> The Peace Rock is an artifact of great cultural and historic importance to the Tlingit people. Upon recognizing its responsibility for site restoration, the Alaska Department of Transportation repaired the artifact rapidly and at low cost. Its restoration was deeply appreciated by the Native community. Today, the site continues to be used for traditional gatherings.

On the other hand, Alaskan humorist Warren Sitka noted that, "apparently in Haines there is more than one way to get stoned."

8
STRANGE BUT TRUE

Joe Flood of Juneau, an old-timer when it comes to radio in Alaska, recalls that in the 1960s "we did rip-and-read news [right off the teletype]. The big thing was to make someone laugh while they were on the air. I remember reading the news one day and watching one of the other DJs set my copy on fire. I had to read the news and keep from laughing before the flames singed my fingers.

"All kinds of things happened in those days. I remember an old alcoholic who died reading the news on the air, and there was a DJ who was reading the news when his secretary held up a sign that read, 'Your fly is open and I love you.' He busted a gut and started laughing hysterically on the air!"

As Joe Flood recalled, the stations were filled with "cowboys." At one Anchorage station he refused to name, "we knew the Big Time was coming when management finally broke down and bought a new transmitter. A new transmitter! That was big time! That was about 1968. We were really thrilled. One of the jocks waited until the three workmen were in the transmitter room sweating and swearing as they were installing the new equipment. Then this guy sneaked into the back room, stripped off all his clothes and walked around the new transmitter stark naked. The workmen looked up in amazement, and without missing a step, this DJ pointed back over his shoulder with his thumb and says 'Locusts!'" (from an interview with Joe Flood).

Ruben Gaines, perhaps the most impressive personality in the history of Alaskan radio, came down to Anchorage from Fairbanks in 1950 to work at KENI which was then located in the Fourth Avenue Theater building in Anchorage. In those days, Gaines and his good friend Ed Stevens were best known for their ability to recreate baseball games.

Gaines recalled, "We had a friend in Cleveland who would listen to a baseball game each week. When it was over, he'd call and give us an inning by inning breakdown of the game. Then Ed and I would recreate the entire game over the next two hours. We'd use a little hickory stick and strike the table for a hit, and then swap an empty toilet paper roll for the ball being caught in a mitt. We had two types of crowd recordings, one for cheering and the other for screaming outrage. After we finished the game, Ed and I would walk downtown for a drink. When we came into the club, everyone would say, Hey! You're supposed to be in Chicago, New York or wherever the game had been played" (from an interview with Ruben Gaines).

On August 9, 1915, the tent city at the mouth of Ship Creek was officially named Alaska City by a vote of the residents. The selection won out over a number of other choices which included Anchorage, Woodrow City (in honor of President Woodrow Wilson), Matanuska, Lane and Gateway. Federal officials did not approve of the name change and left the name "Anchorage" on their maps. Eventually the city changed its name to "Anchorage" to conform to the maps.

Alaska's first mail flight occurred on February 12, 1924, when Carl Ben Eielson took off from Fairbanks with mail for McGrath. The flight was uneventful except for one ironic moment. Eielson spotted Fred Milligan on the trail below and waved to him. Milligan was the man who had the winter dogsled mail contract over the same route. Eielson was going to cover in three hours what Milligan usually ran in twenty days.

When the dog sledder saw the plane overhead, he knew his mail contract days were numbered. "I decided then and there," he later noted, "that Alaska was no country for dogs." Milligan switched from dogs to airplanes and, at the end of the Second World War, was an airport traffic manager for Pan Am (from Jean Potter's *The Flying North*).

In the early 1980s, boxer Hector "Macho" Camacho stopped in Juneau for a tour of the Capitol on his way to a bout in Anchorage. Sitting in a senator's office, he looked out of the back window of the Capitol and commented on the view.

"What's behind that mountain?" he asked an aide. Well, the aide replied, behind *that* particular mountain were more mountains and, about 20 miles away, Canada.

"Canada?" said the surprised Camacho. "Is that the same Canada that's behind Detroit?" (confirmed by William McConkey).

When the "three lucky Swedes," only two of whom were Swedish, made their gold strike, the resulting boomtown was named Anvil because of a large, anvil-shaped rock in the vicinity. In London, a British cartographer who was working on a map of Alaska knew there had been a strike in the Anvil area but didn't know what name had been given to the locale. To remind himself to find the name of this new boomtown, he wrote "Name?" beside the site of Anvil.

The draftsman subsequently forgot to find the name of the boomtown, and the map, with the question mark, went to the printer. The printer looked at "Name?" and read it as "Nome C," or "Cape Nome." Thus Nome was named by accident (confirmed by Albro Gregory, longtime editor of the *Nome Nugget*).

In the late 1940s and early 1950s, hibernation researchers were having difficulty in obtaining body temperatures of sleeping bears. Since body temperatures were taken with rectal thermometers, the device had to be implanted while the bears were asleep. But, as bears had a tendency to sleep with their posteriors against the ground, it was hard to get thermometers implanted. This problem was resolved, reported Walter S. Sullivan, science editor for the *New York Times,* when a hibernation specialist discovered that bears love Maraschino cherries. The researcher would find a hibernating bear, hold a bowl of cherries under the animal's nose and then draw the bowl away. The bear would rise to its feet and move toward the elusive cherry smell. As its tail came up, the thermometer was implanted. The cherries would then be removed and the bear would collapse back into slumber.

In the winter of 1913, severe storms almost obliterated the city of Nome. Towering waves sent tons of water and debris into the ocean-

Summer dogsled. (Courtesy USGS Library, Alaska, Sargent, R.H. 164.)

front community and washed some of the buildings out. The old cemetery was flooded, and many of the coffins were swept out to sea. When the storm subsided and the flood waters passed, the coffin of a well-known dance hall queen (ten years dead) was left on the sidewalk, its lid ajar. An old timer passing on the boardwalk looked into the open coffin and noted with sorrow, "Goldie, you're still the best looking gal in town" (plaque in the entry way of the Nome Nugget Inn).

———

Cliff Cernick, then the editor of the *Anchorage Daily News*, was traveling in Oregon in 1957 when he was asked by a store clerk, "What do you use for money in Alaska?"

"Ivory," Cernick replied with an evil smile on his lips.

"Really?" the clerk replied. "How do you make change?"

"We chip it," snapped Cernick (from *Anchorage, the Way It Was* and confirmed by Cliff Cernick).

———

In 1917, the libelous Juneau scandal sheet *Gleam* was no friend of Charles Sulzer, one of the candidates for the post of Territorial Delegate to the United States Congress. In its October 15th edition, the *Gleam* limelighted Sulzer's allegedly poor ideas as opposed to the superior ones by James Wickersham, the *Gleam's* choice for Delegate. A poem entitled "The Cat Came Back" read as follows:

> Pussy cat, pussy cat why do you screech,
> "I've been to Douglas to hear Sulzer's speech."
> Pussy cat, pussy cat, hat didw [sic] you do then.
> "Went out and shouted for Jim Wickersham."

Neophyte hunter Steven Levi was convinced by his more experienced partner to "bring a huge salmon net" on his first Alaskan duck hunting trip. For hours Levi struggled on the Portage Flats with a 12 gauge shotgun in one hand and a king salmon net in the other. At about one in the afternoon it finally dawned on Levi that there were no pools deep enough to need a net and there were no streams so swift they could not be waded. Only then did Levi ask his partner why he needed the net.

"Well," replied the veteran. "Whenever I shoot a duck I want you to run over and catch it before it hits the ground. The meat doesn't damage that way" (confirmed by Steven Levi and Gary Kremen).

In the early 1980s there was only one person in Alaska who was a worse public speaker than Speaker of the House Joe Hayes. That other person was Representative Al Adams.

Just after the legislative session ended, Hayes, Adams and a host of other dignitaries were invited to Barrow for the dedication of the memorial to Wiley Post and Will Rogers. Hayes, a private pilot, was interested in going but only if he did not have to speak. He was assured by the Master of Ceremonies that no speech would be needed because the Governor, Lt. Governor and at least one high ranking federal official would be there to do the honors.

As fate would have it, when Hayes arrived in Barrow he was told that he was out of luck. The Governor and the high ranking federal officials were weathered in, and the Lt. Governor was stuck somewhere in Southcentral Alaska.

Hayes was furious and started to pull his thoughts together when Al Adams pulled him aside. "I always get rat-holed into giving a speech," Adams told Hayes confidentially. "So I always have my staff type up a few remarks, just in case. Here, use my notes."

A thankful Joe Hayes made a few remarks and, as he was leaving the podium, the Master of Ceremonies said, "And I see we have another legislator in the crowd. Representative Al Adams, would you like to come forward and say a few words?" (confirmed by Al Adams).

In 1940, the race for the Territorial house seat representing Nome and Kotzebue was hot. The candidate from Nome was Frank Whaley. Opposing him was Bess Cross, wife of legendary bush pilot John Cross, who lived in Kotzebue. Cross, intent on winning, had a pamphlet printed containing scurrilous information on Whaley and she demanded that her husband fly over the bush villages in the election district and toss the pamphlets out the window so that they would flutter to the ground like descending leaves.

But John Cross, for whatever reason, didn't like the idea. So he did the absolute minimum. He flew over the remote villages and tossed out the pamphlets. But he did not untie them, so they fell as a bundle, hit the snow and buried themselves. Most of them would not be found until spring—if then.

At Kivalina one of the bundles was recovered. When bush pilot Archie Ferguson flew into town a few days later, he was approached by an old Eskimo who was puzzled by the bundle of election pamphlets. The Eskimo knew that John Cross had delivered the bundle because everyone knew the pilots by their planes. But since the Eskimo could not read, he did not know what the bundle was.

Ferguson knew instantly what had happened. Well, he told the Eskimo, this was toilet paper. Why don't you go use it on your trapline this winter? So the Eskimo did, pleased that John Cross had thought so kindly of him and delivered that bundle personally (from an interview with Fred Goodwin).

In 1982, while examining a bill in committee, a Republican representative from Anchorage noted that there was something suspicious about the content of that piece of legislation. Her comment, on tape, before a full committee, with the press present, was that there appeared to be a "Nigger in the woodpile." Other than being a blatant racist statement, it was incredibly embarrassing because one of the members of the House and the majority coalition was both black and also a Republican. There was a day or two of embarrassing silence and then, on Friday, the black representative's aides threw a party for the rest of the Capitol staff. It offered conversation and wine with "fried chicken, watermelon, black-eyed peas and fritters" (confirmed by staff).

In the gold rush town of Iditarod, it was said that a woman's popularity could be measured by the number of empty beer bottles outside her house.

On March 28, 1983, there was an odd sense of unity in the Alaska House of Representatives. Representative Bob Bettisworth's house resolution passed by a vote of 38 to zero with two absent. Democrats and Republicans, liberals and conservatives, old and young, rich and poor, Native and white, all legislators agreed. They agreed because they all had something in common. They hated Nimbus, the puke green statue of modern art that graced the walkway between the Capitol and the Court House.

"It's so ugly even the pigeons won't shit on it," more than one legislator noted.

Just before the vote, when it was pointed out that the statue was an asset of the State of Alaska and could not be destroyed, it was suggested that the statue be moved to the "Juneau-Douglas Marine Park." When someone asked where that was, an aide replied, "anywhere between here and Douglas where there's water." He paused for a moment and then added: "Very deep water." (The Gastineau Channel divides Juneau from Douglas.)

In the days of the Gold Rush, a local judge made the mistake of sequestering the jury with the evidence in a bootlegging case. After the jury had sampled the wares, they recommended that the case be dismissed because the evidence had disappeared. (This story has been attributed to many locales.)

Representative Dick Randolph, Libertarian from Fairbanks, was on the floor speaking against an amendment when he suddenly realized that he was actually in favor of the proposal he was berating. He apologized by saying that he should have been following his own advice: "Never pass up the opportunity to sit down and shut up when you don't know what the hell you are talking about."

There was a great deal of discussion in Anchorage in the mid–1980s about where to place the homeless shelter. Since the shelter would attract a wide variety of undesirables, no business was interested in having the establishment located near their premises. At last it was decided to place the shelter right next door to one of the mayor's political adversary's jewelry store.

The jeweler immediately realized the fiscal impact of having homeless characters in questionable states of sobriety lurking around his shop day and night. To express his displeasure he went to the mayor's delicatessen where he purchased $1,500 worth of gift certificates for bagels and coffee. Then he walked down Fourth Avenue, the Skid Row of Anchorage, entered bar after bar after bar and handed out the coupons to every derelict he could find. Within a day the mayor's deli was deluged with foul-smelling customers.

The mayor got the message. The site of the shelter was moved.

Since the Alaska Legislature meets in Juneau during the winter, getting in and out of the capital city is exceedingly difficult. Wind, rain, snow and fog can cause planes to alter their destinations so drastically that it is not unusual for Juneau-bound travelers to leave Anchorage and end up in Seattle and then overshoot Juneau the next day and be back in Anchorage, having traveled over 4000 miles without ever having reached their destination.

So many flights "pass over" that it is laughingly said that Juneau is Alaska's only Jewish airport.

One of Alaska's most outrageous characters is William "Wild Bill" McConkey. Best known for his expertise in running political campaigns, he was equally well-known by Alaskan humorists for his bumper sticker. Trying to come up with a bumper sticker that would upset as many people as possible with as few words as possible, his first attempt was NUKE THE UNBORN GAY WHALES. Later he developed a second version which said NUKE THE FEMINIST UNBORN GAY WHALES.

Not content with whales, he branched out. He developed two more bumper stickers. One showed a large baseball bat and, within the outline of the drawing, were the words: I SUPPORT THE PRIBILOF SLUGGERS. The other was created when Democrat Governor Steve Cowper, a Marlboro man character complete with a Stetson, stated that he was a "high plains drifter." At the next Republican gathering, McConkey had a new bumper sticker: THE HIGH PLAINS DRIFTER RIDES SIDESADDLE.

———————

As to the quality of the legendary hooch from the village of Hoochenoo, critics claimed that it "almost kills on sight" and was "certain death to a dog at one hundred yards." One wag suggested that the United States War Department buy it in quantity because it was deadlier than a Gatling gun (from Thayne I. Anderson's *Alaska Hooch*).

———————

It was a tense hearing before the Alaska Public Utilities Commission (APUC). Two garbage companies were fighting over the rights to a new subdivision. Since more customers meant more money, each utility wanted that new subdivision and, of course, rights to the homes under construction farther out of Palmer.

APUC Engineer Irwin Mitchell was called to the stand to explain how utility districts were designed. Mitchell appeared on the stand and explained that districts were designed to make sure that every utility could make a reasonable rate of return. Then he was asked how the Commission staff decided where the end of a utility district would be if there was just wilderness beyond the last house.

Mitchell thought for a moment and finally said, "Well, I guess the utility district ends where you have to start fighting the bears for the garbage."

———————

Once Kotzebue Sound froze for the winter, hunters from around the world would come north to hunt polar bear. As a practical joke, sometimes the Eskimo would drag a bag of garbage far out onto the ice. Back in town, they would sit next to a hunter and say, "There! Penguin!" and point excitedly out the window. Only after the hunter had adjusted his binoculars would the Eskimos break into laughter.

Legend has it that there is no J Street in Anchorage because there was a large Scandinavian population when the town was named. Since Scandinavians have a hard time with the letter "J," it was decided to omit the letter from the city's street map.

Bob Atwood, former publisher of the Anchorage *Times*, once received a letter from a small town in Virginia:

> I am enclosing in this envelope 25 cents in American currency to cover the cost of your sending me via Second Class transient rate mail, one copy of your Wednesday, June 4, 1958, newspaper printed in English.

Then the letter had a set of instructions as to how to remove the quarter from its cardboard backing (from *Anchorage: The Way It Was*).

The gold dredge *Bima* in Nome had difficulties with a 400-pound walrus in 1987 that kept hitching rides on its bucket line (*Alaska Magazines*, December 1987).

In the 1940s, when the English were training Chinese to be pilots, there was some difficulty in translating. When the first Chinese pilot went solo, the last bit of advice given by the trainer was, "When you land, keep your nose up."

The pilot took off and, on landing, kept his nose so high that he crashed and wrecked four planes parked on the runway. The story was retold in Alaska, and thereafter anyone who collided with a plane on the ground was known as a "Chinese Ace."

Merle "Mudhole" Smith became a "multiple ace" when the brakes on the plane he was flying, one of Art Woodley's Travelaires, failed, and the plane smashed into three other Travelaires on the runway. Thereafter, Mudhole's Travelaire was known as the "Yellow Peril" (from Lone E. Janson's *Mudhole Smith*).

Since many of the directors of Bremner Mining Company also sat on the board of directors of Cordova Air Service, it was only natural that Cordova Air Service kept the mine supplied by air. However, the landing strip at the mine was a pilot's nightmare. It was 300 feet long but barely 20 feet wide, had ditches on both sides and enough stones to build a rock wall around Seattle.

After one driving rainstorm, Cordova Air Service pilot Merle Smith arrived at the mine to drop off a load of supplies. As he was loading up to return to Cordova, he was advised to check the landing strip to make certain that he had not dislodged any rocks when he had landed. Merle said he was sure he hadn't, so that wasn't necessary.

He was in error.

As his Stearman started to take off, Smith's left wheel dropped into a mudhole that had been formed when his tailwheel had dislodged a rock on landing. The Stearman buckled and bounced nose down, the propeller boring into the ground at 1,800 revolutions a minute. Thereafter Merle Smith was known as "Mudhole" Smith (from Lone E. Janson's *Mudhole Smith*).

Once asked why he preferred cargo to passengers, Bob Reeve snapped, "Freight don't talk back!" (from Beth Day's *Glacier Pilot*).

In the mid-1930s, in the darkest days of the Great Depression, an old fisherman died in Dutch Harbor. As the body was halfway out the Aleutian Chain, it didn't make much sense to transport the corpse back to the mainland for burial. Thus the authorities had the body buried in Dutch Harbor, searched the fisherman's personal effects and contacted those relatives whose names appeared on any letters or legal documents.

In the case of this fisherman, the burial could not come too soon. He had died of "complicated internal conditions" which required that the body be interred quickly.

In the process of searching the fisherman's personal effects, the authorities discovered a will, in which the elderly man left his entire estate, some $75,000 ($1.4 million in 1990), to a niece in Seattle. The niece, who had probably never even met the fisherman, became instantly and sentimentally attached to the old man.

Not wanting such a valued member of the family to be buried in an unmarked grave in a remote community on a windswept island half-way to Asia, she decided to have his remains brought back to Washington. But she wanted the corpse to return quickly. A barge was obviously too slow, so the niece offered $2,000 cash to any pilot who could arrange transportation of the body back to Seattle.

As a result, there was a "corpse rush" to Dutch Harbor. The first pilot to arrive on the windswept island was Alex Holden of Alaska Southern Airways. When Holden arrived and discovered the body had been buried, he cabled his boss for instructions. The response was short, succinct and left no doubt as to intent: "Get the body."

Holden got a court order by wire for exhumation. As quickly as possible, the corpse was taken out of the ground, wrapped in canvas and given several heavy coats of shellac. When the shellac dried, Holden had a modern-day mummy.

While a mummy of the Egyptian empire came with its own sarcophagus, Holden was not so lucky. Only after the body had stiffened did Holden discover that the corpse would not fit inside the plane. (Even if it had, the stench would have made the journey unbearable.) After he had exhausted all other possibilities, Holden strapped the rigid corpse onto the wing of his plane and flew it to Seward, where a coffin was waiting. From there the coffin went by ferry to Seattle (from Beth Day's *Glacier Pilot*).

A stampeder in 1897, who had not been robbed by Soapy Smith, was asked how he had come through Skagway unscathed. "If you don't get drunk," he replied, "you don't get rolled."

Russian sea otter hunters were alleged to have complained that "the devil must have planted these cursed sea otters in these out-of-the-way regions. As far as we can see land up and down the coast, not a single rum-shop is to be found" (from Anderson's *Alaska Hooch*).

If you are a pilot and are planning on making air drops, make absolutely certain that you and your partner have the signals straight. If you want to know why, ask Doug Geeting of Talkeetna. One Christmas while he was supplying a number of mountain climbers on Mt. McKinley, Geeting received an order for a halibut.

Working with a cargo handler who was inexperienced, Geeting flew out for Mt. McKinley with the requested halibut and an assortment of other goods for other climbers scattered up the mountain. When he arrived at the first encampment, he turned to his cargo thrower-outer and yelled "Halibut."

She thought he said, "All of it." So she opened the fuselage door and proceeded to toss out all of the cargo. It rained supplies on the mountain climbers. The halibut hit a tent and ripped it in two. A case of beer landed between two men inside another tent and sprayed them with foam. Other supplies pockmarked the landscape giving the campsite the appearance of a bomb-testing range.

Feeling the plane unexpectedly light, Geeting turned around to see what the problem was. When he saw the cargo bay empty he asked what had happened to the cargo.

"I threw it out," his cargo handler said. "You said, 'All of it.'"

"No, I said 'Halibut!'" Then he turned his Beaver and went back to see what kind of damage the falling cargo had done. But as he approached the campsite, he saw everyone scattering. They thought he was making a return run (confirmed by Geeting).

Early Alaskan political appointees were hardly the best moral characters or, for that matter, the most competent men to be found in America. Sheldon Jackson claimed that the Territory of Alaska's first District Attorney, E.W. Haskett, was "vulgar and obscene in his conversation, low in his tastes; spending much time in saloons, a gambler and a confirmed drunkard with but little knowledge of the law."

Alaska's first American civilian governor, John Kinkead, had a large, "bulbous nose," which missionaries attributed to his drinking. It was also claimed that Kinkead had come to Alaska with a personal supply of "canned tomatoes [which tasted] like scotch whiskey and produced the same effect" (from Anderson's *Alaska Hooch*).

A bush pilot out of Homer who refused to take live animals aboard received a radio message to pick up a fare on the far side of Kachemak Bay. When he got there, he discovered that his passenger had a cat on her lap. The pilot stated that he had a strict policy of taking no live animals, pets or otherwise, but the lady insisted that she was going to go to Homer with her cat, and that was that.

Thereafter ensued a discussion which was only resolved with the lady absolutely, positively guaranteeing the pilot that this cat was plane-broken and would cause no trouble whatsoever on the short hop over to Homer.

That was not the case. At 3,000 feet, halfway across Kachemak Bay, the cat suddenly went berserk. It exploded out of the woman's lap and began running around the inside of the plane "yowling to beat the devil, too," the pilot said.

As the cat rounded the windshield for the third time, the pilot opened his door, and in the next instant, the cat was gone. "I was just enforcing my no pet rule," the pilot commented (confirmed by the pilot's son, Dave Choquette).

In the early days of the Alaska Gold Rush, "one thirtyish spinster in Nome named Susie Bluenose" entered Nellie Page's roadhouse to give a lecture on temperance.

"You blackguards, you roistering scoundrels," she yelled at the men and women dancing throughout the saloon, "you're all going to roast in Hell! Do you know that?"

Turning to Nellie Page, who was dancing with one of the customers, Susie Bluenose threatened, "Young woman, if this racket is not stopped at once I'm going to have this den of iniquity closed immediately. I'm going to report you to the United States Marshal."

The music stopped and the man with whom Nellie was dancing disengaged himself. Identifying himself as United States Marshal Lamont, the man said, "I am at your service, Madam. Would you care to dance?" (from Albro Gregory's *Tall [But True] Tales of Alaska Sourdoughs*).

As a favor, Alaska bush pilot Mike Hudson was transporting his friend's dog, Queenie. The plane went through some heavy weather, and though Hudson didn't have any trouble, the dog was quite distressed. The dog was so distressed that it was jumping around in the back. The gnarly hand of fate reached in and allowed the dog's paw to strike the door handle. The door popped open and the dog jumped out of the back seat assuming that the plane was on the ground. The dog disappeared into the clouds.

There wasn't much that Hudson could say to his buddy except "Sorry." As soon as the weather cleared, the two men went back to look for the dog's remains, but when they landed, who should come bounding out of the forest but the dog. Apparently the deep snow had cushioned the animal's fall. The animal had a few scratches and a bruise or two, but other than that it was fine.

But they did have a *hell* of a time getting the dog back into the plane to fly home. (Reported in *Alaska Flying Magazine*.)

Occasionally there are times when even the most seasoned of fliers has unforeseen difficulties. Legendary bush pilot John Cross, out of Kotzebue, once went down over the tundra when his gas line became clogged with mosquitoes. How did mosquitoes get into the gas supply? That's a good question, one that John Cross could not answer to the day he died.

One warm winter, Anchorage needed snow for the Fur Rendezvous so badly that it had to be trucked in from the Alyeska ski resort. As the vehicles were unloading their cargo of frozen white crystals, a writer commented to one of the truck drivers that hauling snow was expensive. "Hey," replied the driver enthusiastically, "there's no business like snow business."

Two days before the election, a candidate was being smeared by his opponent for not making child support payments regularly—for two children in two former marriages. The beleaguered candidate tried to explain to the press that at the time the payments were late, his clothing business had been close to bankruptcy.

"I know what it's like to be responsible for children," he said, "I'm a family man."

"You should be," snapped a wag in the audience. "You've got three of them!" (from Mark Hellenthal, political consultant in Anchorage).

While running for reelection, Senator Pat Rodey was walking door-to-door when he was greeted by a stripper wearing nothing more than a T-shirt and smile. She didn't vote, wasn't registered and credited her long career to staying away from politics. She also noted that she worked as a stripper with 20 other women who felt the same way. As Rodey was tall and handsome, the stripper didn't mind standing in her doorway. So she asked Rodey for his position on topless bars.

Rodey replied that he didn't care one way or the other, and then quickly added, "However, my opponent has been endorsed by the Moral Majority."

There was a slight pause, and then the stripper said, "Can you give me twenty-one voter registration forms?" (confirmed by Rodey).

One day in Anchorage, a defense lawyer appeared before a judge with no tie. The judge, no friend of the defense attorney, announced that he would fine any attorney in his court without a tie $100. Thinking quickly, the defense attorney took off a shoelace and wrapped it around his neck. Not to be deterred, the judge then announced he would fine any attorney in court without shoelaces $100.

Glenda Carino had fifteen minutes left on her afternoon radio show in Petersburg. It was Thanksgiving Day in the mid–1980s, and she was missing out on a turkey dinner across town. Since she had nothing to do to fill the time, she decided to call her family, on the air, in the Seattle area. It was a warm, daughter-away-from-home-calling-on-Thanksgiving call, and Glenda said how she missed being away from home.

"If you're so lonely why don't you come home?" her father asked.

"Because Alaska Airlines doesn't fly on Thanksgiving," Glenda responded.

"Oh," said her father who had never been to Alaska, "then why don't you just take TWA or PanAm?" (confirmed by Carino).

———————

A United States Coast Guard Chief on Attu was concerned that his next assignment might be remote as well. But, as he discovered, the Coast Guard assignment personnel in Washington, D.C., didn't seem particularly concerned *where* he went after he left Attu. One day he got a call from his assignment contact. "I'll be in Alaska next week," the Coast Guardsman said. "Why don't you drive down to Kodiak and we can talk about your next assignment?"

———————

Don Gunnette, an avid fish collector, had been warned by his landlord that if he caused one more problem, he would be evicted. His landlord was mercifully out of town one day when Gunnette decided to flush his South American bristle-nosed *plecostomus* catfish down the toilet. This fish was a sluggish, brown-black, armored catfish with what appeared to be a Fuller brush growing out of its snout. It had a face that looked as though it was a cross between a taxicab grill and a rhinoceros. The fish only moved when it burped and in its most active state appeared as a lodestone.

Gunnette flushed the beast down the toilet, but the fish's body jammed in the pipes. Fearful that he would be evicted, Gunnette called a plumber on his own. When the plumber arrived, the veteran of pipe-and-snake simply reached into the back of the toilet to search for the clog. The plumber had been in the business for more than twenty years and, in his words, "had seen everything."

But he had never seen a South American bristle-nosed *plecostomus*. He pulled the fish out, took one look at it and dropped it on the floor.

Gunnette, fearful of being evicted if the truth be known, pointed at the fish and said excitedly, "I'm new to Alaska. Do you get a lot of those here?" (confirmed by Gunnette).

———————

Cutting your own Christmas tree is a tradition in Anchorage. But you have to be careful where you cut. Late one winter in the 1970s, an Anchorage man was looking for the perfect tree. He had been driving for miles through Chugach State Park, and finally, as he was winding up a canyon, he spotted the perfect tree. It was about six feet tall, had branches spaced evenly and symmetrically around the trunk and—best of all—it was twenty feet from the road.

The would-be tree thief (in this case the tree was not under a power line and therefore illegal to cut) left his car running and tiptoed across the snow to the base of the tree. He started his chain saw and was about to cut the tree when he noticed thick branches sticking out of the snow beneath his feet. Looking over the lip of what he thought was a ridge he realized that he was standing on a thin shelf of snow made by snow blowers. He was actually about forty feet above the ground.

In the next instant the tree thief and his running chain saw went through the shelf and began bouncing down through the branches. He ended up hanging onto the trunk of the tree about ten feet off the ground while the chain saw ate its way into four feet of packed snow at the base of the giant spruce.

Four hours later the thief made it back to his car. It was out of gas, and he didn't have a Christmas tree.

At the Kennicott Mine near McCarthy in the 1930s, workmen claimed that it was so cold during the winter that they would "go into the [kitchen's] freezers to warm up."

In the 1850s, one of the best selling products out of Sitka, the "Paris of the Pacific," was ice for the saloons and taverns of San Francisco.

The term *Cheechako*, or tenderfoot, came about as the result of a misunderstanding. A Tlingit in Juneau, legend has it, asked a white man from where he had come. The white man replied "Chicago," and the Native, trying to pronounce the strange word, said "Cheechako." The mistake stuck.

In the late 1970s, Jim O'Meara, a seasoned bush pilot, took off from Lime Village when it was 40 below zero on the ground. "But by the time

I got to 3,000 feet," he said, "it was 30 above. There was a seventy degree difference between the ground and air temperature. On the ground, everything had shrunk because of the temperature. But when I was at 3,000 feet, the paint on my plane expanded faster than the fuselage. By the time I landed in Anchorage, I had lost all the paint off my plane. It had expanded and blown off" (from an interview with Jim O'Meara).

For many men in the armed forces, a year in Alaska meant a year of remote assignment. Stationed in isolated facilities, these men — and occasionally women — spent 365 long days maintaining Coast Guard LORAN stations or Air Force ACWS sites. But no matter how a remote assignment is presented, it was still 365 days removed from civilization.

Gary Hartzell from Riverside, California, was 19 when he was assigned to United States Coast Guard Station Attu, located on the last island of the Aleutians. Like most of the other men, what he missed most was easy to state: "Women. After I leave here there are a lot of things I'm never going to take for granted again. Like the mail coming every day or television stations."

Being one of the younger men on station, Hartzell took a lot of kidding at first. One winter day his roommate woke him up and told him he had overslept. Since it was dark outside almost 24 hours a day, there was no way to tell what time it was by the amount of daylight. Believing him, Hartzell dressed frantically and dashed down the hallways of the station looking for his Chief. It took him ten minutes to realize that it was three in the morning. Later he was almost fooled into believing that a plane was coming in. He thought a C-GULL was something like a C-130.

Another time, after he had been at the base for only a few weeks, he was told the Liberty Barge was coming in to take some men over to Shemya (the closest island to Attu, it is an Air Force Base with women and hard liquor). Hartzell and three other men went out with suitcases to wait for the barge. One at a time, the others drifted back to the base on some excuse or another and left Hartzell waiting for a barge that would never come because it didn't exist (from an interview with Hartzell).

Jim West of Nome, owner of one of the best-known saloons in Alaska, the BOT (Board of Trade) in Nome, is also famous as one of the richest men in Alaska. To impress tourists, he will often pull a wad of cash out of his pocket and show them several thousand dollars in bills folded over and secured with a single rubber band. His secret for success is to "get a rubber band and fill it up" (told to author).

Since commercial space is so limited in Juneau, there is always a mad scramble for legislative offices. As a result, there is an old joke that veteran legislators play on newcomers. Whenever a new legislator complains about his office space, the old timer says, "Well, there's a lot of space down at the submarine pens."

"Really," the newcomer will say, taking the bait hook, line and sinker.

"Yes," will be the response. "But only at low tide."

Before the days of the oil boom, many Alaskan communities had a hard time coming up with critical service equipment, like fire vehicles. In the 1960s, the city of Haines needed an emergency vehicle but did not have the cash in the city treasury to pay for it. Through a federal program, there was a way that the city could buy a vehicle by putting up only 5 percent of the cost.

But 5 percent was still a lot of money. So the city sponsored bake sales, rallies and other fund raisers to pay for its portion. Finally, after months of hard work, the money was raised, and the federal government approved the delivery of the service vehicle.

On the day the station wagon was to arrive in Haines, the entire city was on the dock. The ferry made a sweeping turn and there, framed by the open door, was the piece of equipment they had been working so hard to buy.

Unfortunately the brake on the car had not been set, and, in full view of the townspeople of Haines, the vehicle rolled off the ferry and plopped into 800 feet of water less than 30 feet from the dock (confirmed by DOT/PF).

There is an uncorroborated story that during the Egan Administration the State of Alaska contracted to have a fire station built in Ketch-

ikan. There was some difficulty with the architectural design, and when
the Governor went to christen the structure he discovered the workmen
had constructed a building that had no doors or windows.

––––––––––

Fairbanks was founded by accident. In 1901, suffering a string of bad
luck, Captain E.T. Barnette faced an unfortunate twist of fate. He was
in a wrangle with the stern-wheeler captain of a vessel that was having
a problem with the low water of the Tanana River. Barnette had convinced the captain that it would be possible to navigate the 400 miles up
the Tanana, but now the captain learned otherwise. In a rage, the skipper
offloaded Barnette's 135 tons of cargo.

Barnette watched helplessly as his supplies were stacked on the
riverbank in a pile that "resembled a general store that had gone through
an earthquake." Just then, two prospectors, Felix Pedro and Tom
Gilmore, broke through the underbrush. They had spotted the smoke
from the sternwheeler and hoped that the ship had food to sell. They had
just made a staggering gold discovery and wanted to save themselves the
300-mile walk to Circle. Thus Fairbanks was founded (from Terrence
Cole's *E.T. Barnette*).

––––––––––

The first successful ascent of Mt. McKinley was in the spring of 1910
by four miners, all "older than forty." The men – Charlie McGonagle,
Tom Lloyd, Peter Anderson, and Billy Taylor – planted a flag pole on the
19,470 foot level of the peak. Decades later it was discovered that they
had not climbed to the highest point, which is officially listed as 20,320
feet.

––––––––––

Anchorage poet Steven Levi suspected that the University of
Alaska–Fairbanks' literary journal *Permafrost* was rejecting his poetry
because of his name, not the quality of his submissions. Levi coedited a
literary journal in Anchorage, *Harpoon*, which was the only regularly

published, private, literary journal in the state and therefore in direct competition to *Permafrost.*

To test his suspicion he sent two moose-and-goose-in-the-spruce poems to *Permafrost* under the name Stanley Tarn. But he made the contents so absurd that if a reader was not careful, he or she would like the "theme" of the poem but miss the message. The message in one of the poems was an Eskimo riding an ice cake in the middle of winter on a twelve-foot wave from the Norton Sound to Bethel. Both poems were accepted and published in Volume 4, Number 3, the "All Alaska Issue," in 1981.

Here, for the first time under his real name, is the absurding poem:

BEACHES

Agorapak was sitting on an icecake at the edge
of the spit. Norton Sound was frozen solid,
shore to shore, and just a hint of the sun, sunset red,
dashed along the horizon. The glow of his cigarette
matched the sky. "Eh, Stan." The embers of his cigarette
glowed. "Dinn-tyah know that somewheres got waves here? Big ones.
Ride ten, twelve feet. Think we get wave here?" His arm
swept the horizon as the cigarette glowed. "If do be damn
sure I ride this damn thing well!" he said as he slapped
the icecake affectionately. "Ride all the way Bethel with no
damn plane."

Immediately after the oil spill in Prince William Sound, there was a joke going around that the State of Alaska had agreed to pay Exxon $250 million for the paving of the Alaska Marine Highway between Valdez and Whittier.

When the price of oil went down and the economy followed close on its heels, some Alaskans were driving around with bumper stickers that read, "DEAR GOD, JUST GIVE ME ONE MORE OIL BOOM AND I PROMISE NOT TO PISS IT AWAY LIKE I DID THE LAST ONE."

An Alaska Railroad "rubberneck car." (Courtesy Alaska State Library, C.L. Andrews Collection, PCA 45-564.)

In the early days of the Alaska Railroad, officials ordered the construction of a rail car with seats built in tiers to satisfy the demands of sightseers. These were known affectionately as "rubberneck cars."

———————

For years, the Alaska Railroad engines were known as "moose goosers."

———————

In the early days of the Alaska Railroad, an engineer came across a moose sleeping in the center of the railroad tracks. The courageous man slipped up on the moose and inserted a burning flair under the moose's rump. The moose moved off the tracks quickly.

———————

In some of the two-story brothels, the working women would put the money they earned in a chute that took it down to the bar where their pimp could count it.

———————

In the 1940s, a woman in Hoonah was subpoenaed to come to the trial of her husband. A United States marshal was sent to Hoonah on the ferry to deliver the legal document and escort the woman back to the courtroom. When the wife finally made her appearance before the bar, the judge wanted the reason for her presence noted on record.

"Were you subpoenaed?" he asked the woman.

Not knowing what she was being asked, the woman did not reply.

"Did the marshal subpoena you?" the judge asked again.

"Oh yes," replied the woman, sure she now understood the question. "Once in Hoonah and twice on the boat."

According to the *National Geographic*, May 29, 1891, a group of explorers spotted a *fata morgana*—and not just once, but evening after evening after evening. In their words,

> [W]e would be startled by the site of a vast city with battlements, towers, minarets and domes of fantastic architecture, rising where we knew that only the berg-covered waters extended. The appearance of these phantom cities was a common occurrence during the twilight hours. Although we knew at once that the ghostly spires were but a trick of the mirage, yet their ever-changing shapes and remarkable mimicry of human inhabitants were so striking that they never lost their novelty; and they were never the same on two successive evenings.

According to Gerry Bruder in *Alaska Flying Magazine*, a tourist asked a bush pilot about all the white fish that she saw jumping in the water. Try as he could, the pilot could not see the fish about which she was talking. Finally he came to the realization that she was referring to whitecaps.

In 1971, cabin dweller Ron Rau wanted to bring electricity into his abode. After hooking up the 220 wire to the fusebox on the outside of the cabin, he began looking for a crack in the eight inch log wall through which he could run the wire. But he was out of luck; the cracks were too well filled. Cursing the fact that he did not have a drill, he developed a unique solution. Loading up a 30.06 he shot the "roundest, nicest, easiest wire outlet in the history of non-union jobs."

In the early years of this century, a pair of deputy marshals were called to a lonely cabin on the Chena River where two old prospectors were known to live. When they arrived, smoke was curling from the chimney, indicating that someone had been there recently, and, ominously, there was a human-size mound of fresh earth with a cross and an epitaph written on a piece of paper: "He robbed my camp, so I shot him."

Sure that one of the partners had killed the other, the deputies began digging. Six feet down they found a coffin about the size of a shoebox. Inside was a jaybird, known throughout the Territory as a "camp robber." Only after the sweating deputies finished cursing did the two old-timers come out of the forest laughing (from Gregory's *Tall [But True] Tales of Alaska Sourdoughs*).

During the First World War, Governor J.F.A. Strong established councils of defense across the Territory to keep track of suspicious characters, among other war-related duties. When the Reverend Paul P. Kern of the Church of the Holy Name in Ketchikan was informed that his name appeared on a list of "Anti-Americans," he was not pleased. "A man in my position will not stand for any base underhand[ed] work, nor allow his good name or character to be aspersed by suspicious insinuations or unproven charges," he wrote to the Ketchikan Council. "I am amazed that such an action could be taken by a member or members of the council. To my mind it appears as the insane act of a diseased brain, inspired by ill-advice, over-zealous, ignorant or pinheaded bigotry." He sent a copy to the Governor, the only reason that his correspondence survives to this day.

On June 13, 1992, fishing guide Fred Hall got the surprise of his career. While rowing three clients to a catch-and-release hole on the Kenai River near Crooked Creek, a 38-pound king salmon jumped out of the water and into his boat. The salmon was bleeding, so Hall kept it, with the approval of Fish and Game officers. "I'm fairly amazed," noted Hall at the time. "But if you stay out there long enough, these things happen."

Territorial Attorney General George Grigsby—and later Territorial Delegate to the United States Congress—became tired of the vicious verbal attacks he was underoing from Mrs. Hatcher, the Alaska representative of the W.C.T.U. In a speech in Ketchikan in July of 1918, he referred to Mrs. Hatcher as "a fine old lady with a 60 horsepower tongue and a mule power brain." The *Ruby Record-Citizen*, July 6, 1918, reported that some spectators were "inclined to believe Mr. Grigsby exaggerated the brain power bit."

9
HAROLD "THRILL 'EM, CHILL 'EM, SPILL 'EM" GILLAM

In the heyday of the Alaska bush pilots, there were three descriptions of weather conditions. First there was "Pan American weather," when the sky was clear and visibility unlimited.

Then there was "flying weather" which ranged from good to poor, depending on who was doing the talking.

Finally, there was Gillam weather, conditions that were so *bad* that only Harold "Thrill 'em, Chill 'em, Spill 'em" Gillam would fly.

Whenever there was Gillam weather, bush pilots would sit out the bad spell, primarily because it was too dangerous to fly and, secondarily, because, in their words, "God's plenty busy taking care of Harold."

From the gravel strip runways of the most remote communities in Alaska to the pavement of Merrill Field in Anchorage and Weeks Fields in Fairbanks, there is an old saying that bush pilots understand well. "There are old pilots," the adage goes, "and there are bold pilots. But there are no old, bold pilots."

There was something dramatic, something that captured the attention of the world, about an Alaskan bush pilot. Bush pilots were giants in the world of aviation, the stuff from which legends are made. These were the men, and more than a few women, who flew by the seat of their pants, in open cockpits when the temperature was well below zero, over the roughest terrain in North America, in some of the worst weather on the planet. Season after season, year after year, these pilots loaded their planes, climbed into the cockpit and headed out over the Alaskan bush, that part of the Last Frontier that even today is not connected by road to the Lower 48. Whether it was groceries to remote villages, fur to a rendezvous in Anchorage or the injured to a hospital in Juneau, these pilots were, quite literally, the lifeline of Alaska.

One of the most apparently careless fliers in the early days of Alaskan aviation was Harold "Thrill 'em, Chill 'em, Spill 'em" Gillam. Gillam would fly in any weather. *Any* weather. He had the uncanny ability—not to mention nerve—to fly in the worst conditions that existed. When other Alaskan pilots were grounded because of bad weather, Gillam was in the air.

"Everybody loved Harold," the saying went around Cordova, "except maybe a few husbands." Gillam looked the part of the swashbuckler of the sky. Well-proportioned and blessed with devastatingly good looks, he was also the hero of the younger set. A third grade Native in Cordova, assigned to write a poem about his favorite person, penned five lines that stuck to Gillam like fog to the Thompson Pass:

> He thrill 'em
> Chill 'em
> Spill 'em
> But no kill 'em
> Gillam.

The son of an automobile salesman in Chadron, Nebraska, Gillam ran away from home at 16 and joined the Navy. He mustered out in 1923 and worked in Seattle for a while as a painter. Then, on a construction job, he came north to Fairbanks. When the project was finished, Gillam stayed on and took flying lessons.

Oddly, considering his career, Gillam was the only survivor of Alaska's first fatal air crash. He was aboard a Swallow as a flying student when the plane he was in suddenly spun out of control and crashed. The instructor was killed instantly. Gillam, with his wounds stitched, was out flying the next day, and it wasn't long before he was practicing pulling out of spins—alone.

Gillam entered aviation in a money-making capacity in 1931 in the Copper Mining district inland from Cordova. From a pilot's point of view, the area was cursed. It was overshadowed by a steep mountain that was often blanketed by storm clouds from the Pacific. Turbulent air was more than common, it was routine. Fog was ever-present, and winds were strong and inconsistent. Worse yet, the landing strips were short and, quite literally, hacked out of the side of a mountain or on a plateau. "If you undershot," another bush pilot, Oscar Winchell, recalled with trepidation, "you ran into a bluff—when you took off you hadn't a foot to spare."

It was here that Gillam first made his name. He did not make it, however, without a few mishaps. In his first six months of operation, Gillam had six crack-ups. No one was seriously injured, but he lost an estimated $30,000, which did not put him in good stead with his financial backers.

Harold "Thrill 'em, Chill 'em, Spill 'em" Gillam. (Courtesy Robert C. Reeve Collection, Anchorage.)

But Gillam proved early that he was a pilot with a future. He rapidly acquired a unique reputation. It appeared he could see in the dark and through clouds. On one particularly miserable night, "Honest John" McCreary fell into a cellar and onto a nail. Since there was fear that McCreary would die without a doctor, Gillam flew the man 125 miles through a driving snowstorm — at night — to Kennicott. There the doctor sadly predicted that McCreary would probably not last the night. Gillam went up again, this time flying to Cordova to bring back McCreary's son. McCreary did not die, and Gillam's reputation as a seasoned pilot who had the eyes of a cat was enhanced.

After three years in Cordova, Gillam headed north to Fairbanks. With the money that he had saved in Cordova, Gillam bought a Pilgrim and began flying the Alaska Interior.

Here his reputation grew by leaps and bounds. Unlike other pilots, he would sleep during the day and fly at night — in any weather. He would fly through pea soup fog without batting an eye. Cloud cover and darkness didn't bother him. He would get up, dress and fly.

One incident exemplifies his unique ability. On a singularly miserable night, a group of veteran bush pilots were grounded in McGrath. The storm was so fierce that, as one of the flyers stated, "I wouldn't have whipped a cat out there that night." Yet Gillam flew. The grounded bush pilots were sitting around the fireplace when they heard a plane come in. Gillam entered, said "Hello" to his friends, refueled his plane and took off. Three days later, those men were still in McGrath — and Gillam was back in Fairbanks, safe and sound.

In 1938, Gillam was awarded the mail contract between Fairbanks and twenty bush communities. Unlike Pan American, who had held the contract before, Gillam delivered his mail on time, month after month, with a perfect safety record. Gillam's record of delivery, according to the United States Postal Service at that time, was the best in the United States or any of its territories.

While Alaskan bush pilots found Gillam's flying precision hard to believe, pilots from the Lower 48 did not believe the stories they had heard at all. No one had eyes like that — or good luck that often, for that matter. Hearing of Gillam's exploits, a pilot from United Airlines, Danneld Cathcart, wanted to see for himself. Bracing himself, he rode with Gillam from Fairbanks to Barrow.

Even under the best of conditions this was a treacherous route — the one on which Will Rogers and Wiley Post had been killed in 1935. It was a six-and-a-half hour trip, and Gillam's plane could only carry enough fuel for seven hours. The two men boarded the Pilgrim, and Gillam went up, spiraling his way through several thousand feet of cover. He then proceeded to fly for six-and-a-half-hours over an unbroken sea of clouds. Suddenly Gillam nosed the plane down. Cathcart, undoubtedly sure that his last moments on earth were at hand, later recalled that once into the soup he saw nothing but fog. In fact, the first objects he did see were antenna poles flashing by as Gillam landed in the Barrow lagoon.

Although every pilot in Alaska felt that he "hadn't a nerve in his body," it appears today that Gillam was not just flying by the seat of his pants. In a day when most of the pilots steered by compass alone, Gillam was a technology buff. He established air-ground radio stations in those areas where he flew frequently and had old-timers monitor them when he was in the area. He installed a direction-finder, directional gyro, altimeter and an artificial horizon in the plane, and studied weather and weather patterns assiduously.

But Gillam's good luck was not to last. The Civil Aeronautics Board, forerunner of the Federal Aviation Administration, was not thrilled with his antics and had filed charges against him numerous times for his "bizarre approaches" to landing strips. Before any action could be taken, Gillam took a flying job with Morrison-Knudson. Flying passengers and cargo all over the Territory of Alaska, Gillam was putting in 125-hour work months, far in excess of the 100 maximum. On January 5, 1943, Gillam picked up five passengers in Seattle. A storm was headed in, and after "considerable argument" Gillam was given permission to head north.

Four hours later Gillam entered dense fog in Southeast Alaska and proceeded to grope his way north. What he did not know was that the maps he had been given were obsolete. He became confused and began to circle at 6,000 feet trying to orient himself as his plane began to ice up.

Then things got worse. An engine went out and shortly thereafter the plane was hit with a powerful down draft that caused it to plunge 4,000 feet before Gillam could recover control of the craft. The next thing the passengers saw was mountainside and trees whizzing by the plane's window. Gillam steered for a break in the clouds but he was too low. His wing clipped a tree top and the plane came down very hard.

Since Gillam had not bothered to use the radio to report his position, no one knew exactly where the plane had gone down. Only later was it discovered that they were just sixteen minutes by air from Ketchikan, almost home free. It took more than a month to find the survivors. One of the passengers had been killed in the crash, and the others suffered horribly during that month in the wilderness, but they survived.

But Gillam was not with the survivors. After the plane crashed, Gillam, with just a gash on his head, had headed out to look for help. He had never returned. When his body was finally discovered it was determined that he had tried to cross an ice-covered creek. The ice had not been thick enough to support his weight, and he had broken through the crust and tumbled into the ice water. Apparently he had taken his clothes off to dry them and, in failing to start a fire, had frozen to death.

Thus ended the saga of one of Alaska's most enigmatic fliers. But even today, among the old timers, Gillam weather is still weather that is so bad only Harold "Thrill 'em, Chill 'em, Spill 'em" Gillam would fly.

Note: The bulk of the information in this chapter came from Jean Potter's classic work, The Flying North. Some of the tidbits come from Bucky Dawson of Ketchikan who is writing a book on Gillam.

10
THE ALASCATTALO
DAY PARADE

With the publication of Warren Sitka's *Sourdough Journalist* in 1981, Alaska and the world were reintroduced to one of the world's most unusual mammals, the alascattalo. A legendary animal, the alascattalo is a genetic cross between a moose and walrus, and serves as the symbol of Alaska's unique sense of humor.

It didn't take long for the Alaskan public to express its appreciation for the alascattalo. That winter, the first Alascattalo Day Parade was held in downtown Anchorage. A decade later, the parade is still being held, though the crowds have gotten a bit larger. Though the actual date of the parade varies from year to year, officially it occurs each year on the first Sunday after the third Saturday in November. But the parade route has not changed. Each year the event is held in the alleyway between 4th and 5th and D and E streets in Anchorage. No one is invited; participants simply show up, some in costume, others with floats and none willing to give their real name to the gathered news media.

Outlandish is the best way to describe the costumes and floats that appear in the alleyway each year. One year the first prize went to a frog float. The float in this case was an actual fishing decoy in the form of a plastic frog that had been lathered with ketchup for authenticity. The proud owner won a round-trip ticket to Honolulu. This particular Honolulu, it should be noted, was Honolulu, *Alaska*, a small community on the route of the Alaska Railroad, not the Honolulu of palm trees and hula dancers. Other floats over the years included three people with signs on their backs which read "Frozen" and "Salmon" and "Run." They walked down the alleyway with fishing poles dragging frozen salmon behind them. There was once a root beer cannister for a "Root Beer Float," and a "gar-barge" which was described as a frozen chunk of Fish Creek—complete with cigarette butts, coffee grounds and orange skins.

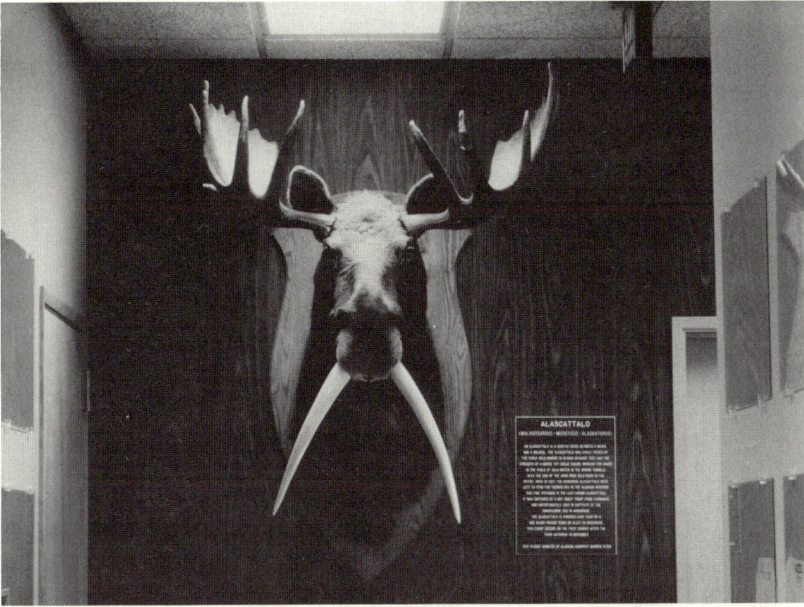

Alascattalo in the hall of the now-defunct Alaska Wildlife Museum in Anchorage. (Author's collection.)

Another year, a participant dragged a fishing line weighted with twenty nuts, because you had to be "nuts" to be in the parade like this one.

Like many other local celebrations, a queen is chosen each year. Being a bit behind the times, the Alascattalo Day Parade crowns the previous year's Queen, who was actually chosen in the current year but was, in reality, the previous year's monarch. Chosen by secret ballot "because no one can be convinced to run for the honor," the only requirement is that the queen know nothing about the parade. "That's because," Warren Sitka commented, "if she knew anything about the parade, she probably wouldn't want to be associated with it."

One of the great moments in the history of the Alascattalo Day Parade came in 1988, when the Alaska Wildlife Museum placed a life-size head of the beast in the entry way to the natural wildlife section. Complete with twin tusks and a plaque authored by Warren Sitka himself, the display garnered more than its fair share of astonished gazes — particularly from tourists who were hard pressed to believe in the existence of the legendary animal. It also attracted the attention of all the television stations in Anchorage, which duly reported its existence to an audience of dubious Alaskans. That the Alaska Wildlife Museum went

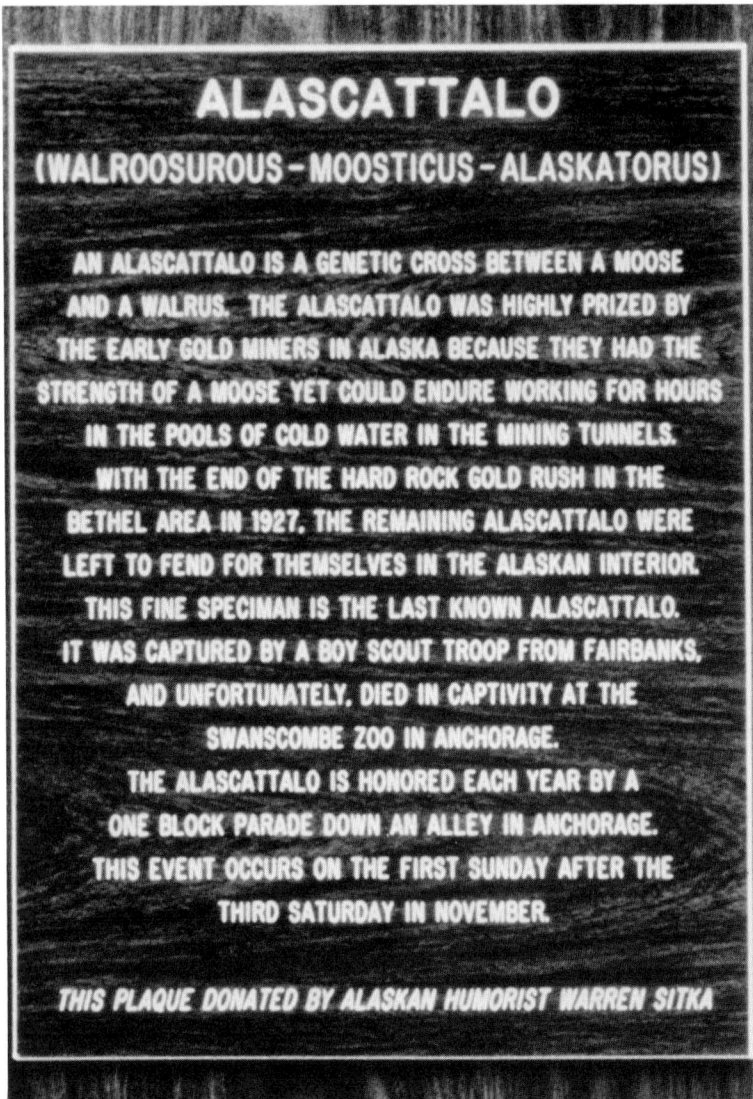

ALASCATTALO

(WALROOSUROUS-MOOSTICUS-ALASKATORUS)

AN ALASCATTALO IS A GENETIC CROSS BETWEEN A MOOSE AND A WALRUS. THE ALASCATTALO WAS HIGHLY PRIZED BY THE EARLY GOLD MINERS IN ALASKA BECAUSE THEY HAD THE STRENGTH OF A MOOSE YET COULD ENDURE WORKING FOR HOURS IN THE POOLS OF COLD WATER IN THE MINING TUNNELS. WITH THE END OF THE HARD ROCK GOLD RUSH IN THE BETHEL AREA IN 1927, THE REMAINING ALASCATTALO WERE LEFT TO FEND FOR THEMSELVES IN THE ALASKAN INTERIOR. THIS FINE SPECIMAN IS THE LAST KNOWN ALASCATTALO. IT WAS CAPTURED BY A BOY SCOUT TROOP FROM FAIRBANKS, AND UNFORTUNATELY, DIED IN CAPTIVITY AT THE SWANSCOMBE ZOO IN ANCHORAGE. THE ALASCATTALO IS HONORED EACH YEAR BY A ONE BLOCK PARADE DOWN AN ALLEY IN ANCHORAGE. THIS EVENT OCCURS ON THE FIRST SUNDAY AFTER THE THIRD SATURDAY IN NOVEMBER.

THIS PLAQUE DONATED BY ALASKAN HUMORIST WARREN SITKA

Plaque of the Alascattalo donated by Warren Sitka. (Author's collection.)

out of business shortly after displaying the alascattalo bust, parade officials have been quick to emphatically state, had nothing whatsoever to do with the Alascattalo Day Parade, the alascattalo or critics of either the parade or the existence of the alascattalo.

Turnout has varied from year to year. At the first parade, the attendance was scant: four people. But, according to parade organizers who refuse to be identified, "attendance has been doubling each year—almost."

One aspect of the parade that is consistent, however, is the starting time. Each year the parade begins precisely at 12:03, three minutes after the noon hour, and usually ends before news people from the local television stations have time to focus their cameras. In fact, the parade is so short that it is often run twice, up the alley and back again.

Zany though it may be, the alascattalo has made a celestial impact. In November of 1991, an asteroid was named after the alascattalo. The asteroid, discovered in 1926 by K. Reinmuth at Heidelberg, was chosen by the Minor Planets Names Commission courtesy of the Smithsonian Institution's Astrophysical Observatory.

Alascattalo, the Most Endangered of Species*

Perhaps one of the most outrageous slaughters in the annals of American history is currently underway and no one seems to care. Currently (February, 1980), all along the Kuskokwim River, there is a ruthless campaign underway to eradicate a species which has taken more than a century to produce. Game biologists contend that if this slaughter is not halted immediately, the alascattalo will be extirpated from Alaska forever.

For those newcomers to Alaska, an alascattalo is a genetic cross between a moose and a walrus. This species was first introduced during the Gold Rush era. The animal was short and stocky and proved to be an excellent beast of burden for both packing and mining. Its stocky legs allowed it to wriggle through the narrower confines of gold and copper mines, and its thick fur kept it warm, even while standing in saltwater pools deep in the earth.

Additionally, the alascattalo proved to be an excellent foodstuff. It combined the delicate flavor of moose with the nutritious base of walrus. And in the genetic recombination, the breeders were able to eliminate the stringiness which characterizes both walrus and moose steaks. This new meat was so popular during the Gold Rush that alascattalo ranches sprang up all along the Kuskokwim River in Interior Alaska.

However, over the years it was discovered that what the genetic breeding produced in meat was lost in the alascattalo's weak ability to

*This article from Warren Sitka's Sourdough Journalist appeared in New England Gentlemen's Magazine, Feb. 23, 1980, and is reprinted by permission.

The Alascattalo was allowed to stock up on Moosecatel, "Alaskan anti-freeze", until his compadre broke the "No Beavers on the Bar" rule.

Alascattalo postcard. (Courtesy Friends of the Alascattalo, Box 110497, Anchorage, Alaska 99511.)

mate and produce offspring. Although they were not sterile, the alascattalo were not known to produce more than one offspring every two or three years.

As the gold began to play out along the Kuskokwim and its numerous tributaries, the miners began returning home. With the subsequent drop in population, there was a noticeable decrease in the need for alascattalo steaks. This, in turn, caused the herd to dwindle. By the early 1920s the number of herds had dwindled to the point that it became a matter of desperation to replenish the stock or lose it forever. At one time it was estimated that there were as few as 100 alascattalo anywhere along the Kuskokwim River.

Fortunately, the federal government stepped into the picture and aided financially when no one else could. Because of the advanced state of the art of veterinary medicine by that date, it was possible to beef up the herds as well as provide the surviving stock with an immunity to the mosquito and no-see-ums which inhabited the same areas. (One of the negative aspects of cross breeding was the alascattalo did not have a thick hide like the walrus nor a dense blanket of hair follicles like the moose.

The Alascattalo took great risks to retain his title as "King of the Forest"
by drawing to an inside straight.

Alascattalo postcard. (Courtesy Friends of the Alascattalo.)

This made them vulnerable to the attack of insects and other parasites.)
With the advent of more selective breeding stock, better graze and
medicine, local ranchers were able to perfect an alascattalo which could
breed two or three offspring every year.

By 1979, there were once again substantial herds of alascattalo from
as far north as McGrath to the Kuskokwim Delta. Smaller herds on the
Yukon were clustered around the mouth of the river near Emmonak and
St. Marys. (The Yukon is a much swifter river than the Kuskokwim and
the alascattalo have a difficult time fighting the current. As a result they
stayed near the mouth of the river where it widens to meet the sea.)

By 1979, another problem arose along the Kuskokwim. Although
alascattalo can walk well, they prefer to stay in the water. Their favorite
foods are the varieties of plants that grow in and around the water,
primarily where there is slowly moving water. (By comparison, the
alascattalo on the Yukon live exclusively on krill, a seafood which is plentiful in the ocean estuaries of the Yukon Delta. Though this puts the
alascattalo in direct competition with the bowhead whale, which survives
on the same diet, the alascattalo population has not yet forced the
bowhead to find another feeding ground.) These plants, however, are the

The declining Alaskan economy had forced the Alascattalo to take a job
for which he was only partially qualified.

Alascattalo postcard. (Courtesy Friends of the Alascattalo.)

only mechanism with which to return oxygen to the waters of the
Kuskokwim. Since Alaska has such lengthy winters, very little time is
available for a growing season. And it has been claimed that as rapidly as
the plants grow to maturity and regenerate the oxygen loss suffered over
the long winter, the plants are eaten by the alascattalo.

At first the fishermen along the Kuskokwim felt that the beasts were
but a minor disturbance. Peacefully browsing, the alascattalo were no
threat to the fish or the fishermen. In fact, in some cases the alascattalo
had to be beaten with paddles to get them to move out of the way of
longboats. The alascattalo are entirely vegetarian and do not compete
with the fishermen for crab, cod or eel. But, as the alascattalo population
increased, the crab and cod takes dwindled, and a very serious problem
ensued. The fishermen blamed the declining catch on the large alascattalo herds. The ranchers blamed the dwindling catch on overfishing and
overcrabbing by the fishermen.

By May of 1979, the situation had reached a critical point. Pitched
battles between ranchers and fisherman were becoming everyday occur-
rences. RECON patrols of fishermen, armed with baseball bats and shot-
guns, were reported moving up the riverbank of the Kuskokwim taking

potshots at all alascattalo that showed their heads above the floating vegetation in the sloughs and eddys. Federal agencies reported at least two massive alascattalo hunts—both illegal—where the spoils of battle clogged some of the backwaters of the Kuskokwim.

At first the ranchers had chased the fishermen out of the estuaries where the alascattalo ate and bathed. But soon there were just too many armed fishermen. Alascattalo herd sizes dwindled, and ranchers faced the possibility of seeing the herds disappear and themselves in bankruptcy.

Then, in a move reminiscent of the Wild and Wooly West, the alascattalo ranchers took a desperate gamble. Rather than face financial extinction, the ranchers decided to start a long drive, moving the alascattalo north to the glacier-fed waters of Lake Minchumina. The alascattalo would be safe there until freeze-up, when the fishermen would be forced to retreat down the river. The ranchers could then return to the banks of the Kuskokwim that winter and allow the alascattalo to breed in their home waters until the next spring. Then, it would be another long drive back to Lake Minchumina. Though this would not stop the problem of marauding fishermen, it would save the herds from extirpation.

As if these problems were not enough, Alaska is expecting an early spring this year. Though the traditional date for the river to break up is late May or early June, this year break-up is expected in mid–May. That means that fishermen in cod scuttles and crab scrounges will be playing the waters of the Kuskokwim as early as the first week in June.

The few fishermen who have been drydocked along the river for the winter have already started in the slaughter. In early February, two Bureau of Timber Reclamation specialists reported seeing piles of alascattalo carcasses on the ice outside of a fishing camp. (Once covered with snow these piles would normally lie undetected all winter long. When spring came, the break-up would carry the carcasses all the way to the ocean, thus hiding the evidence.) When game biologists were called to investigate, they reported finding as many as 250 alascattalo bodies. One fisherman was reported as saying, "This is nothing! Just wait 'till June!"

Aerial reconnaissance was revealed troops of fishermen on snowshoes, trudging in the direction of alascattalo sanctuaries. How many bodies have been disposed of under the ice is unknown. But at least 20 locations of blood on the ice have been located. In one place an alascattalo flipper, dipped in blood, had been used to spell "June" on the ice.

Beginning on March 21, the first day of spring, the days will be longer than the nights. And with each extra minute of light, the ice will melt faster and faster. By mid–May the ice will tear itself free of its mooring

It was love at first sight, but she lacked the rack for which the Alascattalo hungered.

Alascattalo postcard. (Courtesy Friends of the Alascattalo.)

on the banks of the Kuskokwim and will begin gnawing its way, en masse, to the sea. By June 1, the crab scrounges will be on their way north. And that would very well mean the end of the alascattalo.

If something is not done quickly, the alascattalo will be gone forever. Any ideas should be placed in writing and immediately sent to SAVE THE ALASCATTALO, Parsnackle Press, 8512 East 4th, Anchorage, Alaska 99504. If we don't act now, there will be no reason to act later.

Update: Although this editorial was published in February 1980, the plight of the alascattalo remains unaltered. With the change of presidents and the new federal policy under Secretary Watt, there has been a substantial change in the policy of commercial enterprises in national monuments. For the moment this has alleviated the problem of the alascattalo's survival. But the worst is not over. Even with the alascattalo moving north for the summer months, the fishermen are becoming bolder and bolder in their attempts to eradicate the animals. Now floatplanes and hovercraft are being used to exterminate these docile beasts. Without a nationwide campaign to save the alascattalo, this slice of the heritage of Alaska may very well go the way of the carrier pigeon and the dodo.

The True Story of the Most Endangered Species: The Alascattalo

Perhaps the least known, most endangered species in the United States is the alascattalo, *Walroosurous Moosticus alaskatorus*. Originally bred by the early gold miners in Alaska, circa 1900, the alascattalo is the genetic cross between moose and walrus. Highly prized as a mining industry animal, the alascattalo resolved two of the most difficult circumstances of the Alaskan mining industry.

Alaskan mining, unlike that done in the Lower 48, depended on tunnels that slanted down from the surface. In other parts of the United States, miners entered their network of tunnels through elevators and shafts that connected all levels of the mine with each other. In Alaska, a shaft was not possible for a variety of reasons. First, the composition of the soil throughout most of the northland was muskeg, what in the Lower 48 would be called bog or swamp. A mixture of soil, decaying matter, sand and water, this ground had the consistency of a wet sponge. Thus a shaft dropped through bog would have weak walls which could collapse, thus sealing off the mine.

There was another reason a shaft was not feasible in Alaska. Beneath the muskeg are vast fields of permafrost. Permafrost is layer of soil, often thousands of feet thick, which remains permanently frozen. The last remnant of the last ice age, the permafrost is nature's lock on her mineral wealth. Dropping a mine shaft into permafrost was dangerous because once the permafrost layer has been exposed, it would start to melt. Once a shaft was drilled, water from the swamp portion of the shaft would immediately start to trickle down the walls, melting the permafrost as it went. This melting resulted in weak shaft walls and a growing pool of frigid water at the foot of the shaft. If the water was not pumped out regularly, it would freeze. If left for too long a period of time, the shaft would fill and freeze solid.

Because of the muskeg and permafrost layers, Alaskan miners were forced to construct mining tunnels with an eye to entering the permafrost level as quickly as possible and at an angle, so any water drips run down the floor and keep the walls free from any drips. One method was to drill a tunnel in a canyon that had a northern side, that side which is always in the shade. In areas where a river was nearby, miners would drill from the riverbank and allow the natural cooling currents of the river air to cool the permafrost layer at the entrance to the tunnel.

No matter how careful the miners were, however, there was always permafrost melt. The water would seep out of the tunnel walls and collect in low spots on the tunnel floor. If it could not be pumped out fast enough, some of the water would refreeze, making pulling of the orecarts difficult. As more and more water collected, the pools would deepen and spread through the network of corridors. Because the pumping techniques used in Alaska at that time were crude, it was not unusual for pools of water with a thin crust of ice on the surface to infiltrate all levels of the mine.

In some mining tunnels, such as at the Shantytown Mine north of Barsnaggle, the pools of water were often waist-deep and remained that way throughout the mining season—May to September. These pools would freeze each winter and then thaw to just above freezing during the summer. In the deeper recess of the honeycomb of tunnels, miners actually used small "ore boats" to get through the waters. These ore boats, however, were simply the empty orecarts, which could float off the rails if they were not weighted down. (Miners would sit in the orecarts to add the weight as the alascattalo pulled them through the flooded tunnels.)

With both ice floors and growing pools of water, the alascattalo was a valuable animal because it had the strength of a moose and the thick, water-resistant hide of a walrus, which would protect it from the chilling effects of the water in the tunnels. At first the miners had tried to use moose in the mines, but this attempt met with dismal failure. The primary reason was that the animal was so incredibly stupid. Further, the wide rack of the moose proved too difficult to saw free, particularly if the 1,600 pound animal would not remain still long enough to complete the task. It was later discovered, in a most unfortunate manner, that moose also suffer from a form of claustrophobia.

To breed the perfect animal for mine work, the miners cross bred a moose and a walrus. This union, they believed, would produce a dumb, strong animal which had a water-resistant hide and an affinity for humans, so that they could be trained for mine work. The term "alascattalo" was a hybrid itself, combining the words "Alaska" with "cattle."

The genetic hybridization of the alascattalo did not produce a perfect beast of burden for the mines. While the alascattalo was strong and had a water-resistant hide, it was quite unruly, particularly during the rutting season. Though it could work as hard as a mule, the animal was unbelievably cantankerous. It might work for weeks and give its handler no difficulty, and then, one day, turn into an explosive, unpredictable beast. Because of its great strength and limited IQ, the animal was a great danger, not only to its handler but to itself as well. One of the behemoths could easily kick in the side of the ore car or tear out thirty yards of corral fence before it dawned on the animal it could be injured. Worse, when one alascattalo went on a rampage, other alascattalo, depending on their temperment, might join in. The most frequently recorded incident of an alascattalo rampage took place at the Sanderson Second Luck Mine just outside of Bethel in mid–1903.

The stampede began when one alascattalo, cantankerous and sore after its rack had been sawn off, bumped one of its sore stumps on a low ceiling. In a rage, the animal twisted sideways, pulling the half-filled orecart off the rails. The orecart tipped over, and the alascattalo suddenly found itself being dragged down into a pool of water by its leather harness. In terror the animal braced itself and twisted sideways. This action snapped the harness tethers and the animal popped free. Unfortunately it also hit another sore stump on the tunnel wall. Now, with no orecart to smother its rage, the animal exploded down the tunnel deeper into the mine, its bellow echoing through the honeycomb of tunnels.

Among alascattalo, rage is infectious. When one alascattalo is on a rampage, others are soon to follow. Under normal circumstances, a rampaging alascattalo would be left above ground until it became quiet. But at the Sanderson Second Luck Mine there was no way to get the alascattalo above ground—particularly while it was on a rampage. The rest of the alascattalo in the Sanderson Second Luck Mine, also cantankerous from the annual rack sawing, exploded into a mad stampede, which forced some 300 miners out of the deeper tunnels.

Careening from tunnel to tunnel, the rampaging alascattalo knocked out bracing, and sections of the wall collapsed, partially sealing a portion of the mine. All of the miners were able to escape by scrambling through ventilation shafts. The mine remained closed for days as the miners, afraid of being trampled, refused to reenter the tunnel network. When the mine was finally reopened, the miners discovered that the alascattalo had survived for several days standing in shoulder-deep freezing water. The plunge seemed to have caused the animals no harm, and once the humans were back in the tunnels, each animal docilely sauntered back to their respective orecarts. (The Sanderson Second Luck Mine was eventually closed when an underground river was breached and the mine flooded. This fact is only significant in that the miners were forced to ride their orecarts out of the mine like boats, a rarity in mining annals anywhere in the United States.)

To breed a more docile animal, three more hybrids were conceived. First there was what is now called the moosallo (*Moosirous Moosticus alaskatorus*). The moosallo, a cross between an alascattalo and a moose, turned out to be indistinguishable from a moose. It did not have the intelligence of the alascattalo or the water-resistant hide of a walrus. In fact, its hide was so much thinner than that of a moose that it proved to be susceptible to both cold and mosquitoes. The moosallo only differed from the moose phenotypically because it had a vestigial flipper instead of a tail. (An alascattalo has a complete, usable flipper as a tail.)

While the alascattalo is, for all intents and purposes, extinct, recorded sightings of moosallo are made each year. Hunters often report that the moose they shot seemed to have some sort of a flipper-like tail. However, as the years pass, the number of sightings have decreased, and the tail appendage reportedly has been growing smaller and smaller. Biologists feel that, as the moosallo continues to inbreed with moose, within a few more generations it will disappear from the annals of biology forever.

The second hybrid produced from the alascattalo was the so-called walrusurus (*Walrusurus Moosticus alaskatorus*). The walrusurus is a cross between an alascattalo and a walrus. It has a body frame like that of a walrus and is only distinguishable from its marine parent by what appear to be vestigial "legs" on the underside of its flippers. While there may be many walrusuri in existence, it is very hard to tell. Since the animal spends its entire life in the ocean, there is no way visually to distinguish it from other walrus. There have been occasional sightings, but the last one was made during the Second World War, and the carcass of the animal was never examined by marine authorities.

The sighting, interestingly, was made by a group of United States merchant marines who had been temporarily marooned on Unimak Island in the Aleutians during the Japanese invasion of Kiska and Attu. Their small boat had been straffed and sunk by Zeros from the Japanese aircraft carrier *Junyo*. It took the men two weeks to make contact with the United States Coast Guard. During that time the men were forced to survive on a diet of cormorant eggs and fox. The men considered themselves fortunate when they were able to kill what they thought was a small walrus. While slaughtering the animal, they discovered what appeared to be stubby legs on the underside of its flippers. The Coast Guard never investigated the claim, and marine biologists were not informed until after the war. Today, with the passage of the Marine Mammals Act of 1972, the hunting of walrus is now illegal except by Native Americans, and the number of animals taken per year has dropped substantially. If any walrusuri are in existence today, the scientific community is not aware of it.

The third hybrid is the one which has raised the most controversy. Known as a wallaroo (*Walrusurus wallrusus alaskatorus*), this animal is a cross between a moosallo and a walrusurus. The animal, reportedly, has the body and head of a walrus with short, moose-like legs. It has a large, usable flipper for a tail and a rack that appears to be "like a man's hand on either side of its head." It prefers to live in muskeg bogs and, because it does not have the natural oil glands in its skin, loves mud wallows—or, more appropriately in Alaska, bog wallows—and has a pronounced affinity for natural oil wallows. When near the ocean it eats seaweed and crustaceans. Inland it prefers freshwater krill, salmon eggs and small Kuskokwim crab. (The only inland sightings have been in the Kuskokwim River watershed.) Depending on the source, it is claimed that the wallaroo can walk upright for short distances and will also eat the tender shoots from the lower branches of deciduous trees. Hunters allege that wallaroo have flesh that is far tastier and less fiberous than moose and less fatty than walrus.

However, there has been much controversy concerning the wallaroo. While biologists do not debate the existence of the alascattalo, walrusurus or moosaloo, the wallaroo is another matter entirely. Alaskan biologists are unwilling to assert that the wallaroo even exists. First, biologists assert that it would be highly unlikely that there could be a genetic cross between a moosallo and walrusurus. They site three reasons. First, the alascattalo has a very long gestation period (12 months) and thus can only produce one offspring a year. Further, alascattalo adults cannot breed successfully until they are well into their adult years, 7 to 10 years old. These facts would seem to indicate that the hybridization process reduced the fecundity of the animal.

Second, the same biologists contend that it would be physically impossible for an animal with the body of a walrus to stand on its hind legs. Even if the wallaroo had powerful hind legs, it would probably not be able to walk at all. Further, for an animal to have both flippers and legs, biologists say, would defy the laws of nature.

Alaskan historian Dr. Blake Carrigan, in an address to the Arctic Historian Society in Syracuse in 1983, noted that the wallaroo "is, in some respects, an atavistic throwback to an ice age mammal. It has the ability to survive in frigid weather for months at a time and can, like the musk ox, live on lichens it finds by pawing through the snow." At the same conference, biologist Dr. Jerome Sutter bolstered support for the wallaroo by noting that caches of the beasts had been spotted in the Chukchi Sea off the coast of Shismaref. Sutter expected to survey the wallaroo caches during the forthcoming summer. To date, the results of that survey have not been published.

In fairness, it should be added that of the dozen speakers at the conference, only Drs. Carrigan and Sutter spoke in favor of the existence of the wallaroo. It should also be mentioned that Carrigan's doctorate is honorary only, from a McTavish University (?), and Dr. Sutter's scholarly papers have been consistently refused by professional journals because of "the speculative nature of his research data." Many of his colleagues, who did not wish to be named, referred to his theories—and particularly his support of the existence of the wallaroo—as "garbage biology."

11
PORKY BICKAR AND THE MT. EDGECUMBE CHARADE

Throughout the United States, the first day of April is traditionally known as a day of humor and merriment. That's why it's called April Fool's Day. But April 1, 1974, did not start out as a typical April Fool's Day for Sitka, Alaska. After more than 500 year of silence, Mt. Edgecumbe, the extinct volcano at the edge of the city, suddenly started to belch thick, black smoke. While a volcanic eruption in Alaska is rarely cause for much alarm, the smoking Mt. Edgecumbe was an exception. It was located less than 13 miles from the center of Sitka. If the volcano was erupting, it meant a fiery end to the city of Sitka.

"There were a lot of concerned people," stated Oliver "Porky" Bickar, who remembered the day well. "No one knew very much about geology and suddenly, right on our doorstep, was this plume of black smoke coming from an extinct volcano. It did not make for a pleasant morning."

Within twenty minutes, Alaska Airlines rerouted one of its planes over the volcano's cone to take a look. It was probably not a pleasant ride for the pilot. If the volcano had exploded the plane might have found itself blasted out to sea along with two or three cubic *miles* of ash. Or the plane might have been burned to a cinder in a matter of seconds as the mountain spewed molten lava miles into the atmosphere like a gigantic Roman candle.

On this day, however, neither happened. There was too much smoke for the pilot to see anything, so as the residents of Sitka panicked, the Coast Guard was called. A helicopter was immediately dispatched to overfly the cone of the volcano. Everyone was on edge, waiting for the helicopter to report back from its overflight.

Then came the news. When the Coast Guard helicopter came within sight of the cone, the pilot and crew immediately radioed back the fateful words: "We've been had."

89

Porky Bickar's photos which appeared in the July 1974 edition of *Alaska Magazine*. (Courtesy Sitka's Dirty Dozen.)

There, on the lip of the cone, was a sight they had never imagined, even in their wildest dreams. In a large circle were 150 burning automobile tires and stamped out in the snow in painted-black letters 150 feet tall were the words APRIL FOOL.

The "eruption" of Mt. Edgecumbe didn't last long, about thirty minutes. But during those thirty minutes the local police and fire department were deluged with calls. There was near panic until word came back from the helicopter.

It didn't take the residents of Sitka long to figure out who was responsible for the deed. They were the ones laughing the hardest. Led by Oliver "Porky" Bickar, the culprit was actually a group of Sitkans who called themselves the Dirty Dozen, "A group of dedicated citizens for the betterment of the entire community."

Bickar, a long-time resident of Sitka, was well known for his practical jokes. Once word leaked that he was responsible, there was a general sigh of relief—followed by a burst of hearty laughter.

The Dirty Dozen had been planning this particular April Fool's gag for more than three years. Weather had stalled them on two previous occasions but, in 1974, they were finally able to perpetrate the deed. Because they could not find a helicopter locally, they were forced to secure a helicopter out of Petersburg. "We had a local helicopter," Bickar recalled, "but the guy chickened out on us. We even had an FAA approved flight plan, all legal, and this guy wouldn't go. I accused him of being chicken and he said, 'Yeah.' So we got a real daredevil, Earl Walker of Temsco out of Petersburg. He thought it was a great idea, and he showed up ready to haul tires and laugh hard."

The deed took several hours. There were so many tires that the helicopter had to make two trips. On the first trip, Porky went along and began setting the tires in a huge semi-circle. Then, before the chopper came back with the second load, he began stamping out the letters in the snow and painting them black. When all of the tires had been stacked, he stuffed them full of smoke bombs, sterno, and oily rags. After he had ignited the tires, he "laughed all the way back to Sitka."

As the news of the gag spread across Alaska, the rest of the state laughed heartily as well. It was written up in the Anchorage and Fairbanks papers and the story was picked up by the national press. Eventually, even national magazines such as *Sports Illustrated* and *Reader's Digest* ran the story. It was an admirable bit of American humor and a classic Alaskan absurding.

But not everyone was laughing. As soon as it became known that Porky Bickar and the Dirty Dozen were responsible, Porky got a rude letter from the Sierra Club in San Francisco. In no uncertain terms, the environmental group stated that it was going to "take action" against him and the Dirty Dozen for the "desecration" of Mt. Edgecumbe by the "emission of particulate matter by means of combustion."

Four days later Porky Bickar returned a letter to the Sierra Club stating that the release of particulates was justified because it had been an early spring in the Sitka area and "there ha[d] been an unusual amount of sand fleas and tse-tse flies" in the area and, as everyone knows, "the only way to eliminate these critters is to smoke them out." Other parts of the letter cannot be quoted as Bickar, formerly a logger, was not restrained in his opinion of the Sierra Club. As a matter of record, "I never heard back from 'em," said Porky. "I guess they lost my address."

But the saga of the April Fool eruption of Mt. Edgecumbe did not simply pass into the pages of Alaskan history. There was more to come. As a tribute to their exploit, members of the Dirty Dozen immediately began using a drawing of a smoking Mt. Edgecumbe as their stationery logo. Bickar, blatantly violating the rules of the Dirty Dozen, "a secret organization," sent some of his own photos of the deed to *Alaska Magazine*. The photos were reprinted in the July 1974, edition of the magazine. Then Bickar went so far as to appear on a local radio program telling of the deed, yet another blatant violation of the rules of that "secret society."

In mock outrage, the Dirty Dozen called a special meeting on Halloween night, 1975, to "expel Porky" because he was accused "of advertising a secret organization by radio." The expulsion motion passed. It was then moved to "burn and hang Porky in effigy." The chairwoman, however, moved to amend the motion to remove the word "in effigy." She suggested they bypass the effigy and "just use the real thing." There was much "heated discussion," but the amendment was dropped because the Dirty Dozen "might get in some type of trouble with [Porky's] wife." Not to be denied, the chairman offered to call Porky's wife to see if she cared. The motion passed and each of the Dirty Eleven, as they now called themselves, volunteered to light the match. The minutes of the meeting closed with a special thanks to "Chairwoman Revard for buying the beer at the meeting."

Right on schedule, the next day, at high noon, an effigy of "Big Brag Bickar" was hung in downtown Sitka. The balance of the Dirty Dozen, many of them dressed in mock Ku Klux Klan outfits, gathered outside Porky's business, Porky's Equipment Inc., to toss gasoline on the effigy and set it ablaze. It was a fine demonstration and photos of the event were published in the *Sitka Shopper*.

As an interesting historical footnote, Mt. Edgecumbe was named by Captain James Cook on May 2, 1778, probably after a mountain of the same name at the entrance of Plymouth Harbor in England or, possibly, for George, the first Earl of Edgecumbe. But the cape on which the extinct volcano sits had previously been named by F.A. Murelle and Don Juan de la Bodega y Quadra three years earlier, on August 16, 1775. These Spanish scientists named the cape "Cabo del Engano," which translates "Cape of Deceit."

Note: The bulk of the information in this chapter was provided by Porky Bickar. The photos that appeared in Alaska Magazine *can be found on page 18 in the July 1974 issue. The place name information came from Donald Orth's classic on Alaska place names.*

12

FANNIE QUIGLEY, ALASKAN FOLK HERO

Her name was Fannie Quigley and she could out-drink, out-shoot and out-cuss any man in Alaska. She was as tough as grizzly claws even though she only weighed about 100 pounds—including the bottle of home brew called "Kantishna champagne" she always kept tucked inside her boot. And she was the closest thing to a bona fide folk hero that Alaska had in the first half of the twentieth century.

Fannie was born in the Bohemian village of Wahoo, Nebraska, in 1871. A village of immigrants, Fannie, like many of the other children, had no formal schooling. She didn't even learn to speak English until she was a teenager. Though she grew up in a farming community, the tilling of soil did not set her heart ablaze. But the thought of the Klondike did. When news of the gold strike reached Wahoo, Fannie packed her bags and headed north.

Once in the Yukon Territory, she quickly discovered that there was more gold in good meals than in ice cold streams, so she hung a Meals-For-Sale sign in front of her tent everywhere she camped. Walking from strike to strike she served thousands of men hot meals and acquired the name "Fannie the Hike." Her last strike was in Kantishna, south of Mt. McKinley, where she met and married another Alaskan legend, Joe Quigley.

Joe Quigley was a northland folk hero in his own right. One of the few white men to have crossed the Chilkoot Pass before the Klondike Strike, he had been mining in the northland almost a decade before the stampede into the Yukon Territory. He was at Fortymile River near Circle when he heard of the new strike on the Klondike River, and he was one of the few men in the stampede who rushed south to Dawson.

Finding the best sites already taken, Joe drifted down the Yukon River and settled at the mouth of a small creek. Diggings were good but

Fannie Quigley, second from left, and Joe Quigley, first on right. (Courtesy University of Alaska, Fairbanks: Fannie Quigley Collection, ACC# 80-46-242N, in the Archives of the Alaska and Polar Regions Department.)

not exceptional enough to hold him, so he returned to Dawson the next year. There, several friends asked him if they could have his old claim. Joe had no objection, and he drew a map of his find and gave the map away. He never saw those friends again.

Twenty years later Joe was asked to grubstake a miner who swore he had a secret map to a rich strike on a small creek that fed into the Yukon. It was a lost mine, the down-and-outer claimed, that had made at least one man rich. Secretively the miner showed Joe his prized possession, and Joe got a shock. It was the same map he had drawn twenty years earlier!

In 1905, Joe was in Kantishna where he found the diggings fair enough to consider staying a spell. He and his partner, Jack Horne, headed north to Fairbanks for supplies and unexpectedly set off a stampede. Part of that stampede was the woman who was to become his wife: Fannie. The two were married the next year and together worked their Red Top Mine for the next thirty-odd years.

Joe and Fannie were a real Mutt-and-Jeff combination. Joe stood over six feet tall while Fannie was under five feet. But size didn't mean much to Fannie. Whether it was hunting moose, working in the Red Top or dog mushing supplies into Kantishna, Fannie was as adept as any man in the rough-and-tumble early days of Alaska.

Because of the unique location of the Quigley cabin near Mt. McKinley, the pair were known worldwide. Over the years they hosted the outdoors set of the rich and famous who came to study or climb Mt. McKinley. Scientists, nobility and big game hunters, as well as grubstakers, park rangers and geologists all came through Kantishna. The Quigley cabin was hospitable to them all. Though Fannie had not learned to speak English as a child, she showed no lack of understanding of the language and became well-known and highly regarded as a true conversationalist—though she was known to swear frequently.

She was also renowned for her cooking. Even in the harsh conditions of Kantishna, Fannie grew her own vegetables. Her garden included a wide variety of vegetables that many Alaskans only dreamed of: rhubarb, celery, potatoes, carrots, beets, turnips, onions, lettuce and radishes. That she found time to tend the garden is surprising considering that Kantishna only has ten weeks of growing weather. She was also adept at adding wild fruits and berries to her menu. Those berries the Quigleys did not consume raw were turned into jams, jellies and pies.

When it came to meats, Fannie was without peer. She shot and butchered her own meat and used the tunnels of the Red Top Mine to keep the carcasses frozen year round. Here the vegetables were kept fresh as well. The tunnels served this purpose well, for more than one traveler reported being surprised to be served what appeared to be a fresh vegetable salad in the middle of winter.

Since supplies had to be hauled by dogsled from Nenana, Fannie made certain that every ounce that was carried was consumed. Tom Markham, a well-known Alaskan attorney at the time, happened to be eating at the Quigleys' when Fannie noted that he had left a small bit of butter on his plate.

"What are you going to do with that butter?" Fannie asked quizzically.

"I've had more than I can eat," Markham said being polite.

"Don't you know we have to haul our supplies a hundred miles by dog team? You eat that butter, or you'll get the same plate with the butter still on it for breakfast!"

"All right," Markham said. "I'll eat it with my pie."

Another time Fannie entertained some city-folk who commented on how good her "grouse" had been. The meal had actually been of porcupine, but Fannie agreed that yes, it had been a grouse. Later she commented to another guest who was familiar with Fannie's ways, "If I tell her it's porcupine she'll probably get sick and die on me."

One winter when game was scarce, Fannie and Joe went hunting in different directions. When Joe came back empty-handed, he found Fannie dressing her game: two caribou, a bear and a moose. Joe was embarrassed, and Fannie wouldn't let him forget it.

"You ain't fit to go huntin'," she said as she tossed him her skirt. "Here, you do the housework today. Gimme your pants."

One day Fannie was out hunting and spotted a moose. Suddenly she was faced with a dilemma. She was far from the cabin and in the high country, so there wasn't any cover she could use to keep herself warm during the night. And she did not have any sleeping gear with her. But if she shot the moose, left the carcass on the ground and went back to her cabin to spend the night, by the next morning wolves would probably have devoured the moose. If she let the moose go, she might not be able to find it again.

So she nailed the moose, gutted the animal on the spot and spent the night *inside* the warm carcass. Unfortunately, it got so cold during the night that the carcass froze solid with Fannie inside and, as Fannie told many travelers, she "had a heckuva time" hacking her way out. This story was vintage Fannie Quigley and was recounted to author Edna Ferber who used it in her classic novel, *The Ice Palace*.

Grant Pearson, a park ranger at McKinley in the '20s and '30s, remembered a time when he visited Fannie and found her drying her clothes. When asked how her clothing had become soaked, Fannie told a story that will live forever in the annals of hunting in the last frontier. Spotting a caribou bull she had taken a shot. The bull jumped into a clump of willows. Absolutely certain she had hit the bull, Fannie was surprised to see it walk out of the other side of the clump as though nothing had happened. She took a second shot and hit the bull again. Then she got a surprise: there were two bulls and both were wounded. In a rage both animals charged, splashing across an ice-choked creek toward her. But they didn't run far. Midway across the stream they both died.

Not about to let the meat go, Fannie waded into the frigid, thigh-deep water and roped the carcasses so they wouldn't float away. Then she dragged them ashore, one at a time, dressed them, and carried the meat back to the cabin.

Fannie wasn't only adept with firearms. In a land where doctors were few and far between, she was the next best thing to a medical practitioner. One day Joe was involved in a plane wreck near the cabin, and when Fannie found him, his nose was completely split open.

Inside the cabin, Fannie washed the wound and stitched it closed with catgut.

"That was the first time I ever sewed up anyone," Fannie later recalled. "I sewed it the same way as I do my moccasins, which is what I call the baseball stitch." The doctor in Fairbanks wasn't thrilled with the stitching, but Fannie felt otherwise. The stitching hadn't given Joe any trouble, so Fannie said, "I guess the baseball stitch is as good as [the doctor's] new fangled sewing."

Perhaps the most humorous incident in Fannie's life was the week she hosted Father Fitzgerald and his pilot. Weather had forced their plane down, and the two spent a few days in Kantishna.

The first night the men were there Fannie offered them caribou stew. The pilot ate hungrily but the priest just looked at his plate.

"Don't you like my cooking?" Fannie asked.

"You know today is Friday," the man replied. "I don't eat meat on Friday."

"Oh," she replied and left the table. A bit later she came back with a bowl of lettuce. "Here," she said, "eat grass. All the rabbits do."

The missionary and Fannie got along well, and when the weather broke they were good friends. Before the two men took off, Fitzgerald offered to pay Fannie for their keep. Fannie turned them down. "You don't owe me anything," she said. "Your money's no good here."

"Well, then," said the priest. "My pilot will be flying back here. What kind of chocolates do you like?"

Fannie's reply was quick, "Schlitz."

Joe Quigley sold the Red Top Mine in the late 1930s and moved to Seattle, but Fannie stayed in Kantishna. She died in her sleep in 1944.

Note: Source material on Fannie Quigley is hard to find. This information came primarily from two articles by Grant Pearson, who knew Fannie personally. These articles appeared in the Alaska Sportsman, in August of 1947 and March of 1950. Pearson's book, My Life of High Adventure, also includes material on Fannie. In April of 1970, Ruth Carson wrote an article on Fannie for Alaska Magazine which was based on personal interviews, and JoAnne Wold's The Way It Was has a short chapter on Fannie as well.

13
STRANGE BUT TRUE, TOO

Much to the chagrin of the male *muckers* (miners) at Vault Creek in the early 1900s, one of their number was the handsomest ladies' man in the locale. He got all the women, and in those days, there were not that many women to get. The rest of the men rued the day he had ever come to Vault Creek and decided to even the score.

They took their time and waited for the right idea and the right moment. It came at a dance during the summer. Halfway through the dance, the ladies' man suddenly realized that none of the women would dance with him. He would ask for a dance, his partner would take one step toward him and then say no. He "smelled a rat," and then he smelled something else. Outside, after removing his shoepacks, he found that his fellow muckers had filled his shoes with Limburger cheese, which his hot, sweaty feet had activated.

From that day forward, he was known as Shoepack (from Gregory's *Tall [But True] Tales of Alaska*).

In the 1960s, the Alaska State Troopers flew out to the Bush in the dead of winter to retrieve the body of an old miner. The corpse had been frozen in a sitting position, so the Troopers just slipped the cadaver into one of the back seats of the plane and strapped it in.

As the Troopers were about to take off, a drunk came stumbling up and asked for a ride into Fairbanks. "Sure," said the pilot, "climb into the back seat." The drunk crawled in the back, introduced himself to the corpse and carried on a one-way conversation all the way to town. Right after they landed, the drunk leered at the pilot and said, "Wassa matta w' that ol' guy in there? He acts like he's dead or somethin'."

Another version of this story, which also cannot be verified, told a similar situation in which a woman hitched a ride seated next to a corpse that was belted into a rear seat of a plane. The ride was exceptionally bumpy, and on more than one occasion the pilot was not sure that he would make his destination. But the woman sitting in the back seat didn't bat an eye. When the plane arrived at its destination, the woman was asked if she had been frightened. "Well, I was at first," she replied, "but [my fellow passenger, i.e., the corpse] was taking it so calmly I didn't think we had any reason to be concerned."

Tony Schwamm, well-known bush pilot in Southeast Alaska, once landed his plane on what he thought was deep water. Much to his surprise, as he was gliding to a stop he cleared the water on the back of a whale.

Homesteader and pig rancher Clifford "Moosemeat" Johnson was known as an eccentric around Anchorage in the 1940s. One day he decided to add a bit of color to his life, and he painted his outdoor table with stripes of red, yellow, green and blue. The table did not last long, for a marauding bear tore it apart before the paint was dry.

Johnson's luck didn't seem to be getting better any faster either. The next day he spotted a bear on his property. The bear had one of Johnson's pigs in its mouth and was about to make good its escape. Johnson shot the bear, saved the pig and, on examining the bear, discovered that its paws had residue of red, yellow, green and blue paint.

On September 15, 1902, a masked bandit entered the Skagway Branch of the Canadian Bank of Commerce and demanded $20,000. To show that he meant business he had a bundle of dynamite sticks in one hand and a revolver in the other. Just as the "transaction" was about to take place, John G. Price, a Skagway attorney, came through the door with $350 to deposit. The bandit became nervous and fired. Whether the shot was intended for a bank employee or Price is not known. The slug hit the dynamite, which immediately exploded. The bank employee was blown out the back door and Price was pelted with glass fragments, his $350 blowing all over the street. The bandit died in the hospital several hours later.

The bank was wrecked, and some $2,800 in gold dust was scattered. The military cordoned off the area and used hoses to wash everything down. Then the top six inches of soil from the area was shoveled up and put in barrels. The barrels were then dragged to a creek where they were sluiced. "The panning efforts resulted in the recovery of more than was believed on hand in the bank at the time. John Price recovered all of his bills, not losing a single one."

(As a macabre historical tidbit, the severed head of the bandit was a popular town exhibit for years.)

In the April 1976, edition of *Alaska Magazine*, page 66, there is a photo illustrating the dangers of being a stupid skipper. When the captain docked his boat in Homer at high tide, he made the mistake of securing the boat to a piling instead of the floating dock. As the tide went out — all 18 feet of it — the boat ended up hanging from the piling. When the tide came back in, water rushed over the gunnels and filled the back of the boat while it was still hanging vertically.

In 1941, an Alaskan was accidentally killed when he was mistaken for a moose. A manslaughter charge was not pressed, but the accused was jailed for 90 days. He was charged with hunting during closed season.

In the early days of Anchorage, the CAA — now known as the FAA — had its offices in the Federal Building — now known as the Old Federal Building. Whenever a pilot had an accident, he had to go to the CAA headquarters and fill out piles of paperwork. After filling out page after page of details of the aeronautical mishap, the final question was usually answered with a single word. The question was "General ability as a pilot?" and the usual answer was "Excellent."

Once Merle Sasseen, a bush pilot with a sense of humor, was in the CAA's office for third time in only a few weeks. He had survived the mishaps on the old Anchorage airfield — now known as the Park Strip — and was dutifully filling out the CAA paperwork page by page by page. When he came to the last question, he wrote, "I used to think I was pretty good, but lately I've begun to wonder" (from *Anchorage: The Way It Was*).

In the 1960s, two bank robbers from the Lower 48 held up a Juneau bank and tried to make their getaway by driving out of town.

On December 22, 1989, a Thai Airlines 747 was detected by an Anchorage air traffic controller heading *east* due south of St. Paul. The air traffic controller called the airliner, and the pilot said no, he was headed *west* on a flight from Seattle to Tokyo. Wrong, said the traffic controller, and he was right. The Thai Airlines flight was *six hundred miles* off course and flying 180 degrees different than what the plane's instruments were telling the pilot.

When Judge Moody was in private practice in the 1940s, he was appointed by Judge Dimond to a criminal case. The suspect he was to defend had been found hiding under a car with a sizable amount of cash on his person. Since this man fit the description of a bandit who had just robbed the newly-opened Traveler's Inn and the money on his person was identified as having come from the Traveler's Inn, the prosecution believed that they had an airtight case.

The suspect, however, swore to Moody that he had not done the job. He had been under the car because he had had trouble with the police before and hid when he saw them approaching. As for the money, "some other guy must have left the money behind."

"What do you think of my story?" the suspect asked Moody.

"I don't think it's worth a damn," replied Moody. "I think they'll convict you."

"Maybe you can come back tomorrow and I'll tell you another one," replied the suspect (from Pam Cravez's *Seizing the Frontier: Alaska's Territorial Lawyers*, Alaska Historical Commission, 1984).

Lawyer George Grigsby was once cross-examining a well-known Anchorage madam, Marie Cox Chili, when a comical response took him by surprise. Chili used her parlor as a front for prostitution, and Grigsby was defending a man who was accused of stabbing one of her "clients."

For some reason Grigsby was intent on establishing that the door of Chili's establishment had a bearing on the murder trial in progress.

Focusing on the door, he asked a string of questions such as which way the door opened and whether it had windows and, if so, how many. Finally he asked one question too many.

"Is the door knob on the right or the left?" the lawyer asked.

Irate at the string of questions, Chili snapped back, "Mr. Grigsby, why are you asking me all these questions about the back door? You know that back door as well as I do. You're in and out of there every night" (from Cravez's *Seizing the Frontier*).

Jimmy Ing had been found guilty of forging 200 Morrison-Knudsen checks and cashing them through his underworld connections. Anchorage Federal District Court Judge L. McCarrey, Jr., gave Ing ten years on each of 20 counts and ordered them to be served consecutively.

After the verdict, a newspaper reporter commented to Jimmy Ing, "Two hundred years! What in the world are you going to do?"

"Well," the unfortunate man replied, "it looks like I'll just have to do as much of it as I can" (from Cravez's *Seizing the Frontier*).

In a dispute between two Juneau residents over storing a vehicle, one hoisted the other's car high into a tree with a crane. (A photo of the dangling car can be found on page 26 of the September 1976, *Alaska Magazine*.) Later the man who hoisted the automobile stated that the car now served as a weather vane. When the car was sticking straight out from the tree, "you know the *taku* wind is blowing like hell."

Flamboyant Edgar Paul Boyko once made a bet with fellow attorney Roger Cremo that he could win a case before Judge McCarrey by using some of McCarrey's buzz words, "exhaustion of administrative remedies." Cremo took the bet.

At that time Boyko was representing a privately owned and privately insured bus company. Boyko then filed a motion to dismiss, using as the excuse that the plaintiff had "failed to exhaust her administrative remedies" because she had not gone to the bus company's Board of Directors. McCarrey granted the motion, and Cremo was furious. (Only a

government agency has administrative remedies. There is no such
mechanism in the private sector.)

It has been reported, but not confirmed, that in the early days of
bush flying, a plane carrying chicks in cages was weathered in at a remote
location. The cold front lasted almost a week during which time the
chicks grew so large that they broke the cages and the pilot was forced
to abandon his cargo.

In Fairbanks, District Court Judge Harry Pratt was famous for wearing green eye shades and fiddling with his hearing aid in court. On hot
summer days, he would often wear Hawaiian shirts. Members of the Bar
in Fairbanks were also convinced that if an argument bored him, the
judge "turned off his hearing aid, pulled down his eye shade, and dozed
off" (Cravez's *Seizing the Frontier*).

In the late 1960s, Nome District Attorney Fred Crane invited the
Alaska Bar Association to have its annual convention in his jurisdiction.
Sadly, a few months before the meeting was to be held, Crane died. But,
since all the arrangements had been made well ahead of time, the convention was held on schedule.

The Saturday night before the banquet, many old friends of Crane's
were drinking and playing poker when someone remarked that in Nome
no one was buried in the winter. The bodies were kept in storage until
the thaw made it possible to dig graves. Someone then suggested that
they prop up Fred Crane for one last night of merriment.

According to Bob Erwin, the former District Attorney for Nome,
Crane's body was taken out of the freezer at the morgue and transported
to the BOT (Board of Trade).

In his early days of flying, Sam Shafsky worked on a gold dredge pulling seven twelve-hour shifts. This job didn't leave a lot of time for flying.
Shafsky made the best possible use of his free hours, which did not come

without a price. One day on the gold dredge he fell asleep, and while he slumbered, tons of icebergs came up the bucket line, filling the interior of the dredge. It was only when the dredge starting listing badly that the captain knew something was amiss below decks (from an interview with Sam Shafsky).

At Tatalina Air Force Base in the mid–1970s, a group of airmen decided to photograph a bear *inside* the ACWS station. They set a trail of raw meat to lure the animal into the station's nightclub and up onto a stool. Then, as the bear devoured steak bits, the men snapped pictures through an open but barred window.

An unforeseen problem occurred when one of the men took a flash picture of the animal. The bear jerked back and fell off the stool. Disoriented, it ran through the first doorway it happened upon—which was not the doorway through which it had entered—and began making its way into the hallways by going up a flight of steps toward the main hallway that connected all parts of the base.

Just as the bear was halfway up the stairs, two officers from operations came around the corner. They stalled. The bear stalled. Then the bear went back down the stairs only to find his way now blocked by the photographers who had come running through the nightclub. The photographers stalled. The bear stalled.

Then the bear took the only option open to him: through an open door into the station's crowded movie theater.

In the early 1980s, the state prosecutor out of Anchorage, Steven Branchflower, was in Juneau to supervise a very sensitive investigation. Since Juneau was so small and he didn't want anyone to recognize him until the indictments were delivered, he went to the State Courthouse very early, left very late and spent all day in the bowels of the building, not daring to be seen on the street.

But dating was a problem. He did have a girlfriend in Juneau who was a legislative aide and lived with two other aides and a television reporter. Not wishing to be recognized and still wanting to see his girlfriend, Branchflower resolved the problem by driving to her house and waiting for her in his running car—with a bag over his head.

In 1989, an East Coast company began buying up grave sites in Barrow so they could resell them to Easterners who were interested in being frozen and possibly brought back to life at some future date.

In the 1930s, Richard Davis of Cordova discovered a bleached human skeleton on the beach of Southeast Alaska. A prankster at heart, he collected the bones in a gunny sack and kept them under his boat's sink for several years, often using them to frighten his procession of girlfriends. When he finally decided to dispose of them, no law enforcement official wanted to be responsible for the paperwork, so he just buried them in the Cordova area. Unfortunately where he buried them is now a lawn, and one of these days, Davis noted, someone is going to dig them up accidentally while planting flowers (from an interview with Richard Davis).

According to *Roadhouse Tales*, it is alleged that in the winter of 1901 a live mammoth was shot by hunters outside of Nome. Apparently the beast had become enraged at the presence of the campfires of Eskimos and had "stamped them out like flies." Naturalists were called in, and with Winchester at a safe distance, they fired on the animal. "The bullets glanced from the beast's hide as if it had been steel armor plate," the book reported dutifully.

Next the naturalists employed a Gatling gun—though there is no reference as to where they got such a weapon—and they "brought down the game. It was a huge beast and was believed to weigh at least thirty tons."

Jack London, whose books symbolize Alaska for the world, actually wrote of the Klondike Strike, a gold rush in the Yukon Territory of Canada. London spent all of 21 days in Alaska, going down the Yukon River bound for St. Michael where he was to take a steamer back to Seattle.

Robert Service, a Canadian poet who was only in Alaska later in life when on tour selling his books, is honored by having a high school in Anchorage named after him.

In 1976, the Forest Service came to the aid of a young black bear who had lodged its head in a coffee can. The bear wandered into a campsite with its head in the tin can, and concerned campers made the call. On page 24 of the November 1976, edition of *Alaska Magazine,* some of those concerned campers can be seen fleeing from the scene as the Forest Service rangers hog-tie the bear before forcibly removing the coffee can.

———————

In the early days of the Klondike Rush, a 20-year-old lad died of natural causes in one of the boomtowns. Searching his personal effects, the address of his parents in Boston was discovered, and his personal effects were sent back east.

The boy's parents, well-heeled, wanted their son's body back in Boston, so they arranged to have a lead coffin shipped across the United States by rail to San Francisco and then by steamer to Dyea. From there the coffin was carried up over the Chilkoot Pass to the boomtown.

When the coffin finally arrived, eighteen months had passed since the youth had died. No one in town remembered the incident, much less where the lad might have been buried. But since the parents had paid for the transportation of the coffin both ways and the townspeople did not want to disappoint the parents, they found a convenient collection of human bones, loaded them into the coffin and sent it back to Boston.

For the second time the coffin went down the river, over the Chilkoot Pass, on a steamer to San Francisco and then across the United States by rail.

But it did not take long for the family to learn of the deception. The family doctor opened the coffin, examined the remains and stated that they were Indian bones. Realizing that they would never get their son's body back — and that they could not bury an Indian in Boston — the coffin was then resealed and, for a third time, crossed the United States by rail, was placed on a steamship for Dyea, was transported over the Chilkoot Pass and floated down the river to the boomtown.

This time the family did not want the coffin returned. After the bones were disposed of, there was a question as to the ownership of the coffin. No one owned it, yet it was too valuable an item to be thrown out. Thus is was put up for auction and, after several owners, it was sold to a roadhouse on the American side of the border where it became Alaska's first bathtub.

———————

In 1981, KTVA reporter Mary Fondahn forgot the basic rule of television reporting: the camera never blinks. She was clowning around and pretended to interview a paper bag in the same manner that a well-known newscaster on a competing station had interviewed a murder suspect. It was her birthday, and as a gift, the television crew sent it aloft to the state satellite as a feed. That evening, anyone with a satellite dish anywhere in Alaska picked up Mary Fondahn interviewing a paper bag.

In 1989, Fifth Avenue Auto Body in Anchorage needed a sign that would attract attention, so they sawed a car in half and hung the rear portion on their outside wall so that it looked like the car had smashed into the building.

Legendary bush pilot Archie Ferguson was a great one for a story. Once, he told a friend, he had a cargo of turkeys to transport from Nome to Kotzebue. Because the cages were too large to fit into his plane, he took the turkeys out and put them in the cargo hold individually.

As he started to take off, he realized that the combined load of turkeys was too heavy so he frightened some of the birds into flying around in the cargo hold. This, he claimed, lightened the load enough for him to take off.

In 1901, G.W. Blankenship, a sourdough in search of new diggings, was paddling away when he was suddenly blown out into the Arctic Ocean by a fierce storm. He claimed that he was directed back to land by a "spook guide," the ghost of his father-in-law, who "sat in the stern of the boat, and by motioning with its hands, directed [Blankenship] to steer while [the ghost] pulled at the oars."

Not only did the ghost of his father-in-law save his life, Blankenship also claimed that the "spook" directed him where to "find gold." Following the instructions of his deceased father-in-law, Blankenship filed claims in Candle Creek, "many of which were valuable."

Supposedly the Eskimo word for whiskey is "tonak." The origin, it is claimed, began with a white sea captain who spent the winter on St. Lawrence Island. Every time he mixed a drink and offered it to his Eskimo companion, he said "Well, Joe, it's time for us to take a tonic."

The Native thought the term "tonic" meant "whiskey" and the name stuck.

In January of 1990, the Anchorage Police were called to a laundromat. A customer complained that a slot machine had not paid her any winnings. Since gambling was illegal in Anchorage, the police were very interested.

But the police were in for a surprise. Although the laundromat advertised that the machine *did* pay off, the slot machine was rigged so it would *never* hit a winning combination. Thus, as the police decided, it was legal to advertise that a machine *could* pay off and then rig the gambling device so that it would *not* pay off.

When the State of Alaska established the Status of Women Commission, the originators didn't think through the acronym. Only after the Commission was established and the stationery printed was the error realized. For years, to the mirth of male chauvinists, the organization was known as the SOW Commission.

When Mt. Redoubt erupted in January of 1990, there was a great concern in Southcentral Alaska as to the impact of volcanic dust on Alaskans' health. One OB/GYN received a call from a concerned expectant mother who asked, "Is there any danger to my baby if I breathe?"

"No," replied the physician. "The greatest problem will come if you don't breathe."

Complaining to some outsiders about Alaskan's lack of sensitivity for national problems that existed in their own community, a legislator noted in frustration that "most Alaskans think that crack is something in a sidewalk."

Drue Pearce, running for a seat in the State Senate, found that one of the issues she hadn't counted on fighting was her being female. "I couldn't vote for a woman," said a male chauvinist, who also happened to be a legislator, to Pearce's male campaign manager. "You know how women are. At that certain time of the month there's no *way* of knowing how they'd vote."

When the conversation was repeated to Pearce, she was quick to snap, "I vote better on those three days than he does the rest of the month."

A lucky photographer in 1976 got the snapshot of a lifetime. Standing at the Ship Creek fish ladder, he was waiting to capture a jumping salmon on film. When a salmon finally leaped out of the water, the photographer triggered the shutter and caught the fish slamming head-on into a cement piling. The photograph was reprinted in *Alaska Magazine*, November 1976, page 28.

Juneau gadfly Jeff Brown, also known as Joe Gorilla of Gorillagrams, published a "concise reference guide" for Outsiders having difficulty with Alaskan terms. Some of the gems in the *Dictionary of Alaskan Terms* include:

> **blanket toss**   what most Alaskans do with their bed coverings after a winter without a bath.
> **bottomfish**   where most of them are in Prince William Sound.
> **fishwheel of fortune**   Eskimo game show.
> **fjord**   Alaskan vehicle similar to a Cjhevy.
> **hooligan**   see "Legislators."
> **tar balls**   what oil company executives have.

The 1964 earthquake caused an unexpected complication in Valdez. The earth tremors caused a submarine earthslide of an estimated

98 million yards of material right at the waterfront. When the land fell away, water rushed into the gap creating a tidal wave which hit the city. Then the water retreated across the bay and rebounded up the mountains on the far side and came back across the bay to hit the town a second time. The same scenario was repeated twice more with the town of Valdez hit by the same tidal wave *four* times.

Since 1964 the site of the city of Valdez has been moved.

An environmental attorney in Anchorage in the late 1970s wrote to the State of Alaska Department of Fish and Game and demanded that the oil companies be ordered to take down all unused drilling rigs because ducks were colliding with them in the fog (confirmed by O.K. Gilbreth, Executive Director of the Alaska Coalition for American Energy Security).

In the late 1970s, Native groups and the oil industry had a standoff over drilling on the Barrier Islands. Even though the water between the coastal plain and the islands was no deeper than 12 feet, many Natives claimed that the drilling activity would frighten the whales. Intrigued that a whale would frequent 12 feet of water, an oil company representative asked how many whales had ever been seen between the mainland and the islands. "One," replied an Eskimo. "But it was dead."

In October of 1988, gadfly Jeff Brown sponsored a rain festival in Juneau complete with alleged works of art. Brown himself entered a sculpture titled "Alaska Roadkill," which showed a salmon partially flattened by a tire tread. A second Brown entry included a collage of tuna, salmon and other sea creatures talking. For "realism," Brown hooked up a speaker to the collage and broadcast "fish jokes" during the exposition.

In the late 1930s, there was lively debate in the Anchorage Assembly chambers as to whether prostitution would be allowed within city limits. It was finally decided that while the brothels could remain open, there would be no toleration of pimps. Mayor Bubendorf, who spoke with a thick accent, summed up the meeting by stating, "...then it's settled. The girls can stay but no pimples."

On August 3, 1908, a group of citizens in Nome founded a social organization they named the Radiator Club of Alaska, which would meet periodically at the Golden Gate Hotel. As part of the rules and bylaws, it was agreed that every member must "elevate himself above work of all kind, and must under no circumstance *sweat*." Further, members must never refuse to drink but must never *treat*, and no member was allowed to tell the truth. And, if any of the rules were broken, the transgressing member was under obligation to "buy a round of drinks for all present."

Finally, the secret high sign was given by placing one's thumb at the end of his nose, opening his hand and then extending his four fingers. This was also a recognition sign among members. To do it with both hands meant that the member was in distress and needed a drink.

When the Natives of Kotzebue were taught the white man's religions, the men and women of God had a hard time explaining the concept of the Second Coming of Christ. Finally they settled on explaining that Jesus would "come from the sky." This was an adequate explanation until the arrival of the first airplane whose pilot, naturally, was treated as if he were Jesus.

In the fall of 1989, an Anchorage police officer "kicked a rooster to death in the line of duty." Officer Robert Heun was investigating a domestic squabble when a large chicken attacked him. The rooster lunged for a second try when, according to the police report, Heun "took the offensive and struck out at him with two, size 10 Vibram soles." The suspect, the report concluded, "was reduced to a pile of black feathers."

James Bernard "Ben" Moore, the founder of Skagway, figured he had beat the high cost of dogsledding. He used sled teams of Angora sheep.

The animals didn't get cold and could forage for food by themselves along the trail. This saved the musher from having to pack food for his team.

For a few years, there were three or four teams of Angoras that were quite popular with the photographers. The end to the Angora teams came sadly. "They used to wander up in the hills," Moore lamented, "but six were shot by a fool who took them for wild goats." That ended the saga of the most unusual dogsleds, er, sheepsleds, in Alaska history.

In 1989, the North Slope village of Atqasuk introduced a novel way of keeping kids in school. Those students who showed outstanding citizenship and attendance were awarded a barrel of heating oil, worth about $100. For exceptional students, there was a shot at a school-year-end prize of a round-trip ticket to Anchorage.

Did it work? For the first nine weeks of the school year, attendance was at 91 percent, 30 percent higher than the previous year. It would have been even higher if two students had not come down with the chicken pox.

"By golly, if it takes $100 and a barrel of oil to get kids in school," Principal John Hetherington said, "it's worth it."

In the late 1970s, one of the most respected members of the Alaska House of Representatives was Ernie Haugen from Petersburg. Among the aides, he was best remembered for some of his personal antics. Every day at 4:30 he would look out of his fifth floor office window and watch the bureaucrats explode out of the SOB (State Office Building) and loudly yell, "There go the leeches!"

One of the most popular places for legislators to keep food cool, winter or summer, was on the outside window sill of the Capitol. Over the years, pigeons learned that anything in paper or plastic on the ledges was edible. Legislators who are more interested in beer than soda pop learned early that ledges allowed them a haven for their beverage without breaking the rule of no alcohol "in" the Capitol.

One of the most prized possessions of early Alaskan bush pilots was their "short snorter." Each pilot carried a ten dollar bill which all his buddies signed. The point was to force each pilot always to have enough money to buy gasoline. Pilots would often show each other their bills and talk about the antics of those who had signed their respective currency. To be caught without your short snorter meant you had to buy drinks for the house, a time-honored pilot's tradition. Being without a short snorter is grounds for withdrawing a pilot's license today.

While driving up the Alaska Highway north from Seattle, Randy Comer surprised his girlfriend by stopping the car occasionally and dashing through the forest and climbing trees. When asked what he was doing, Comer replied that he was practicing for when he met his first bear.

Arctic Village has two streets. One is named for a highly respected chief of the area. The other is Rock and Roll Avenue.

When environmentalist writer Art Davidson went on his first camping trip in Alaska, he carried an armful of rolled newspapers and a box of matches. Expecting to meet a bear, he planned on lighting the newspapers and using them as flaming torches.

As he settled down for his first night in the wilderness of the northland, off in the distance he heard a sound that could only be described as "rrrrrrrrrrrrr." In an instant he was wide awake and lighting his newspaper torches. As the sound grew louder, Davidson began tossing fuel on the campfire.

"RRRRRRRRRRRRRR."

Davidson finally located the source of the noise. It was above his head. Looking up into the night he saw the red light of an airplane crossing the sky, "RRRRRRRRRRRRRR."

A close friend of Roy Corral had a dog with two names: Chinook and Smiley. When Corral asked why the dog had two names, he replied that in the remote village where he and the dog lived, all the whites called their dogs names like Kobuk or Karluk. The Natives called their dogs names like Spot or Harry. So he had decided to have a bicultural dog.

During the Exxon *Valdez* oil spill, the editors of *Alaska Magazine* were approached by a cartoonist who was interested in putting one of his drawings in the magazine. A well-done cartoon, it showed oil spill workers holding up the small, dead body of a midget with a conical hat. The script indicated that this was the first dead ELF the oil workers had found.

Alaska Magazine declined to use the cartoon. While Alaskans know the ELF as the Economic Limit Factor, legislation that was killed as a result of the outrage from the oil spill, there was a fear that many Outsiders would believe that one of Santa's workers had become trapped by the goo and drowned.

The residents of Valdez had more than the oil spill to concern themselves with in 1989. By January of 1990, 158 inches of snow had fallen on the city, a record. Then the news got worse. On January 16, the city received 47½ inches in just a few hours. Homes were buried up to their second story windows and plows turned walkways and roads into white trenches.

The greatest danger was the buildup of snow on the roofs. To remove the weight, every able-bodied person in Valdez had to get up and shovel snow. Diane Skodinski, who was spending her first winter in Valdez, was amazed to see the people attack the snow with "shovels, scrapers, blowers and chain saws. I've never lived in a place where they had to use chain saws to cut the snow."

As a humorous aside, one enterprising businessperson cleared off a parking lot and used the twenty-foot pile of snow for a drive-in movie backdrop. What was the movie? "Back to the Beach," of course.

When Joan Daniels came to Alaska in the late 1960s, she arrived broke, her dreams of building her own cabin wrecked on the jagged rocks of reality. But rather than abandon the dream, she became a night club dancer to earn money for building materials. She referred to herself as a "stripper for boards and nails."

Evan Swensen, editor of *Alaska Outdoors* and producer/director/writer/actor of his own series on the Alaskan outdoors, remembers one time when he had to reshoot a scene. The fish he had caught was so rambunctious that it was all he could do to keep it on the line and avoid bumping into the cameraman on the small boat. The next day, the video crew decided that they would have to reshoot some of the action because they did not have establishing shots.

But they needed something to use as the "fish." Rather than try to catch another large one, Swensen tied a lead pipe at the end of his line and danced around in the boat "battling" the fish. The video crew took the establishing shots. When the filming was through, as a gag, Swensen reeled the pipe in and netted it for a humorous out-take video. As he lifted the pipe aloft gleefully, one of the cameramen on shore yelled, "And there you have it, ladies and gentlemen, the Great Northern Pipe."

During the Second World War, Quartermaster Louis Zomparelli and some of his buddies in Cold Bay were complaining about the poor quality of the GI food. The cook apparently took their words to heart and several days later served a delicious meal of chicken. When Zomparelli went to compliment the cook on the chicken, the cook replied, "Chicken? Those were seagulls" (from an interview with Louis Zomparelli in the possession of the University of Alaska, Anchorage).

Climbing Mt. McKinley is quite different than climbing other mountains in the world. The summit is not difficult to reach because the route has a smooth, 40 degree angle. The problem is in coming down. If someone slips and starts to slide, they cannot stop until they reach the 14,000 foot level. A former Park Ranger who remembered picking up the remains of a British team that tried to slide down from the summit recalled, "There were bones sticking through all of the parkas and equipment." Then he humorously added, "We couldn't sell any of it."

In December of 1987, a mouse chewed into a bag of marijuana at the Alaska State Troopers office in Palmer. When Trooper Lt. Jay Yakopatz discovered the culprit, the drugged mouse lurched out of the box of pot at him and scampered away.

It was "the mouse that roared," Yakopatz said laughingly of the "half-crocked mouse." When last seen, the suspect was moving "very fast" with "dark beady eyes and dilated pupils."

In January of 1912, Frank Lewis of Juneau went to court because it was alleged that he did

> wilfully, maliciously and feloniously injure and destroy one chair, one iron grating and one iron steam radiator, each and all the personal property of the United States, by then and there maliciously dashing and pounding the said chair against the concrete floor of the United States Jail, in the said town of Juneau, and thereby and in that manner breaking and destroying said chair, and by then and there maliciously twisting and bending said iron grating, tearing the same loose from the window casing of said jail, and by maliciously twisting the said radiator and tearing the same loose from its connections.

He was sentenced to six months.

14

THE ARCTIC COMPASS

One of the many difficulties faced by layman when it comes to understanding the Arctic is the concept of direction. In the Lower 48, as a geographic example, the direction "North" is very easy to ascertain, even if all you have is a compass out of a Cracker Jack box. In the Arctic, things are a bit different.

In reality, what Americans in the Lower 48 call "North" is not really the North Pole. It is actually magnetic north, a spot on the earth about 1000 miles south of the North Pole. This geomagnetic spot, interestingly, "slowly and continuously changes its position, following a roughly circular path that has a diameter of about 100 miles," according to the *Encyclopaedia Britannica*.

From a purely practical point of view, what this fact means is that the further north you go, the more inaccurate your compass becomes. As you progress north in Alaska, the needle in your compass that is supposed to be pointing north, will actually be pointing east, then southeast, then south southeast, and, finally, when you arrive at the North Pole, due south. (At the North Pole, every direction is south.)

While the actual geographic location of magnetic north is only a question of academic concern to people in the lower latitudes, for map makers etching cartographic renderings of the earth with a polar view, the concept of direction is difficult to convey. On a conventional map, north is almost always oriented to the top of the sheet of paper. Somewhere on the map there will be a rendition of a compass with the Cardinal points labelled: west to the left of north, east to the right and, finally, south at the base of the map.

When it comes to the same compass drawings on a map of the globe with an Arctic perspective, direction becomes a problem. From the North Pole, at the center of the map, *all* directions are south. Further complicating the navigational issue, east and west are then directions of lateral motion. The traditional means of guidance are also skewed. While

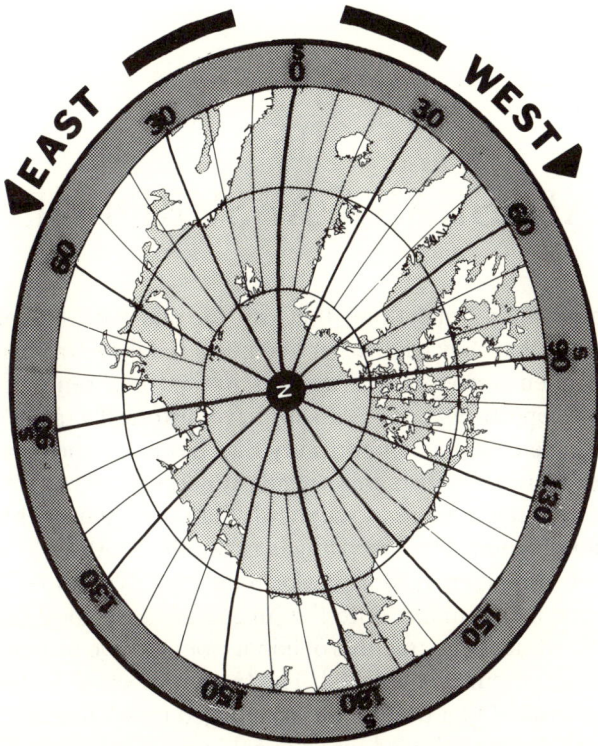

Arctic compass. (Author's design.)

the expression, "exactly eight miles south of here" has a specific meaning in Des Moines or Phoenix, at the North Pole, there are 360 degrees of possibility.

To resolve this difficulty, a new compass format had to be designed. The rendering had to contain all of the traditional direction-finding logic but, at the same time, explain pictorially the concept of lateral directional movement — that is, east and west between the two known points of the compass — that is north which was a single spot at the center of the map and south which was 360 degrees of possibility. The result was the Arctic compass, designed by Steven Levi of Anchorage.

15

ALASKANA ABSURDITIES

If there is any one thing that can be said with certainty about Alaskans, it is that they have never been slow to take entrepreneurial advantage of their surroundings. Alaska is, in the truest sense of the word, the land of opportunity, and Alaskans have historically taken advantage of every single economic opportunity that has come their way.

Take tourism. Tourists are so regularly fleeced that many tour operators view themselves more as shepherds than merchants. This is hardly a new phenomenon. The first Tlingits in Southeast Alaska undoubtedly viewed the white men as tourists worth fleecing. When Joe Juneau and Frank Harris first stumbled into the Juneau area, the local Indian chief was able to extract large amounts of liquor from the two sots on the promise of showing them yellow metal. The two prospectors, history reports, were so inebriated that they had to be dragged up what is now Gold Hill and have their noses shoved into the gold vein to see it.

Alaska's history of absurding has hardly been without its celebrity, both sung and unsung. Another misapplied bit of Alaskana is scrimshaw, the etched drawings on ivory that are associated with Alaskan Native art today. In reality, the first people to do scrimshaw were white whalers who sometimes had days of slack time on their hands. The whalers would take a whale tooth and slowly scratch drawings in the surface with a knife. Once the drawing was completed, the tooth was lathered with charcoal. When the tooth was wiped clean, the only coal left was that which had been trapped in the scratches. Thus the drawings were visible as black etching against the pale white of the whale's tooth.

But it took the Alaska Gold Rush to popularize this art form. Angokwazhuk, better known in Alaskan history as Happy Jack, was introduced to the art form when he was invited to join the white crew of a whaling vessel going down the West Coast of North America. He returned to Alaska the next year and began carving scrimshaw in the same design as the whalers. The pieces were immensely popular (not to

Anaktuvuk mask. (Courtesy Danny Daniels.)

mention profitable), and soon many Eskimos were following in his footsteps, or at least his handiwork. As the whaling industry faded into obscurity, scrimshaw became more popularly associated with the carvings of the Eskimo and remains that way today.

Happy Jack is also famous — or infamous, depending on one's point of view — for making the billiken part of the heritage of the Northland. A small, Buddah-like figure with a foolish grin, the billiken is sold in many tourist shops across Alaska, often with a scrap piece of paper which reads:

> Just rub his tummy
> or tickle his toes,
> He brings you luck,
> so the story goes.

Happy Jack saw the billiken in the United States and brought the concept back to Alaska. He made the first one in 1909 at the suggestion of a Nome merchant, and it was dubbed Kopturok, or "Big Head."

In the Lower 48 (the Lower 46 at that time), the billiken had already been patented by Florence Pretz in October of 1908. It was an instant hit in the United States, and the small figurines appeared as dolls, incense burners, salt-and-pepper shaker sets, hat pins, watch fobs, belt buckles and a wide variety of other household items. But by 1912, the billiken craze had faded — except in Alaska.

Today, only in Alaska does the billiken still have a grip on the commercial market. While many merchants sell the item, few know its history. Some claim that it is "an Eskimo god," while others say that it was a means of using every possible portion of the walrus tusk, "even the tip." The actual fact of the matter is that the billiken is carved because it can be sold.

Another example of a unique, Alaskan, nontraditional art product is the Anaktuvuk mask. One winter, three men — Bob Ahgook, Justice Mekiana and Zaccharias Hugo — were working a trap line and decided to liven up the Christmas celebrations in their home of Anaktuvuk Pass. They planned to come back to the village in disguise, wearing masks they had constructed out of caribou hides and bits of fur. The masks were such a hit that local schoolteachers urged the community to start producing them for sale to bolster the local economy. The idea took hold, and today Anaktuvuk masks are one of the most easily identifiable geographic artifacts of all Native arts and crafts.

There are also other artifacts that are quite identifiable as Alaskan — though many Alaskans cringe at the idea. Take, for instance, moose

The Giant Igloo, generally regarded as the ugliest building in Alaska. (Courtesy Jimmie Froehlich.)

nuggets. Known by a variety of names including moose pecans, moose beans and just plain scat, the nuggets are collected and used to make unique earrings, swizzle sticks, tie tacks and other commercial items.

Oosiks, the bone that walrus and seals use to erect their penises, are also understandably popular items among the earthy. Mosquito memorabilia, including traps, T-shirts, and hunting signs attract the attention and dollars of tourists, and coupling ivory bears grace many of the windows of gift shops.

But this is not the extent of the commercialization of Alaska. In Fort Yukon, for example, there is a large plywood circle nailed to a tree. Since Fort Yukon is on the Arctic Circle and many tourists fly north from Fairbanks for the sole purpose of being on the Circle, the tourism people in Fort Yukon decided to give the tourist that for which they were looking. This came in the form of a plywood circle with the words "Arctic Circle" prominently displayed in the center. Does it work? The people in Fort Yukon seem to think so, and the fact that tourists are still coming north to Fort Yukon is reason to believe they are correct.

Perhaps the worst form of Alaska art commercialism comes in what many Alaskans believe to be the ugliest structure in the state. Located on the Parks Highway 188.5 miles north of Anchorage and 169.5 miles south of Fairbanks is the Giant Igloo. This monstrosity is a multi-floored

Moose and carriage. (Courtesy University of Alaska, Fairbanks: R.D. Pinneo Photograph Album, ACC #73-23-1 in the Archives of the Alaska and Polar Regions Department.)

structure designed like an igloo but with dormers, little windows that project out of the sloping roof, for each room. The Giant Igloo is such a stunning sight that few can resist bursting into hysterical laughter when the building is spotted from the Parks Highway.

Then, of course, there is the public art that has broken out like a rash across the state. Perhaps one of the most "interesting" examples is in the Federal Building in Anchorage. Visible from the Seventh Street entrance is a piece of artwork described as an "untitled light sculpture." It is actually a single green neon light in a glass-covered aluminum case that runs diagonally down and along the length of a wall at the 7th and C entrance. The cost for this piece of artwork—paid to artist Dan Flavin of Anchorage—was $80,000. In the Federal Building pamphlet which describes the works of art, Flavin is quoted as saying, "I want installational-architectural coordination in that lobby. I want a total artistic realization, even if I have to sacrifice relatively—the private artist at work and play in the public sector."

Not many people know what Flavin meant.

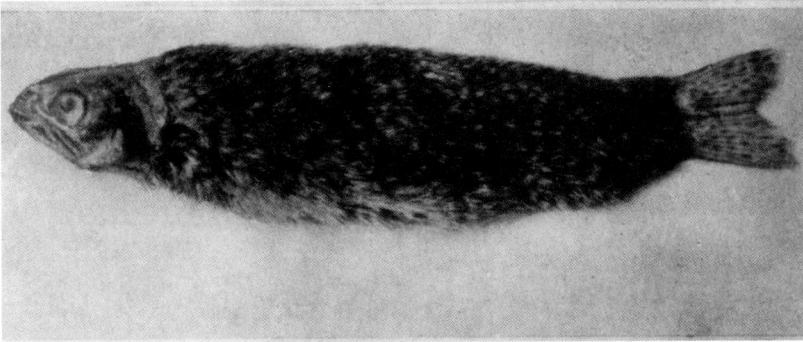

Alaska Fur Bearing Trout (postcard). (Courtesy Anchorage Museum of History and Art, B83.146.103.)

There have always been entrepreneurs who have taken advantage of Alaska's heritage of humor by adding their own particular fillip. Note some of the photographs and postcards that can be found in the archives of the Anchorage Museum of History and Art. These represent different methods used by photographers with an exquisite sense of humor. The razorback clam, of course, is a double exposure, while the "moose cart" is a staged picture.

A sterling example of Alaskan absurding is the "Alaska Fur Bearing Trout." The trout is actually a postcard, and there is no doubt that this photo convinced more than a few Americans that Alaska did indeed have furry fish. Though not inspired by this postcard, it is alleged by Alaska's greatest living poet, Ruben Gaines, that at one time a furry fish did indeed live in Alaska. This, it should be added, was part of a collection of poems by Gaines of the legendary Chilkoot Charlie.

While the creators of the furry fish, the razorback clam and moose cart are lost in the mists of time, that is not the case with current classics of Alaskan absurding postcards. Today there are three standouts in the field, Jimmie Froehlich of Anchorage, Jeff Brown of Juneau and Tom Sadowski of Anchorage.

Jeff Brown of Juneau, also known as Joe Gorilla of Gorillagrams, has produced a set of postcards which are specific to Southeast Alaska. Most notable are the "Record Catch in Southeast Alaska" and the "Cleaning of the Mendenhall Glacier." Juneau has almost become accustomed to the antics of Jeff Brown. Among his other credits he claims to have recorded a tape of elevator noise which was "originally broadcast to aliens" and published an irregular, irreverent, zany tabloid called the *The Juneau What,* which included such headlines as "VEGETARIAN EATS GREEN-

Top: Cordova Razorback. (Courtesy Anchorage Museum of History and Art, B71.X.5.19.) *Bottom:* A postcard by Jeff Brown. (Courtesy Jeff Brown.)

Another Jeff Brown postcard. (Courtesy Jeff Brown.)

More absurding postcards. (Courtesy Tom Sadowski.)

HOUSE!" and "CITY OF FOOL'S GOLD DISCOVERED, Archaeologists amazed 'Even the skeletons look stupid!'"

Froehlich has been in Alaska since 1975 and has held jobs as varied as home builder, photographer and waiter. Besides his postcards, his most talked-about project was the production of *Trailer Court*, a campy, bizarre 15-minute film of life in a trailer court in Spenard. When asked for the source of his sense of humor, Froehlich stated he did not understand English.

Tom Sadowski has a similar story. When reached for comment, he refused to admit any postcards were his in spite of the fact that his name was printed on the back of each one. "It's just a figment of your imagination," he snapped, "or a cup of bad coffee." Bad coffee or not, Alaska's heritage of humor and absurding continues to be strong and bountiful.

Note: The definitive source on billikens is Dorothy Jean Ray and her article "The Billiken," in the Alaska Journal, *and* Alaska Sportsman *goes into great detail on the history of the artifact. The quote from Dan Flavin appeared in the brochure "Art in Alaska," released by the General Services Administration. Brown, Froehlich and Sadowski were interviewed for this chapter, though it is doubtful any of them will admit it in public.*

16
BERING SEA GOLF CLASSIC

Having trouble with the fairways in Palm Springs? Think the 14th Green at Pebble Beach is a pain in the rickshaw? W-e-l-l, then you should try the course in Nome. Nome? Nome, *Alaska*? Nome has a golf course? Yup, and it's an easy one. There are only six holes and the par is 41. There's only one problem: you can only play golf once a year.

Since 1984, Nome has been sponsoring the strangest golf tournament in the world. Known as the Bering Sea Golf Classic, it's a course of six greens scattered along a mile on the frozen surface of the Bering Sea. Since the ice is about two feet thick, there's very little chance of falling into the drink. The Classic is held each year around St. Patrick's Day and is a fundraiser by the Bering Sea Lion's Club.

The course starts behind the Bering Sea Saloon where fluorescent orange balls are passed out to all golfers. The greens are exactly that, green, which makes them very easy to see against the white of the ice and snow. The flourescent balls are supposed to be easy to spot against the same ice and snow. They are supposed to be but are not, confirmed Lois Wirz of the Nome Visitors Bureau, a veteran of the course. "It's easy to lose your ball. Sometimes it just keeps bouncing, thirty, forty yards beyond the green. Or it falls into a hole or crack and you have to be almost on top of it before you see the ball."

Rules? Yes, believe it or not, there are rules. Five of them, in fact.

Rules

1. If you hit a polar bear with your golf ball (endangered species list) you will have 3 strokes added to your score. If you recover said ball, we will subtract 5 strokes.
2. No poaching crab from crab holes. If you get caught bending over a crab hole, you might get kicked in the ice hole.
3. You are not required to replace ice or snow divots.
4. Swimming in water holes is prohibited.
5. Standard rules of golf apply.

Amid the fun of the Bering Sea Golf Classic, however, there has been a sense of anticipation. As the Bering Sea Lions will tell you, there is an unknown person in Nome who has sworn that he/she wants to make headlines in the *Nome Nugget* by being the first person to streak the event. With temperatures at ten or fifteen below zero, *that* will be something to see!

17
ALASKAN GHOSTS?

In May of 1973, the chief mate and two sailors on the Alaska State ferry *Malaspina* saw a sight about which they are undoubtedly still telling their grandchildren. On a clear Sunday morning near Twin Island in the Revillagigedo Channel north of Ketchikan, a huge vessel suddenly appeared dead ahead. Lying broadside to the path of the ferry, it was about eight miles away and was an "exact, natural and real" ship.

The three men, in two different locations on the ferry, reported the same sighting. With binoculars they scanned the strange vessel and saw sailors working on deck. The ferry crew watched the strange ship for ten minutes and then, just as suddenly as it had appeared, it vanished into thin air.

Alaska, just like every other state, has its share of ghosts. Alaskan ghosts are no different than those in the Lower 48. They walk through walls, talk to themselves, appear and disappear at will and generally upset quite a few people in the process. But in Alaska, ghosts are viewed more as a part of the northland's rich heritage rather than evil spirits that are doomed to haunt the world of the living for eternity.

Take the ghost in Room 5 of the Gakona Lodge. This spectral being is known to stomp up and down stairs, turn down music, frighten dogs, slam doors, talk to itself and even blow pipe smoke in people's faces. John and Jerry Strang, who own the lodge, started a list of the ghost's idiosyncrasies but stopped when the list became too long.

Under normal circumstances, one would assume that the ghost would dissuade people from spending the night there—particularly in Room 5 where the ghost "hangs out." To the contrary, business at the Gakona Lodge is booming, probably due to the ghost. In fact, John and Jerry feel that the ghost is such a draw that when a woman from the University of Alaska, Fairbanks offered to hold a séance for the purpose of ridding the lodge of the spirit, the brothers turned her down.

Who is the ghost? That's a good question. No one knows for sure. The brothers did find an old photo in the lodge of a man with a pipe who they think may have been the human husk of the ghost. There's no reason for the Strangs to be concerned. As long as people come to the Gakona Lodge and ask to spend the night in the garish yellow room Number 5, the ghost is good for business and a bona fide part of Alaska's heritage.

Fifty miles south of Gakona is Tonsina Lodge. Here "The Ghostly Bartender" resides, occasionally walking between the old lodge and a tavern, The Mangy Moose Saloon. This ghost also has a favorite room, Number 18. Maids have occasionally found the door to that room locked from the inside, though no one spent the night there, and, on more than one occasion, an indent on the bed where someone or something had sat, though no one had rented the room.

The ghost apparently doesn't like people in its chambers either. In 1981, four members of a road crew rented the room. Before morning all four were sleeping in their trucks, and none of them would say why. When the maid went to clean the room the next morning, it was bolted from the inside.

Unlike the spectre of the Gakona Lodge, this one is visible. Described as a "tall, thin man with longish hair, a black tie and mustache" he also displays facial expressions. A courteous ghost, he has opened doors for women with their arms full of groceries. Though no one knows who the ghost is or why he is there, the lodge did receive an anonymous letter in 1985 containing a poem which offers a possibility. The poem reads:

The Ghost of the Tonsina Lodge

He escaped from a place
that was lower than Hell
through the swamps and the hate
of a Louisiana jail.
Under the Big Dipper
among the ice and trees
he found a place called home
where his soul ran free.
He stayed to himself
cutting a stake from the land
working through the Roaring '20s
as a railroad man.
In the Tonsina Lodge
as night settled in

two Canadian Mounties
closed in on him.
In final desperation
at the point of a gun
he committed his soul
to the land he loved.

Each part of Alaska has its own heritage of ghosts. In the Interior, there is the "Ghost of Fort Yukon," recorded by William Healy Dall in the 1800s. Dall wrote that in Fort Yukon knocks would be answered to empty doors and cooking utensils would move from hooks without human hands. Strachen Jones, the post trader for the Hudson's Bay Company at the time, professed ignorance of the strange happenings, even though everyone at Fort Yukon had witnessed at least one eerie event.

Oddly, in the spring when Jones and his men headed down river with furs, "at the nightly bivouac, to the astonishment of the voyageurs, the noises continued." Raps and scratching were heard on the boat's mast and men who slept around the camp fire swore they heard Jones talking to "a voice unknown to any of the party."

There have been two reported ghosts in the Aleutians, though there is no documentation by which they can be traced. One is "Jake," who supposedly walks the beach below the Scotch Cap lighthouse/foghorn on Unimak Island. On April 1, 1946, a tidal wave crested at Scotch Cap and five Coast Guard lighthouse personnel were swept to their deaths. Today Scotch Cap, which overlooks the confluence of the Pacific Ocean and the Bering Sea at the southern end of Unimak Pass, is an automated lighthouse. Though there is nothing on paper, some of the Coast Guard personnel at the old LORSTA (LORAN Station) Sarichef have sworn to have seen Jake, or at least his footprints, on the beach below the lighthouse at Scotch Cap. The second ghost is that of a Japanese Colonel on Attu who has been seen by only one credible witness.

In Southeast Alaska, Skagway has a gold rush ghost and it, like the ghosts of Gakona and Tonsina, haunts a specific room in a hotel. "Mary" the friendly ghost, lives in Room 24 of the Golden North Hotel. She's a shadowy figure that floats through the air and can sometimes be seen near the window of the room where she resides.

As the story is told, Mary came north at the request of her Klondike Rush sweetheart, who swore he was going to marry her. She arrived in Skagway and rented Room 24 in the Golden North Hotel. The wedding was never to be, though, for he had been killed in a landslide on his way to her side. Mary refused to accept his death and continued to wait. She soon developed consumption and became very ill. One day the doctor stopped at her hotel room to check on her condition and found her dead. Perhaps appropriate for a ghost, she was completely dressed in her bridal outfit.

Mary likes to wander the Golden North Hotel and occasionally turns on lights or pulls drapes shut. In 1983, a family reported that "someone opened [the door to their room] and sat down on the edge of the bed. They saw the door open and saw the indention on the bed. They saw the indentation leave and the door close."

Mary is not the only ghost in Skagway. It is said that there is a ghost "lingering" in the Pullen House, a deteriorating boarding house, and one that bellies up to the bar in Skagway's best-known saloon, the Red Onion.

The oldest known white man's ghost in Alaska is also in the Southeast and is said to have haunted Baranov's castle in Sitka for 50 years. Don't look for Baranov's castle today because it was destroyed by fire in 1894. But in the 1800s it was the most impressive building in Sitka — though it was built of logs, not stone — and was situated on what is now Baranov's Hill.

The ghost of Baranov's Castle was romanticized and popularized in a 1911 book, *The Lady in Blue, a Sitka Romance*, by John W. Arctander. How true the story is is not known, but the names in Arctander's book have a historical basis. There really was a Governor Adolf Etholen and a Father Veniaminoff who later became Bishop Innocent. But the authenticity of the story is murky.

According to the story, Princess Olga Feodorovna was in love with a Russian naval officer by the name of Victor Gregorovitch Schupkin. Though he was of noble birth, he was neither old enough nor rich enough to suit the ambitions of Olga's rapacious uncle, Count Adolphus Paulovitch Etholen.

Count Etholen was the Governor of Sitka at the time and thus the leading political figure in Russian America. A more suitable mate, the Governor thought, was Prince Ivan Sergovitch Peploff. Peploff was wealthy, powerful and had excellent political connections. On the other hand, he was "old and ugly, selfish, rude, a gambler and drinker who had already driven one wife to suicide."

But Peploff had other problems. He was infatuated with the Princess but couldn't win her heart as long as Schupkin was in Sitka. Therefore, to remove his competitor from the scene, he conspired with the Governor to have the young officer deliver a letter to a ship anchored in Sitka's harbor. When Schupkin went aboard the *Ouropa* in September of 1843, he was knocked unconscious and locked below decks. The ship immediately left for a secret mission north of the Yukon River.

When it became apparent that Schupkin was missing, many of his friends feared that he had been lost while hunting or killed by the sometimes hostile Tlingit Indians. The Princess was distraught. The Governor told his niece that the naval officer was surely dead and that she should marry his coconspirator, the evil Prince Ivan. Father Veniaminoff, the Russian Orthodox priest of Sitka also urged her to marry Ivan. There was another reason, the priest told her. Ivan was blackmailing the Governor, and if she failed to marry Ivan, her uncle would surely be ruined and their family name besmirched.

Alone, thousands of miles from any other relative and under pressure from both her uncle and the priest, Olga agreed to marry Ivan on March 18, 1844 — but only if her naval officer had not returned by then. Prince Ivan rubbed his hands in glee and counted the days. Princess Olga spent each night with a candle in the cupola on top of the castle looking for the lights of any incoming ship.

Finally the day of her wedding came. The Princess, wearing a blue gown, was married to Prince Ivan by Father Veniaminoff in the Russian Orthodox Church. Then a wedding feast was held at Baranov's Castle.

But the feast was interrupted by the booming cannons of an approaching ship. Prince Ivan wasn't concerned; after all, he was now a married man. But Olga felt that her lost love was aboard that ship and slipped out of her own wedding feast. At the door she was met by her aged nurse, who told her Schupkin had returned to Sitka and was waiting for her in her bedroom. There she confessed her love to him and killed herself with Schupkin's dagger. Schupkin followed suit and the two lovers were found dead in each other's arms.

For fifty years, residents of Sitka reported a strange light from the cupola of Baranov's castle on the 18th of each month, the last time being on March 18, 1894, fifty years to the day that Princess Olga had married the evil Prince Ivan Sergovitch Peploff. On that final day, Baranov's castle burned to the ground, and no cause for that fire was ever discovered.

This is a fine story but the facts are a shade different. There was a Governor Etholen but his middle name was Karlovitch, not Paulovitch. Neither he nor his wife had a niece by the name of Olga. The castle actually burned to the ground on March 17th, and although no one knew how the fire had started, eye witnesses agreed that it was "first observed in the glass cupola on the roof."

Interestingly, in 1883, Eliza Ruhamah Scidmore, in her book *Alaska,*

Its Southern Coast and the Sitka Archipelago, reported that Baranov's castle was empty except for a signal officer and the

> ghost of a beautiful Russian, whose sad story is closely modeled on that
> of the Bride of Lammermoor. She haunts the drawing room, its north-
> west chamber, where she was murdered, and paces the governor's cabi-
> net, where the swish of her ghostly wedding gown chills every listener's
> blood. Twice a year she walks unceasingly and wrings her jewelled
> hands.

One of the most unusual tales of the supernatural in Alaska is that
of the steamship *Eliza Anderson.* On August 10, 1897, the *Eliza Anderson* left Seattle for St. Michael. The Klondike Rush was on and men from
the four corners of the earth were rushing north to the gold fields of the
Yukon. The most commonly used route was by steam ship up the Inside
Passage from Seattle to Dyea or Skagway, and from there on foot over
the Chilkoot or White passes into Canada. A far less strenuous route,
though more expensive, was via an ocean voyage to St. Michael and then
up the Yukon River to Dawson.

There were problems, however. Ship owners constantly overbooked
the vessel so that there were more passengers than there were berths
available. The *Eliza Anderson* was no worse off in that circumstance than
any other ship. That was the good news. As Pierre Berton noted in his
classic work, *The Klondike Fever,*

> The *Eliza Anderson* seemed to lack every item necessary for a sea
> voyage. She had no propellor, no up-to-date boilers, no water con-
> densers, no steam hoisting tackle, no electric power, no refrigeration,
> and, incredibly, no ship's compass. Her coal bunkers were makeshift and
> totally inadequate, a factor that almost proved her undoing.

The vessel was traveling with four other ships, none of which could
be called sea-worthy, and the voyage also started poorly. Rough weather
at Dixon Entrance tested the endurance of the ships, and the four-and-a-
half days across the Gulf of Alaska to Kodiak must have put more than
one passenger's head over the rail. In Kodiak, the *Eliza Anderson* took
coal aboard. Then, while the ship was delayed in port, the rest of the expedition fleet went ahead to Unalaska, the next coaling stop.

In Kodiak, just before he was to leave, the skipper was warned that
an "equinoctial gale" was brewing and if the weather got worse, his ship
would probably founder in the turbulent Pacific and sink. Violent storms
were common this time of year, and many a sturdy craft was already on
the bottom because the skipper had been too hasty in setting to sea. The

Eliza Anderson would be particularly susceptible to storms, it was noted by many mariners in Kodiak, because she was a river steamer, not an ocean-going vessel. With a shallow draft, she would be very unstable in the churning sea. Throwing caution to the wind, Captain Powers scoffed at the gloom-and-doomers and stated, "Hell, I promised them in Seattle that I would get this ship to her destination, and I don't intend to let a little breeze make me break that promise."

Thus Captain Powers set out, and within a few hours the *Eliza Anderson* was battling for her life. Hugging the Kodiak Island shoreline, violent waves crashed into the stern wheeler. The wind tossed the ancient vessel about violently, sometimes rolling her so far on her side that her paddlewheels almost cleared the water.

Feeling that the ship was in danger of being swept ashore and ground to splinters on the rocks, the captain speculated that his chances of survival were better on the open sea. This might not have been the best decision. Away from the coastline the ship started lurching immediately and almost listed completely over.

Then, as if by magic, all the kerosene lanterns were extinguished, throwing the ship into utter darkness. The passengers undoubtedly felt that their last days on earth had come. Being tossed about like so many rag dolls, they were sharing the floor with dishes, chairs, bedding and all other shipboard articles that were not nailed down.

All night long the *Eliza Anderson* fought for her life. The decks were awash. All but one of her lifeboats had been swept overboard and her life rafts were gone as well. Flooding was common, and doors were swinging and banging with each roll of the ship.

Realizing that their only hope of survival was to keep the *Eliza Anderson* headed into the waves, Captain Powers ordered a sea-drag tossed overboard. A sea-drag, or a sea anchor, is a large canopy of canvas, like a parachute, that is secured to the back of a ship with a steel cable. Tossed overboard, it billows full and serves to give the ship a steadier ride, though it slows the ship down.

But even with the sea anchor, the *Eliza Anderson* was in trouble. The ship was making little, if any, headway, even with the engines going full force. Then the rudder chain broke. As the ship foundered in the water, each wave threatening to roll the ship over, the crew scrambled quickly to install relieving tackle. Then there was a report of flooding below decks. When the pumps were turned on, it was discovered that they were clogged with coal dust and were thus inoperable.

Ordering everyone into life jackets and sending out signal flares — not that they would do any good considering that any vessels in the area would be in the same distress — the captain and crew prepared for the end. The Reverend Hawkins calmly walked among the passengers and was credited with stopping a panic while other passengers "were intoxicated to a stupor, having fortified themselves with liquor from their private stock in an effort to bolster their courage."

Then, as if the situation were not bad enough, Lady Luck turned over another bad card. The *Eliza Anderson* was out of coal! A lazy crew had hidden half the bags of coal on the Kodiak dock rather than haul them aboard. Now the ship was going to pay for that error in judgment: without power she would surely be swept sideways and rolled. To survive, it would be necessary to burn everything on board: chairs, tables, bedding, molding and even personal possessions. In a frenzy, the passengers immediately began ripping apart the interior of the ship and handing the burnables down a line of men into the boilers.

It didn't take long for all the burnables to be consumed and then there was nothing left to rip from the walls. The pressure in the boilers was falling and the captain knew that he had no choice now but to abandon ship. Ordering the passengers and crew to grab anything that would float and prepare to abandon ship, the captain was about to give the order when he got the shock of his life.

The door to the wheelhouse was violently pushed aside and a stranger stood before the captain, a man he had never seen before. The ghostly figure was more than six feet tall, "gaunt of features with glittering gray eyes which peered unblinkingly through the misty spray. He wore oil-skins and high rubber sea boots. A sou'wester covered a mop of greyish-white hair. A flowing white beard gave his leathery face the aspect of a Viking from out of the dim past."

Seizing the wheel, the gaunt stranger said to the captain, "Your ship is in great danger, Skipper! Let me take the wheel and I will try to save her!"

Ordering all the power that the *Eliza Anderson* had left, the gaunt stranger demanded that the sea anchor be cut free. Then he turned the ship back toward Kodiak. A giant of a man, he was handling the wheel alone, a task which had required at least two men to control only moments earlier. The boat wallowed as she turned and then raced with the wind. Moments later the crew saw the rocky shore of Kodiak Island uncomfortably close.

Despite the pleas from the crew to let them resume control of the ship, the captain let the stranger wrestle the wheel. The rocks drew closer and closer until it appeared that there was no way they could avoid a collision. Then, just before the *Eliza Anderson* struck the shoals, the stern-wheeler rounded a point and a sheltered cove appeared. The gaunt stranger pulled the ship into the cove. The wind and waves blocked, for the first time in hours the *Eliza Anderson* was safe.

Profusely thanking the gaunt stranger, the captain escorted him to his own cabin and then went below to see what damage had been done. When the passengers learned what had happened, they raised several hundred dollars among themselves to present to their unknown benefactor. But, when the captain returned to his cabin, the stranger had disappeared. A thorough search of the vessel failed to produce the man. Since the only lifeboat left was in use at the time and the ship was well off shore, everyone was baffled as to who this mysterious stranger had been and how he had disappeared so quickly.

The *Eliza Anderson* also had another bit of luck. There was an abandoned cannery on the island which had a supply of coal. This the passengers and crew quickly seized and used to power the ship the rest of the way to Unalaska. In Unalaska, the tale of the "stranger who came aboard" spread quickly.

Though many stampeders believed what they heard, the United States Coast Guard was not particularly impressed with the story of a gaunt stranger suddenly appearing and saving a ship. Ghosts may haunt hotel rooms and saloons, but rarely do they save ships. While the captain, crew and passengers may have gone to their graves believing that divine intervention had given them a new lease on life, the Coast Guard was unimpressed with that explanation. To investigate the matter, it ordered the Revenue Cutter *Corwin* to proceed to the area and find the alleged "gaunt stranger."

It was not until 1946 that the *Alaska Sportsman* revealed the truth. Visiting the cove where the *Eliza Anderson* had been sheltered from the storm, the Coast Guard encountered two tall Norwegian brothers, Erik and Olaf Heestad. The brothers lived in the area but had gone broke when their small salmon cannery had been squeezed out of business by the larger companies. They then made their living hunting and fishing.

One of the brothers, Erik, had been in the city of Kodiak on the day the *Eliza Anderson* was in town and decided to stow away. He needed to get to Unalaska to see if he could get a loan from his uncle who had made a fortune in the sealing business. Once onboard, Erik had hidden with the cargo below decks.

In spite of the fact that the ship was in trouble, Erik had been afraid to come out of hiding. Being an expert sailor, he figured that the ship would be able to weather the storm, and it was not until the flooding began that he realized how critical the condition of the ship was. Only then did he reveal his presence.

As to his disappearing act, the explanation was simple. After he had accomplished his amazing feat, he left the captain's cabin and went down on deck. Nervous about accolades and concerned that he would be questioned about his unexplained presence on the ship, he wanted to get ashore. As he lived on the shore of this very cove, he was close to home. Getting ashore proved to be quite simple.

While the captain, crew and passengers were huddled on the sea side flank of the *Eliza Anderson,* Erik went to the land side. Spotting his brother looking at the ship through binoculars, Erik waved to Olaf to pick him up. Olaf rowed out and picked Erik up while the passengers and crew were on the far side of the ship. Then the brothers hid in the forest until the *Eliza Anderson* left the cove.

Thus ended what was considered by many Alaskans to have been one of the most tantalizing tales of the high seas. Here was a gaunt stranger coming to the aid of a ship in danger of sinking and then disappearing as mysteriously as he had appeared. It had all the trappings of a visit from the supernatural and, undoubtedly, more than one passenger chilled his children and grandchildren with the story of that grave night in August of 1897, when a spectre from beyond this world came on board the *Eliza Anderson* and saved his life.

Note: *Source material for this chapter came from a wide variety of sources, including* Bits and Pieces of Alaskan History, *1973; Debbie McKinney's "Alaska's Ghost Tales," in the September 18, 1986,* Anchorage Daily News *and "Roadhouse Attractions," in the August 17, 1985,* Anchorage Daily News; *Richard A. Pierce's "The Ghost of Baranov Castle,"* Alaska Magazine, *May, 1970; William Healy Dall, "The Ghost of Fort Yukon,"* Alaska Journal, *1981; Carol Murkowski's "The Lady in Blue" and Paul Fattig's "North Spawns Spooky Stories," in the October 29, 1985,* Anchorage Times; *and Thomas Wiedemann, Sr.'s "A Stranger Came Aboard,"* Alaska Sportsman, *April, 1956, and Pierre Berton's classic work,* The Klondike Fever.

18
UNUSUAL OR HUMOROUS ALASKAN PHRASES

absurding Alaska's unique form of humor. Absurding is the taking of a ridiculous idea, treating it as though it were true, and then enhancing it. For example, if a tourist were to ask an Alaskan where one might see a penguin, an Alaskan (with a straight face) might reply, "Well, you can usually see them down on the parkstrip early in the morning. Park over by the igloos about 6 am and you can see 'em looking for worms."

alascattalo a legendary cross between a moose and a walrus, honored each year with a parade. One block long down an alley, the parade is in Anchorage and is held on the first Sunday after the third Saturday in November. Awards are given for the smallest, ugliest floats.

Alaskan business card the act of making an absolute fool of yourself on an airplane or in some other public place and then handing out someone else's business card.

Alaskan daisy a 55-gallon drum, so-called because they seem to "sprout" everywhere in Alaska.

Alaskan fur snake the cloth covering for steering wheels.

Alaskan guarantee *see* "tail light guarantee."

Alaskan insulation *see* "insulation, Alaskan."

Alaskan martini an open can of beer.

Alaskan nightingale frog.

Alaskan raincoat a large plastic garbage bag which has holes ripped in the bottom and sides to allow your head and arms to be stuffed through. Alaskan sportsmen often carry several of these "raincoats" because they are light and durable *and* can be used for a myriad of other functions, including transporting water, packing dirty diapers and stinky garbage out of the bush, or wrapping fish with wet leaves

142

for the trip back to civilization. Cross-country and downhill skiers often keep a spare garbage bag in their back pockets because they are light, flat and are absolutely necessary during an unexpected chinook.

Alaskan suitcase   a cardboard box.

Alaskan tuxedo   grey quill pants and jacket with a bolo tie.

Alaskan yacht   a sailboat of any size or description.

Alaskan year   a year composed of 9 months of winter and 3 months of relatives.

alphabet soup   the Alaskan term for the myriad of Federal agencies in Alaska that are referred to by their acronyms such as EPA, DEC, DOT, DOT/PF, DNR, OSHA, HUD, and APUC.

Arctic Bump   a tall tale told by Alaskan bush pilots which alleges that the air above the Arctic Circle is thicker than that below the Circle. Because of the differential, when a plane cross the Circle, there is a slight bump. Today, commercial airliners cause their planes to "bump" when they pass over the Circle—for the sake of Alaska's humorous heritage.

barnette   Because E.T. Barnette (*see* below) had apparently absconded with the money from his own bank and left the city of Fairbanks broke, the *Fairbanks Daily News-Miner* used the founder's name as a verb to mean "to rob." This is an historical tidbit and the term has meaning to Alaskan historians only.

Barnette, E.T.   founder of Fairbanks.

bazooka   one of the three weapons guaranteed to stop a wounded, charging brown bear. The other two weapons are a howitzer and a flamethrower.

bear insurance   a large caliber gun, most often a .357 magnum.

bearflanks   an Anchorage term for Fairbanks.

"Bible leaf"   term for the chunks of whale flesh which were boiled down to oil by the whalers in the last century.

billiken   figurine patented in 1909 by Florence Pretz of Kansas City who was a schoolteacher in Alaska. The billiken is as Alaskan as the hamburger is American.

Blue Ticket   a one-way ticket out of a community given to a lawbreaker whose crime was not serious enough to consider hanging. In the early days of Alaska when there were few jails, a Blue Ticket meant leaving town on the first available means of transportation regardless of direction or destination.

Bourbon flu   a hangover.

box rushing   during the Gold Rush, prostitutes would entertain their clients in "boxes" on the balconies of saloons. The men were expected to buy liquor, where the establishment made its profit, and the prostitutes were expected to sell the most expensive liquor possible. This was known as "box rushing."

boxes   *see* box rushing

break   an ice lead; also what happens to your fingers in a Gustavus poker game when you fill your inside straight with a card from your sleeve.

bug   "to have the bug" or "be infected with the bug" means to have gold fever, an irresistible desire to search for gold.

bug juice   insect repellent.

bullchitna   the quality of most bear stories told by Alaskans.

bunnyboots   large, air-insulated boots which are used by the military in snow country. When worn in an airplane, a valve in the boots must be opened to allow the boots to "breathe."

cabin fever   an ailment which strikes during the winter in Alaska. In the old days, when Alaskans spent the seven cold months in a cabin, sometimes a man would go stir crazy.

cache   pronounced like the word "cash," a verb that means to hide an object so that it can be retrieved later. As a noun, the term means a small structure where goods are stored. Usually this structure is built high off the ground so bears will not devour the food left there. Cache is one of the few Alaskan terms that have made it into general American English usage.

calf   in terms of a glacier, an ice chunk that falls off the face of the glacier. When the calf falls into the water, it is then called an iceberg.

calving   how a glacier "gives birth" to a calf.

camp robber   a species of jays which descend on a campsite and steal everything that is edible, often right off someone's plate.

carpenter bear   a bear which, once inside a cabin, makes his own door out.

cheechako   (chee-chahk-ooo) or (chee-chahk-er), tenderfoot or newcomer. Originally it meant someone who had not been in Alaska from freezeup to breakup. Today it is a derogatory expression used by Alaskans to refer to a person who presents ideas which Alaskans do not like and is usually preceded by the adjective "Damn" or "$#%&*@$." Supposedly the term is a Tlingit interpretation of the midwestern pronunciation of the city "Chicago."

Chinese Ace   a pilot who lands his aircraft so poorly that he hits a parked plane.

clear shot   any shot an Alaskan says he could make if he were shooting while his hunting buddy is drawing a bead on the target.

continental United States   all states of the United States on the North American continent. This includes Alaska.

Creek Street   famed, picturesque wooden walkway in Ketchikan. It is also the site of the last legal brothel in Alaska. It was said of the creek after which Creek Street was named that here both salmon and miners went upstream to spawn.

dirty berg   an ice berg formed from the medial morraine.

dog salmon   a species of salmon. It derives its name from the Indians' belief that the fish was only fit for dog food.

double digit midget   someone who is leaving a military base in Alaska in less than 100 days. The name comes from the numerical count-down. With one year left, for instance, the count would be 365. When the count drops below 100, it goes into double digits.

Dunlop's Disease   an Alaskan affliction in which one's belly "dun lops" over one's belt.

"edge of the wilderness"   a description of the Anchorage bowl's location, in the pocket formed by Knik Arm on the north, Turnagain Arm on the South and Fort Richardson Army Base and the Chugach Mountains on the east. Because the city ends so abruptly at the "edge of the wilderness" it's often said that Anchorage's greatest charm is being so close to the wilderness.

"end of the earth"   the tongue-in-cheek description of Fairbanks' location on earth. When Fairbanksians reply in rage that "Fairbanks is *not* the end of the earth," people from Anchorage usually respond by saying, "Well, you can see it from there."

Eskimo ice cream   a mixture of berries, seal oil and snow.

Eskimo yo-yo   a toy made of two weighted puffs of fur at both ends of a piece of string. The object is to cause both puffs of fur to rotate in different directions, never colliding with each other.

"face like dog salmon, breath like husky"   description of a person lacking in facial beauty and hygienic concern.

fatboy pants   down insulated pullover pants for snow country.

flamethrower   one of three weapons guaranteed to stop a bear. The other two are a bazooka and howitzer.

flushies   toilets that flush.

galloping glacier   a rapidly moving glacier, sometimes covering hundreds of a feet in a day. A glacier that moves faster than a galloping glacier is called a river.

Gama Land   the legendary island in the Bering Sea where the walrus go to die.

Gillam weather   weather so bad that only Harold Gillam would fly.

granola chic   a style of food, store or community that is expensive, hip and environmental, the naturalist strain of yuppies.

grub   food.

grubstake   an amount of money or collection of supplies given in exchange for a percentage of a claim to be made. A hardware store owner, for instance, might give a miner equipment in exchange for 30% of any gold the miner discovered.

gullwing   Stinson aircraft made in the 1930s and considered one of the sturdiest bush planes ever built. It is said that the gullwing was "built like a bridge and flew like one too."

gunpowder proof   in the Gold Rush days, homemade liquor was said to be "proofed" if gunpowder mixed with the concoction would burn with a steady glow.

gussak   derogatory Yupik (Eskimo) term denoting whites. It is believed that this word is a corruption of the Russian word "cossack."

hog ranch   derogatory term used in Territorial days to describe any settlement near United States Army posts where "watered whiskey" and women of low morals could be found. A hog ranch was also called a "ranch" or a "rancherie."

honeypot   a toilet used in the bush consisting of a large trash can which is lined with a plastic garbage bag.

hooch   booze, usually rotgut.

Hoochenoo   Tlingit village in Southeast Alaska. Originally the word meant "bear fort" but has since come to be associated with an alcoholic beverage distilled by the local natives through a method taught them by white soldiers. This brew was called "hooch."

howitzer   one of three weapons guaranteed to be effective against a bear. The other two are a flamethrower and a bazooka.

ice crispies   the sound of decaying ice when it breaks apart. A more sophisticated way of describing the sound is that similar to the delicate tinkle of a crystal chandelier.

Icebergia   one of the derogatory terms used to describe Alaska by Americans who were not in favor of its purchase.

iceworm   in biology, a worm which lives immediately beneath the surface of a glacier. (The iceworm is from the family *mesenchytraeuf*.) In literature, of Robert Service origin, a piece of spaghetti with eyes inked in and dropped into the bottom of a shotglass was a practical joke on a cheechako. In honor of this tale, each February the city of Cordova hosts an Iceworm Festival complete with a 150-foot Chinese dragon-style iceworm which weaves through the city streets.

insulation, Alaskan fat, as in the human fat that insulates an Alaskan's stomach.

Irish lord a trash fish.

Jewish airport the Juneau airport because, during the winter, so many planes headed there "pass over" due to inclement weather.

Ketchikan small community in Southeast Alaska whose name comes from the Tlingit word meaning "eagle wing." Ketchikan is the "Wettest City in the World" with an average rainfall of 160 inches.

Klawock town in Southeast Alaska whose name is the sound made by a raven.

lake-hopping a canoeing term meaning to paddle across a lake, portage, paddle across a lake, portage, etc.

"Live on the snow, not in it" advice to a cheechako which, translated, means to live with the environment rather than trying to fight it.

loaded for bear, to be to be armed with a loaded gun, safety off, looking for and expecting trouble.

Los Anchorage a Fairbanks term for Anchorage.

Lower 48 the contiguous states.

middle of nowhere for an Alaskan, Iowa.

moose nuggets moose droppings, also known as moose pecans or moose beans.

"Moosegooser" the colloquial name for the engines of the Alaska Railroad.

mosquitoes large, voracious, bloodthirsty insects of the Alaskan interior which attack in clouds without mercy.

nakhani Athabaskan equivalent of Bigfoot.

Nanook polar bear in Yupik.

"Nantucket sleighride" in whaling terms, the ride the small whaling boats were given when a whale was harpooned and sped through the water.

Native Alaska has four classes of aboriginal peoples: Inuit or Eskimo, Athabaskans (Indians), Aleuts and Tlingt or Tlingt-Haida.

Nome gold rush city on the Norton Sound. Originally named Anvil, the current name of the city came as the result of an accident. British cartographers, while putting a map of Alaska together in 1900, knew there was a gold strike boomtown on the cape where Nome stands, but didn't know its name. To remind themselves to find the name of the town, the cartographers wrote "Name ?" They subsequently forgot to find the name of the town and the printers interpreted the handwriting as "Nome C." or Cape Nome.

no-see-ums   small, gnat-like insects which bother Alaskans mercilessly in the bush. These insects are so small that they can barely be seen, thus their name.

old pilots   part of the bush pilot adage which states that "there are old pilots and there are bold pilots but there are no old, bold pilots."

oogrook   Yupik term for the bearded seal.

oosik   bone in the penis of a walrus or seal.

Outside   anywhere in the United States except Alaska, usually used in reference to the Lower 48. (*See also* "We don't give a Damn how they do it Outside.")

PanAm weather   in the heyday of the bush pilot, weather that was so clear that even Pan American would fly.

panhandle   southeast Alaska.

pencil miners   mining claims filed under fictitious names.

penguins   none in Alaska.

pie-in-the-sky   an unrealistic project, proposed by someone who does not know what he/she is doing, involving money he/she does not have, which he/she plans to get on promises he/she cannot keep, which will be repaid by revenues that cannot logically be determined, which will produce a benefit that cannot be calculated. In Alaska, pie-in-the-sky projects usually begin with the phrase "If the State of Alaska would give us . . ." and end with the phrase ". . . benefit all Alaskans."

Quivit   wool of the musk ox.

rail fever   sea sickness.

ranch   *see* hog ranch.

rancherie   *see* hog ranch.

roadkill   an animal killed on the side of the road, usually butchered and given to charity.

sailrabbit   an animal which has been run over so many times that it can be pried loose and tossed like a frisbee.

September   late September and early October. This term is used to describe the time of year when the snow dusts the tops of the mountains but not the city streets. Alaskan artists like this time of year because the snow makes the texture of the mountains stand out.

Seward's Folly   *see* next term.

Seward's Ice Box   derogatory term for Alaska used by those who did not favor the purchase of Alaska.

short snorter   a bill, most often a $10 bill, that a bush pilot kept as emergency fuel cash. Short snorters were usually signed by other bush pilots so the older they were, the more names were scrawled on both sides of the bill.

short timer someone who is about to leave the state, usually within three or four months.

Sitka slippers rubber boots with thick, removable wool linings.

skookum originally the Pacific Northwest term meant strong or serviceable, but over the years the Alaskan meaning of the term changed to mean smart, as in "street smart."

slickum a chemical additive to petroleum in the TransAlaska Pipeline which reduces friction between layers of oil and thus allows the oil to travel down the pipeline faster.

snakes none in Alaska.

snowgo snowmachine.

SOB State Office Building, the structure in Juneau where the bulk of the State workers spend their time.

socked in fogged in, usually meaning that planes could not fly.

Sourdough an old timer, traditionally someone who had been in Alaska from freezeup to breakup.

Southeast Southeast Alaska, i.e., all of Alaska south of Yakutat. This area is sometimes called the "Panhandle."

spare tire large accumulation of insulation; *see* "insulation."

spearchucker a very derogatory term for a Native.

Spenard a rather seedy section of Anchorage named for Joseph A. Spenard, 1879–1934, who homesteaded on the lake which now bears his name.

Spenard cadillac a four-wheel drive truck with four flat tires, no windshield, and a pair of foam dice hanging from the rear vision mirror.

Spenard credit card gas siphon.

Spenard divorce a divorce in Spenard in which dissolution is achieved when a person shoots his or her spouse.

Spenard marriage any marriage performed by a bartender or bellhop.

Spenard martini glass of beer with a peanut in it.

Spenard suitcase cardboard box; also known as Spenard Samsonite.

spit a very narrow peninsula of sand or earth.

square tires as the temperature drops, car tires lose pressure, creating flat surfaces on the bottom. When the car is driven, it takes a few hundred yards for the tire to warm up. But, until the tires get warm enough to expand to their normal size, every time the frozen flat portion hits the ground, the tires will bump. Seasoned Alaskans can tell the temperature by the amount of time it takes for the tires to "thaw" and become "round."

Squarebanks term for Fairbanks used by people who do not live in
Fairbanks.

squaw candy smoked salmon.

sun dogs pillars or circles of rainbow which appear around the sun during the winter. Usually this occurs when there are ice crystals cir-
culating high in the sky.

surimi a fish fiber protein cake currently made from pollock. Surimi has
no fat content and no taste. Thus it can be mixed with other foods,
such as beef sausage, without altering the taste of the other foods
and, at the same, reduce the percentage of fat content. A 20% surimi
beef sausage, for example, tastes like a 100 percent beef sausage but
is 20 percent fat-free. Perhaps best known in the supermarket as "im-
itation crab," surimi can also be reduced to a flour and stored.

Susitna "Sleeping Lady," the mountain due west of Anchorage. Once
upon a time, the legend goes, an Indian maiden was waiting for her
brave to return from battle. Unfortunately he died in battle. When
the other Indian maidens went to break the bad news, they found
her asleep. Rather than wake her to bad news, they let her sleep. She
has been asleep ever since, and over the years, leaves and snow have
covered her, forming the mountain that can be seen today.

tail fire a fire made by lazy campers. After a fire has been started, logs
are placed across the fire so that their center burns first. When the
log burns through, the long log has become two logs which are added
to the fire. The two new logs are then placed over the fire in the same
manner as the original, long log. Eventually, all that will be left are
the "tails" of the logs.

tail light guarantee an Alaskan guarantee that is good as long as you
can see the car tail lights of the salesman who made the guarantee.

termination dust first snow of the season in Anchorage which dusts the
top of the Chugach Range. In the old days it was the first sign of
winter and meant that construction projects were about to ter-
minate for the season. Today, for the Outsider, the appearance of
termination dust means that it is time to pack up and leave if they
want to avoid the winter snow.

Thompson Pass the mountain pass on the highway between Tok and
Valdez. It is alleged that there is a pass here but few Alaskans have
seen it. It's usually socked-in.

toothpick forest the term used to describe the fringe of dead trees
along the northern shoreline of Prince William Sound. As a result of
the Earthquake of 1964, the land on the north side of the Sound fell
six feet. Trees which had been growing on the edge of the Sound on

the north were suddenly submerged and subsequently died. Many of these dead trees still stand, giving the impression, at a distance, of a fringe or forest of toothpicks.

tube   part of a parka. A parka that has a "tube" has two very wide collars with tufts of fur on the edges. When the collars are zipped together they form a tube. The creation of this tube leaves a space of air between the face and the outside environment where the warm breath can gather and keep the face warm. The tube will keep the face warm even in a high wind.

Turnagain Arm   the arm of water which forms the southwest boundary of the Municipality of Anchorage. It was named by Captain James Cook when he sailed up this stretch of water in search of the legendary Northwest Passage. The tide went out and left Cook on a siltbar. When the tide came in again, Cook decided to "turn again" and come out of the arm.

visqueen   a large, thick sheet of black plastic. Visqueen can be used to do everything from keeping heat around drying cement in the middle of the winter to covering an outhouse in the bush.

Walrussia   derogatory term for Alaska by those who opposed the purchase of Alaska.

"We don't give a Damn how they do it Outside."—a phrase made famous by a beer brewery in Anchorage which captured the Alaskan sentiment that "things are different in Alaska" and Alaskans don't "give a damn" how anything is done Outside. The downside of this attitude is that Alaskans often end up making the same mistakes that Outsiders do in trying to solve the same problem. (*Also see* "Outside.")

"We don't tan; we rust!"   lighthearted statement made by Southeast Alaskans because the sun is such an infrequent visitor.

white movie   an Alaskan absurding tale invented by Warren Sitka. Sitka claims that during the winter Alaskan movie theaters will host a "white movie" in which the lights of the theater are turned on to simulate daylight. This will help, Sitka claims, alleviate Cabin Fever.

white socks   voracious flies known as "white socks" because they have white markings on their feet that appear as tiny socks. They do not play baseball.

whiteout   conditions where snow is falling so heavily that visibility has been reduced to a few feet.

windshield appraisal   an appraisal by an Alaskan realtor during which he drives by the property and estimates the value of the property.

windshield visitor   a tourist who sees Alaska through the windshield of his car and doesn't go into the bush.

"woman behind every tree"   statement made of the flora and fauna of the Aleutian Islands, an area devoid of both.

Xerxes   famous Persian Emperor and included in this phrasebook to make certain that there was a listing under "X."

Zulu Time   the time in Greenwich, England, which is necessary for LORAN navigational calculations.

19

"HEY BUDDY, CAN YOU SPARE A BINGLE?"

Did you ever wonder what Alaskans used before they had cash? To most Americans this is a ridiculous question. Of course Alaskans use American money. They used American money before statehood, probably all the way back to the Russian era, because Alaska was part of the United States. What else would they use? The answer to that question is actually not that simple.

Initially, of course, Native Alaskans had a subsistence lifestyle that did not require money. With the coming of the white man, that changed. The Russians had supplies the Natives needed, and the Natives had furs the Russians wished to buy. But without some medium of exchange, bartering was the only way a transaction could be completed.

That led to problems. The Russians didn't always have what the Natives wanted when furs were available. Or the Natives wanted an item from the store at a time when they had no furs to trade. To resolve these problems, the Russians established a credit system to provide a primitive form of what economists today call "cash flow."

But the extension of credit quickly proved to be a nightmare. Although keeping track of large amounts of money was easy, recording very small sales kept the bookkeepers working late into the night. This led to errors in the records which eventually became so numerous that the Russian-American Company was losing money. To end the morass of paperwork, Russian Governor Baranov proposed a clever solution to his superiors in St. Petersburg. He suggested the printing of money for use in Russian America.

The board of the Russian-American Company liked the idea and issued Alaska's first scrip, called *marki*, which was first made of parchment and later walrus or sea lion skin. In 1804, Baranov's superiors sent

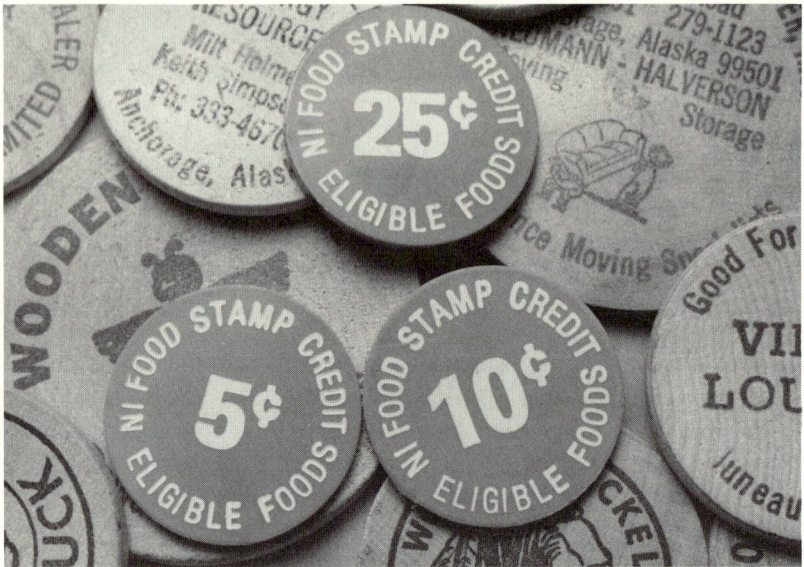

Bingles. (Courtesy Danny Daniels.)

him 50,000 rubles on parchment, most of which was to be paid to the Russian-American Company employees as wages.

It was a brilliant scheme. By paying for everything in *marki*, all the money eventually flowed back to the company store. This scheme worked until 1869, when Alaska was transferred to American hands. Then, as the Russian-American Company was disbanding, all *marki* were collected and destroyed. Today there are only about a dozen *marki* notes left, most of them in museums.

From the end of the Russian occupation to the beginning of the 19th century, a wide variety of objects were used as mediums of exchange. Gold nuggets and dust were most common, but fur, beads and skin were also negotiable. There is even some evidence that fish tails sometimes were used in lieu of cash.

The Klondike Strike, and thereafter the Alaska Gold Rush, didn't change things much. Though thousands of men rushed north, the standard was still gold. Nuggets and dust were used for almost all transactions as the gold could be weighed out for both large and small purchases. But when the boom played out, Alaskans were once again left with the problem of how to transact "nickel-and-dime" business without coins.

Thus was born the bingle: a coin or token imprinted with the name of a business. The coin could come in any denomination, but almost all of them were in values of a dollar or less. Bingles were of wood, metal and paper. Most likely the paper scrip was produced at local print shops, while the coupon books were printed by outside firms. The metal and wood tokens were stamped out at stamp and die companies in Seattle, Portland and San Francisco and perhaps a few others.

Oddly, Alaskan bingles were printed without dates. Why, no one is certain. There were also some bingles that were "mavericks," tokens with no store name attached. Needless to say, cashing a maverick was difficult. While bingles were supposedly only good at the store where they were purchased, many merchants offered reciprocity.

Kaye Dethridge of Sitka, the largest merchant of Alaskan bingles, is unsure where the name originated but has found the term used as early as 1916 in Petersburg. Other token collectors believe that the term originated with the Reverend Bingle, who was active in the development of the Alaskan Interior in the 1930s. Regardless of the origin of the name, the term was cemented in both Alaskan history and vocabulary when the Alaska Rural Rehabilitation Corporation (ARRC) issued tokens to the Palmer colonists which were called "Alaskan Bingles."

The ARRC followed the same scheme as the Russian-American Company. If everyone had bingles and everyone spent time at the company store, there would be cash flow within the colony.

Unfortunately, it didn't happen that way. As soon as the merchants near the colony realized they were losing cash customers, they began accepting bingles at their establishments in lieu of hard cash. This created too many problems for the Palmer Colony, and the bingles were phased out in 1938.

But the end of the bingles in the Palmer Colony did not mean an end to the tokens throughout Alaska. Bush communities still needed the metal discs because there were too few U.S. mint coins in circulation. In communities such as Shishmaref, Kotzebue, Noorvik, Gambell, Savoonga and Kivalina, a bingle was still the only reasonable way to handle small transactions.

Interestingly, Dethridge believes that the bingles for the Palmer Colony were issued and controlled by the Department of the Interior. But the bingles used in many of the Native stores were issued and controlled by the Bureau of Indian Affairs. This is unusual because coinage is constitutionally handled by the United States Department of Treasury. Bills and coins not issued by the Treasury are known as "counterfeit."

While the United States government was well aware of the bingles, little was done to stop their use. But the government was not pleased with the practice. According to Howard Thew, who owns one of the largest

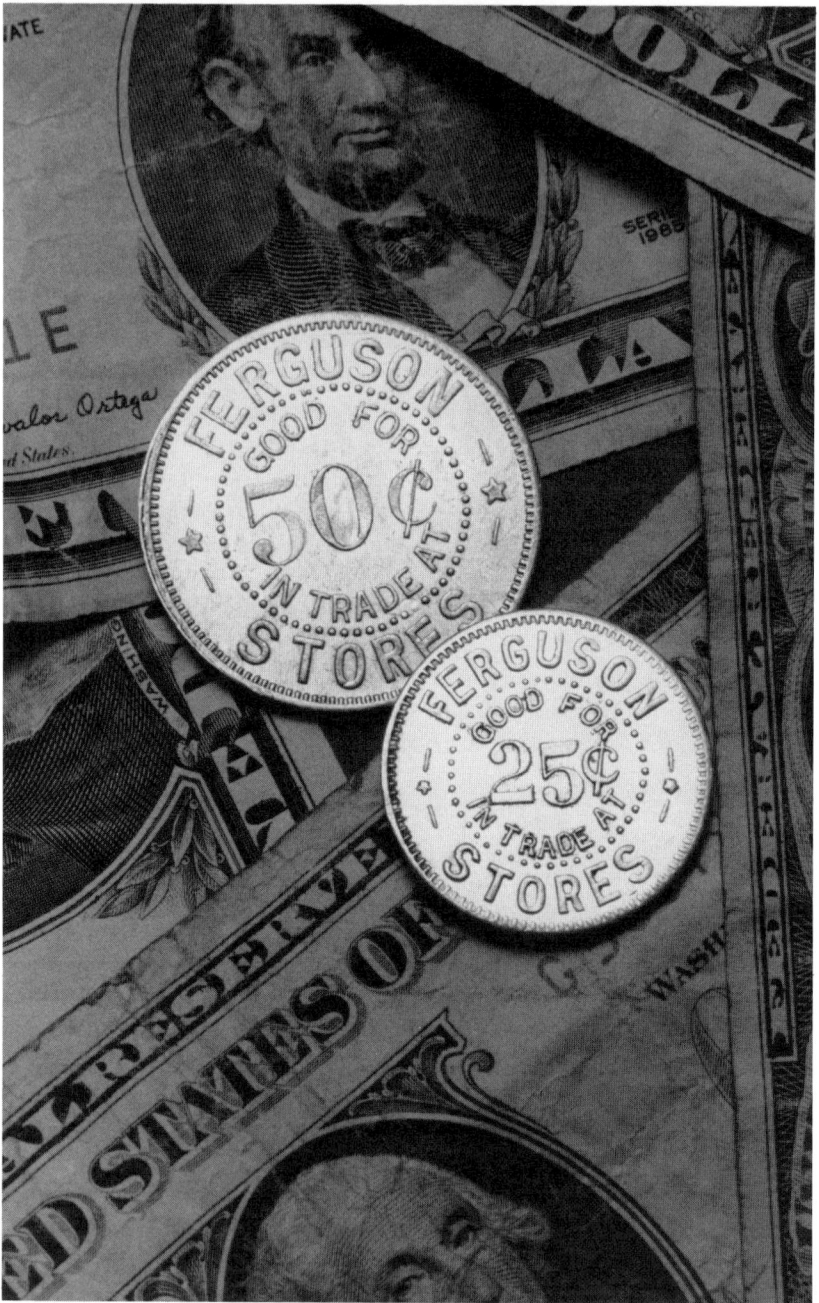

Bingles. (Courtesy Danny Daniels.)

collections of tokens in Alaska, the question of the legality of the bingles came to head in the early 1960s when Natives tried using the bingles "at the Post Office in Seattle. After that the government said 'no more bingles.'" The ensuing uproar effectively finished the widespread use of bingles in Alaska.

No one knows for sure how many bingles were coined, primarily because new ones are always turning up. "Today those bingles are collectors items," Dethridge notes. "There were about seventy-five businesses across the state that issued the bingles, and there are at least a few samples for all of them. Some are wooden. Others are colored. There are those that are intricate and others that are plain. The value of those tokens today depends on supply and demand. Some you can buy for a few dollars."

Then there are others which are rare and therefore quite valuable. The rarest of all bingles is known as the Priesner dollar. Only one is known to be in existence — owned by Kaye Dethridge — and it has a story that is as unusual as the coin.

The bingle itself is an ordinary-looking, well-worn coin, except that it has a gold nugget imbedded in its back. Issued by Gustave Priesner for his McCarthy drug store about 1910, it became a piece of treasured Alaskana when it was connected with the paperwork which has made it famous.

Priesner, who had the status of an enemy alien during the First World War, was well-known around McCarthy as much for his girlfriend as for his pharmaceutical enterprise. His femme was Rose Silberg, who ran a "resort" which catered to the booming population of men who were working in the Kennicott copper mine. Silberg was saving her money and keeping the horde in Priesner's safe. All went well until Silberg found herself a new boyfriend.

With a new beau, Silberg wanted her money, about $20,000, from Priesner's safe. The druggist refused to relinquish the money and harsh words were exchanged. The next time Silberg was seen it was in a mutilated state on the floor of her resort, the Chili Con Carne Parlor. The room had been ransacked, and an empty pocketbook was found on the table.

The murder must have created quite a stir in the small town. The *McCarthy Weekly News*, whose specialty heretofore had been grocery specials, political announcements, local fillers and business shorts, dedicated the center of the front page to the crime. "Literally Hacked to Pieces," one of the subheads screamed, and the paragraph below provided grisly details of the stabs, gashes and cuts on the "body in a nude condition." The only detail left out, which was provided to the readers

by the Cordova *Daily Alaskan* two weeks later, was the presence of "many
bloody finger marks" on the floor.

The last man known to have seen the victim alive was Gustave
Priesner. He had been seen by Joe Petrie, owner of the Golden Saloon.
Petrie told a few people what he had seen, but when the Marshal went
to take a deposition, Petrie could make no comment. He was found dead
in his room at the Golden Hotel. Murder was suspected and an autopsy
ordered. Priesner was an obvious suspect since Petrie's death could have
been by poison, a substance a druggist could easily obtain.

From here the record gets sketchy. In 1963, a woman searching for
bottles in the McCarthy jail happened to come across a bundle of papers.
In them was a telegram dated April 12, 1918, ordering the arrest of
Priesner for murder. Another document in the bundle was a letter dated
October 28, 1918, from the United States Marshal in Valdez to the Deputy
U.S. Marshal in Cordova regarding the sending of "eight jars containing
the stomach of Petrie, who died at McCarthy last spring under suspicious
circumstances."

While these documents made interesting reading, they were still just
historical tidbits. Ten years later, in 1973, when the *same* woman returned to McCarthy to look for bottles, she accidentally uncovered a
purse with three Priesner coins: five, 10 and 25 cent pieces. She sold the
coins to a Juneau token dealer who tracked down the famed $1 coin. To-
day that coin is worth $10,000.

And what of Priesner? Unfortunately, the historical record is thin.
The last newspaper reference to the druggist was in the April 15, 1918,
Cordova paper. Priesner, the Cordova paper recorded, had been arrested
in Fairbanks with $20,000 on his person. But he had not been detained
for murder. He was being held because he had failed to register as an
enemy alien. He was taken into custody as he was heading for the
Chandelar district where it was his intention to open a trading company.
Then, "under telegraphic instructions," Priesner was "taken back to
Chitina."

The charges against Priesner must have been dropped for there is
no record of a murder trial. There is also no further mention of Priesner
in the Cordova or Fairbanks papers, though many of the issues are missing or unreadable on microfilm. Priesner apparently spent the years of
the First World War in a detention facility for enemy aliens in Salt Lake
City. What happened to him after the war is not known. The last mention
of Priesner in historical documents is a civil suit filed against O.W.
Brehmer of McCarthy in 1920. Thus, at least in 1920, Priesner was still
free in McCarthy. (Howard Thew believes that Priesner eventually went

to Siberia, but there is no documentary proof to support that contention.)

While Priesner's fate remains unknown, the place of the bingles in Alaska's history is secure. They are more than pieces of metal, paper or wood. They are part of the rich heritage of the northland.

20

THE CORDOVA
ICE WORM FESTIVAL

Perhaps the most well-known Alaskan animal — right after tourist-eating brown bears and mosquitoes large enough to carry off small children — is the ice worm. Supposedly this animal lives in the year-round ice and snow of Alaska and can be harvested by intrepid entrepreneurs who use them to eat the sediments in the bottom of the bottles of Alaskan whiskey much the way larvae are used in good Mexican tequila. Of course, the fact that there are no Alaskan distilleries has not put a damper on this legend.

Oddly enough, though the ice worm is part of the heritage of the northland, the ice worm was never an Alaskan story to begin with. One of the originators of the myth was Robert Service, a Canadian poet writing poems of the Klondike Rush in the Yukon Territory of Canada. Service's tale of the ice worm cocktail tells of a *Cheechako* who was bamboozled into believing in ice worms when a sourdough put a stump of spaghetti with red ink eyes in the bottom of his shot glass.

The myth was further enhanced by legendary Alaskan newspaperman Stroller White. As a cub reporter in Dawson, Canada, White expanded the legend as part of a joke. Responding to his editor's demand that he "go out and rustle up some news," he did exactly that. He immediately went to a bar, and after long and involved deliberation over several glasses of elixir, he came up with an ice worm story. Returning to the newspaper office he set down a classic of northern tall tales.

In a straightforward manner he reported that the extremely low temperatures combined with the "recent heavy fall of blue snow" had brought thousands and thousands of ice worms out to bask in the "frigidity."

Because there were so many worms and all those organisms were "chirping," the story ran, the good people of Dawson were unable to

160

sleep, and serious debate was under way as to how to resolve this lamentable situation.

While the readers in Dawson were thrilled with the tale, the rest of the country was enamored. The article was reprinted again and again until Stroller White's fame as the world's ice worm specialist was worldwide. Correspondence from the four corners of the world came to White's office, and he responded to each letter with lies, lies, lies. He even received a letter from the United States Department of Agriculture asking for more information on the beasties and from the Scientific Research Society in London, which requested specimens.

From such humble beginnings, the legend of the ice worm grew by leaps and bounds. Within a decade, ice worm memorabilia was being sold across Alaska. Perhaps the most famous was the postcard of a miner harvesting the animals as they hung from the lip of a glacier. What the ice worms were used for was never stated on the card, but the can in the harvester's hand suggested fishing—perhaps for ice fish.

Myths aside, there really are such things as ice worms. While it is hard to believe, these worms do live in the uppermost crust of glaciers. When it is cool—whatever that means to an ice worm—the worms come out and feed on the red algae that accumulate on the surface of the ice floe. Quite a bit smaller than the ice worms of Alaskan lore, these pin-thin annelida are dark and on warm days can be so numerous that they appear to carpet glaciers.

True to the Alaskan tradition of not allowing the facts to derail a good story, the ice worm of lore is now an Alaskan institution. Ice worm pins, postcards and T-shirts are sold across the state, and each year in mid–February the city of Cordova holds an Ice Worm Festival.

The Ice Worm Festival began in 1961 when the community of Cordova decided that something was needed to accent the city's existence. The Ice Worm Festival was an attempt to publicize the name of Cordova and enhance tourism—a non-polluting, renewable resource which Alaskans have been harvesting since the turn of the century.

The first festival was a "grand success," according to the *Cordova Times*. In addition to the 150-foot long, "One and Only Cordova Iceworm" with its 37 pairs of legs—courtesy of the high school band and honor society—there were a host of other activities for the locals, including a peripatetic "Court of Injustice" where beardless men were sentenced by the "hangin' judge." Awards were given for the largest, funniest, and scruffiest examples of male plumage. There was also the usual assortment of foot and bike races.

A staple of all community fairs since the dawn of time, a cake

Harvesting the legendary ice worm. (Courtesy University of Alaska, Fairbanks: Alywin Humphries Collection, ACC #83-148-182N, in the Archives of the Alaska and Polar Regions Department.)

Top: Ice worms in their natural state. (Courtesy Alaska State Library, Winter and Pond Collection, 87-1899.) *Bottom:* The "One and Only" Cordova Iceworm. (Courtesy Cordova Historical Society.)

contest, was also held. In 1961, first prize went to a chocolate cake, of course, and second prize to the apple pie. Where one would find fresh apples in Cordova in the winter was a mystery. Third prize went for a Polka Dot Candy Roll. As a note of humor, the first prize in the adult parade award category went to a "Lady with a Chihuahua dog." Why, much less how, a Chihuahua would be in a winter parade in Alaska is an interesting thought.

Since 1961, quite a bit has been added to the Ice Worm Festival. Ice worm eggs are regularly "hatched" with aid of a heat lamp and the "Ice Worm Wiggle," a dance honoring the beast of yore, was introduced to the festivities in the 1970s. But, from the point of view of Cordovans, the most important aspect of the parade has been achieved: Cordova is no longer a forgotten town.

21

S. LUNDBLAD
AND THE FISHY POEM

With anti-German hysteria running rampant through the Territory of Alaska during the First World War, Alaskans were seeing spies everywhere. No one was above suspicion, least of all anyone who had any characteristics that were, appeared to be, or were suspected of being, Teutonic — and to many Alaskans, "European" or "Scandinavian" was the same as "German."

More than once, the misguided instincts of a citizen just trying to do his duty for his country went awry. Take the case of S. Lundblad, a fisherman and seafood entrepreneur in Seward. Lundblad, because of his Scandinavian background and peculiar friends, seemed a likely German spy — at least to the eyes of E.W. Swayer, Jr., the editor of the *Seward Gateway*.

Swayer, in his capacity as a good citizen, was suspicious of Lundblad and, in writing, confided his feelings to the local military intelligence establishment.

Lundblad, the editor reported, had three suspicious associates: Captain S.S. Johnson, "Peterson," and Ed Jacobsen, and a more conspiratorial crew one would have been hard-pressed to find. According to Swayer,

> Lundblad, who is known as the "Swedish Poet" hereabouts, is violently pro-German. Prior to the declaration of war, he regularly received letters and papers direct from Sweden. He has lived in Germany and is well acquainted with German philosophy and teachings. Lundblad is exceptionally well-educated. He speaks all of the language of western Europe, including Russian, Norwegian, Swedish, German and French. He associates with other pro-Germans and of late is rooming with a man of military bearing and of decidedly Teutonic appearance, although he has been known for some years in Alaska as "Peterson" and as a Swede.
>
> Peterson claims to have been a ship master, who on account of bad eye sight was forced to give up the sea and take to carpentering. . . . On

165

arrival he got in touch with Lundblad and now rooms with him. [Peterson] has peculiar habits in that he is constantly on the move about the street at night, being found walking back and forth near his home at 3 oclock [sic] in the morning. He has such a decided military bearing and Teutonic appearance that mention has been made about it by several people.

Capt. S.S. Johnson has long been in Alaskan waters and is a mariner of no mean ability. He owns a very small fishing schooner, the *Hannah*. He is a giant physically, has little to say, makes long trips in his boat and does not catch very much fish. He was gone 10 days recently and came back with only 800 pounds of halibut, a catch which it would be possible to take in five hours.

Ed Jacobson is a silent chap, keen witted and apparently the only one of the four who is always on his guard about what he has to say.

The four men started a "first class deep water fish" industry in Seward in the June of 1917. To announce the formation of the venture, Lundblad submitted a letter to the general public and a poem, both of which he expected would be published in the *Seward Gateway*. Swayer and a local United States Army Captain looked over the letter and poem and felt they

may contain a message concerning the value of [Seward] for [German] submarines and advice as to how much gasoline or fuel could be found here. The letter may also tend to show that nothing can be done here until an *agreement is reached* [note the words *we cannot agree* in the poem] or until certain conferences are held, etc.

The letter and the poem "'What D'ya Mean He Miss'd His Boat" were not published. Swayer did publish an announcement of the new business and another poem by Lundblad. After the poem was published, Swayer became suspicious because Lundblad complained that the word "than" in the last stanza should have been "then" and that the poem "should not have been divided into stanzas."

Lundblad tried to get a poem published and complained about the misspelling of "than" which should have been "then," causing the informant to believe that the poem was actually a secret message "concerning the value of Seward as a possible temporary base for a submarine raid by German craft."

The poem in question, "'What D'Ya Mean He Miss'd His Boat" was not published in the *Seward Gateway* but remained in the War Department file along with a letter from Lundblad announcing the formation of his new company to provide "first class deep water fish" to citizens of Seward. Another poem by Lundblad, praising fish as a food, was published.

Swayer, who did not sign his name to any of his memos, was named in correspondence to Major Van Denman by the Department of Justice. Swayer further informed the War Department that

> I respectfully submit that there is a posibility [sic] that a German radio station may exist in western Alaska, that it might bepossible [sic] to send code messages disguised in published matter, which would otherwise escape detection and that it is possible—shoudl [sic] submarines leave Germany for the Pacific for them to seize and operate for a number of days from this port.

Both of Lundblad's poems and letter, written in an elegant hand, are on the following pages in the hopes that some retired cryptographer may, after more than seven decades, be able to break Lundblad's sophisticated code.

Letter the *Seward Gateway* refused to publish:

June 1, 1917

To The Public

Undersigned and Capt S.S. Johnson and his partner Ed. Jacobsen, the energetic and persevering fisherman, the forerunner of the new fishing era in Seward have this day formed a combination to furnish the citizens of our town with first class deep-water fish of all the varieties most liked. Each season brings its own kind. Now on hand from the cold storage of Seward Fish Company's place of business, which has passed into my hands, you will find principally halibut and red snapper at the price of 15 cents a pound.

Against cod fishes from deep water nobody should have any prejudice. Cooked and served with stirred butter it is a veritable delicacy. It can be obtained if notice is given a few days before delivery desired. It sells at 10 cents a pound. Salt cod and salmon billies (?) are on hand. If somebody should have a preference for ooligan I have a small quantity in just in absolutely first class condition at the price of 5 cents a pound. About razor back-clams and crabs I wish to confer with the public I hope to meet.

My endeavor will be to handle fish in all directions and to try to develop the opportunity this locality undoubtedly has as a fishing center. Though without the determination of the community to help along, such endeavors would be wasted energy. I therefore sollicit [sic] the good will of everybody, my own desire being to please everybody who enters my door. Neither the fishermen, nor the dealer, nor trading of any kind can thrive if such relations are not established.

Yours truly,

S. Lundblad

Note: In the original letter, many of the words were underlined, and there were small marks that the author took to indicate paragraph breaks. These were not reproduced. If this letter had been printed, the underlinings would not have been used in the *Seward Gateway*.

Poem by S. Lundblad that was published:

> On folks who have not wit enough
>> To know that fish is good;
> Is wholesome, not at all as tough
>> As meat oft used for food
> I do not figure, not at all;
>> They cry, "No fish for me,
> My means are as yet so small.
>> Fish! We cannot agree."
>
> Some think the fish goes to the brain
>> I am afraid my cure,
> However willing, were in vain,
>> Could not be perfect, sure.
> All those the fact do not deny
>> That people eating fish
> Life's hardships do quite well defy,
>> Leave naught for strength to wish.
>
> I welcome on my silv'ry ware
>> A course of fish, than meat.
> Is style that here should not be rare'
>> Fish makes your temper sweet.
> To those who have our place at heart
>> I say: Eat lots of fish!
> It gives our industry the start.
>> At least a week a week a dish.

Poem by S. Lundblad that was not published.

> "What D'Ya Mean He Miss'd His Boat?"
>
> The bay was peaceful thru' the night
> Yon' mountain, with twin peaks alike
> Majestically frown'd, while moon wink'd
> And seem'd to smile in solitude,
> As if to intimidate, his domains were waste—
> The slightest ripples, lapping on the crag
> Did agitate the down-cast spirit more;
> Of a sad-faced mortal, multitudes would note
> His incapacity for mirth—
>> He miss'd his boat.

I too; have wander'd to this land of wealth untold,
I too; have sunk a shaft, in search of gold.
I turn'd out frozen muck, there in the night
And forgot starvation, and my youth did blight.
"I struck it," but 'twas not the stuff I sought
The myriads of old Neptune laid the plot.
And while I've ponder'd and on the subject dote
My friends tell me, sure
      You miss'd your boat.

They've fought and muck'd for wealth
That lies beneath the knolls of Koyukuk;
They curs'd the country, call'd it, "land that God forgot,"
The best stuff in them, seem'd to wither up and rot
They've stuck till destiny has snag'd the end.
When now they reach the last league
Down lifes' beach afloat,
Yet still, the same voice calls,
    "You've miss'd your boat."

The deep, dyed Borealis in it's frantic flight
Would fain out-do the meteoric spectrum of this sight.
The Royal robes of Grand Ancestral Patriarch
Their entity, on traditional fashions gloat;
But fain would they chide, until the spirits flight
Of some ones' brother who had miss'd his boat.

The old hydrallic'r, from Placer ground
Not in his wildest dreams would get beyond
The wine-cup sparkling—nor the vine.
He weighed out virgin gold
For vintage rare,
To soothe his crippl'd conscience.and his throat [sic]
The throng he elbows thru', take up the air
And chorous [sic] here and there,
    He miss'd his boat.

Good people here, we all share destinies 'like,
Here fifty-fifty chances, take we all:
Ah, thee and me—thrust not your broad-sword
No—eloquence nor desire
Observe ye, then, procrastination—"thief o' time,"
Idcntified, be all—success; not doped with wine
Preserver your possibilities, retain your land
To a fallen brother, always lend a hand—
Leave him robed; or say, spare him a coat,
Make him to smile—real smiles, just say
    There'll *be* no boat.

Note: This story and the supporting documentation came from the Office Chief of Staff, War College Division, War Department, June 28, 1917, Document File 10080-119 from the National Archives in Washington, D.C. Also included in the file was a copy of a news article from the Seward Gateway, *June 1, 1917, entitled* "Swedish Poet and Associates Deal in Fish."

22
WARREN SITKA AND
SOURDOUGH JOURNALIST

Perhaps the best example of Alaskan absurding can be found in the classic work by Warren Sitka entitled *Sourdough Journalist.* Written as a tongue-in-cheek exposé of some of the allegedly juicier bits of Alaskan history that had been "roundly ignored" by traditional historians, the book presented stories that were so absurd that no one should have believed any of them.

That was not the case. Shortly after the book appeared, a tourist showed an Alaskan acquaintance of Sitka's a copy of the book and asked if it were true that Bethel had an annual Kuskokwim Crab Roundup. The Alaskan being questioned looked at the story, immediately recognized the handiwork of Warren Sitka, and stated with a straight face, "they did a couple of years ago but I don't know if they're still doing it." What is surprising is that the story of the Kuskokwim Crabs was written to be so outlandish that no one could possibly believe it to be true.

This chapter is composed of a brief biography of Warren Sitka, a portion of which appeared on the back of the original volume, and four of his stories from *Sourdough Journalist*. (Another of his stories appears in the chapter on the Alascattalo.)

Sitka, one of Alaska's most notable bush columnists, came to the northland in the spring of 1937 as a roustabout. Since that time he has worked as a lumberjack, teamster, farmhand, teacher, poet and physicist across the Territory and later the state of Alaska. He settled in Barnsnaggle in the early 1940s where the local *Barnsnaggle Gazette* drew upon his talents for his noted column "Alaskan Graphorrhea."

Sitka rose to national prominence in the fall of 1962 with the discovery of gold in the Barnsnaggle region. The city, which increased from a sleepy population of 135 to a booming 6,000 virtually overnight, made headlines around the world when it was discovered that the gold was actually iron filings that had been planted in local streams to stimulate the tourist trade. Although Sitka does not claim credit for this blaze of publicity, he is generally acknowledged as the brain behind the scheme. Sitka, now retired, continues to live in Barsnaggle.

The 17-Pound Blueberry

The other day I read in the *Wasilla Register* that a Mr. Harold P. Krebs of Delta Junction had successfully farmed a seven-pound blueberry ("World's Largest Blueberry Grown in Delta Junction," *Wasilla Register*, September 15, 1978, p. 15). Although I agree with the *Register* that the blueberry was "substantially larger" than the normal blueberry which one finds in the wilds of Alaska, I dispute the contention that this was the "World's Largest Blueberry."* Though it is not a well-known fact, the Matanuska Valley has a species of blueberry which has been recorded at 35 inches in diameter and with a weight of 17 pounds!

The Natives of the Matanuska Valley knew of the blueberries that reached this size and used them to their own advantage. As long as they harvested the berries before they reached eight or nine pounds, the blueberry meat was edible. Usually they sliced the meat into steak-like slabs. Then, with the proper seasoning, the steaks could be quickly broiled over an open fire.

But the Natives also learned that after the berries had reached ten or eleven pounds, the skin became so tough that it was almost impossible to chisel through. Even if they could skin the berry, the water content was so high that it was almost like eating a watermelon. Though a blueberry of this size is not what one would consider tasty, it is still nonetheless edible. Dr. Vorpal, Captain Cook's personal physician, reported that one of the men from Captain Cook's colony, Endeavor II, stayed alive for three days living on nothing but giant blueberries. The survivor, one Daniel Dafoe of Crusoe, Sussex County, even reported that he was able to keep the large, local mosquitoes away with a mixture of blueberry juice and salamander milk.†

There has been some research on blueberry size, most notably John Barimore (the elder) and his co-author Saradenzia Manzanilla in their classic work Berries of the World; Size, Weight, Structure and Uses, *Quince Press, South Braintree, MA, 1956.*

   †*Dr. Vorpal reported that although the Natives treated this local fruit with great respect, the English colonists were not averse to disrupting the natural habitat of the species. On more than one occasion Dr. Vorpal had to stop some Englishmen who*

Dr. Vorpal also reported that the Natives found the blueberry patches an excellent place to hunt for moose. Because of the tremendous size of the blueberries, the patches offered the moose an easy feast. Moose have the dentition to nibble through the thick skin of the blueberries and did not appear to mind the watery content of the interior. Even though there were plenty of smaller blueberries available, moose appeared to have a preference for the largest blueberry in the patch. Evidently the moose preferred one large meal to several smaller ones.

While the moose browsed, the Natives found them an easy target. When the moose had bitten off the top layer of the skin and stuck its snout into the confines of the berry skin, the Native could slip up on the unsuspecting creature. Often the berries were so large that the moose's head would completely disappear into the berry, leaving only its twitching ears exposed.

During seasons when the blueberry crop never attained a size larger than eight or nine pounds, the Natives had to stalk the moose through the undergrown patch. Over the years they learned that the best means of concealing themselves was to don a costume which looked as though it was part of the scenery. Usually this required skinning a dozen blueberries and sewing the skins together as a shirt and trousers. The berry skins worked well as long as the Natives staked them out in the sun for a while to loose the ragged tags of meat which had been left on the inside during the cleaning phase of the tanning. Then, dressed in clothing that blended into the patch, the Natives would stalk the moose as they browsed.

The Natives also found that the hides, when twisted together, made excellent rope. Eventually, the men of Endeavor II showed the Natives how to grease and wax the strips to make them water repellent.* With this innovation the Native culture was dramatically changed. Prior to this

---

were actually trying to distill the blueberries with the skin still on. This rotgut brew, known euphemistically as "Matanuska Brandy," came directly from the berry and was therefore of a poorer quality than that from the moose hide. Usually the men could drink their fill of the brew before the fire ate through the bottom of the blueberry. Then the juice would put the fire out. If, however, the skin of the blueberry proved to be tough, the berry distilled even more than anticipated. This pleased the Englishmen but created an added danger. When the bottom of the berry finally burned through, there would be a sudden blaze. Several men had to be treated by Dr. Vorpal for flashburn. Dr. Vorpal also reported that some of the men used the heavier berries as "medicine balls" to improve their strength. Another man collected the huge fruits to drop on the unsuspecting fresh water sharks and giant salamanders which lived in the borogroves surrounding Endeavor II.

*Dr. Vorpal also showed the Natives that the thinner berry skins, when waxed, were good for sewing, hanging trinkets and extracting pieces of meat which had become lodged between their teeth.

time the berry hides would not be used for fishing because they came apart in the water. Now the Natives could supplement their diet with fish. (Prior to this time they simply stepped into the stream and grabbed whatever fish happened by.)

The greasing and waxing of the skins also changed the Natives' clothing style. Formerly the Natives used moose and caribou hides to construct their wickiups, which are small, rounded living structures. But with the discovered impermeability of the blueberry skin, the Natives could replace the heavy moose and caribou hides with the blueberry skins. This made for lighter structures and freed the moose and caribou hides for use as clothing.

There was also another advantage to using the berry skins for wickiups. They were thin enough that they could "breathe," allowing a layer of moisture to form on the outside of the primitive structures. During the winter this layer froze and gave the wickiups a thin mantle of ice which acted as insulation against the bitter winds of the Matanuska Valley. Dr. Vorpal reported that the ice gave the wickiups an "ice-blue" tint. Undoubtedly this led later explorers to belive that there were igloos in Alaska.

Naturally, however, the greatest benefit that the Natives and later the white reaped from the large blueberries was a drink of the distilled meat of the fruit. The Natives had learned that crushing the smaller, eight-pound blueberries and boiling the liquid in a moose hide (which was kept soaking wet to keep it from igniting) would produce an intoxicating concoction. This liquid was then allowed to pass through a maze of "green" yet hollow caribou rib bones. The distilled brew would permeate the calcium structure. Then the Natives would freeze the ribs. At their convenience they would then thaw out a rib or two and get pleasantly inebriated. From this process comes the term coined by Captain Cook's men, "ribbed" or "to take a ribbing," meaning to get drunk, be drunk or be in the process thereof.

The English, however, loathed to chew on rib bones, and usually just drank the brew directly from the moose hide. Eventually the term "moose hide" became synonymous with "ribbed" and came to mean a primitive drink or binge as the case may be. Later Americans in Tennessee revived the word in the more familiar "moonshine."

World record blueberries are hard to come by these days. Though they were plentiful in the early days of Alaskan settlement, today the berries are few and far between. The constant encroachment of urban society has all but eliminated them from the Matanuska Valley. Before the editor of the *Wasilla Register* makes any further rash statements about world record blueberries, however, I suggest he take Seed Road 5.37 miles south of Deception Creek. This is in the direction of Bench Lake. And I would also suggest that he take a camera and scale.

Kuskokwim Crabs

In addition to some of the most unusual geologic and meteorological phenomena in the world, Alaska is also famous for its wildlife. From the grizzly to the alascattalo, the Northland boasts some of the most unusual beasts in the world. But perhaps *the* most unusual is the Kuskokwim crab.

Known throughout Alaska for its fine meat—rivaled only by that of the Alaskan king crab—the Kuskokwim crab is also known for its voracious appetite and predatory nature. It is one of the few varieties of freshwater crab in the world, not to mention one of only a handful of crab species that have the ability to survive out of the water for lengthy periods of time.

Originally the Kuskokwim crab was a saltwater dweller. Fossils of the crab from the Holocene show that the Kuskokwim crab was a resident of the waters of the oceans off the coast of Alaska in the Bristol Bay region. It lived side by side with the Alaskan king crab through at least two glaciations. Then, for some unknown reason, possibly because of population pressure, the crab moved up into the headwaters of the Kuskokwim. Amazingly, it survived the change from salt to fresh water.

Not only did the crab survive, but it seemed to thrive in the fresh water. Over the eons the Kuskokwim crab was able to populate most of the waters and tributaries of the Kuskokwim watershed, pushing deeper and deeper inland wherever there were river holes deep enough to allow them to overwinter. Varieties of the crustacean have been taken as far north as Lake Minchumina, leading scientists to believe that at one time the waters of the Kuskokwim and the lake were one and the same.

To survive in the chilly waters of the Kuskokwim River, the Kuskokwim crab had to undergo certain evolutionary adaptations. First, because the Kuskokwim was a freshwater source and the species of flora and fauna for foodstuffs were somewhat limited, the crab had to develop an omnivorous diet. During the salmon runs, of course, the crab could gorge on the dying fish and later on the slower swimming smaller fry. But during the "off season," the crab was forced to make do with a selection of indigenous water plants.

Further, since the Kuskokwim was frozen over from September to

May, the amount of food which fell into the water was extremely limited during that stretch of the year. Consequently, the crabs developed a somewhat comatose state during the winter. Had they been land dwelling animals, scientists would have called this hibernation, but since this metabolic state was — and to a certain extent still is — unknown in water-related animals, scientists simply called it a "comatose state." But this state of pseudo-hibernation did allow the crabs to survive the long winters until the warmer weather broke the back of the ice and allowed foodstuffs to fall into the river.

Even the ability to hibernate did not seem to be enough. Eventually population pressures forced the crab to seek food elsewhere — specifically, out of the water. It has been suggested that at one time the crabs turned cannibal and devoured each other, a practice sometimes observed in the waters of the Kuskokwim.*

At some point in the holocene, just as it appeared that the organism would go the way of the sabre-tooth tiger and the lagartosaurus, the Kuskokwim crab achieved a remarkable adaptation: it learned to survive out of the water for short periods of time. Since there was never enough carrion and vegetation in the water, at some moment in its ancestral history the Kuskokwim crab left the water to forage for food along the riverbank.

Over the centuries the crab was able to refine further its survival abilities on land so that it can forage for as long as four hours before it has to return to the water.

These extended periods on the land also helped the crab develop other adaptations. Since the water supports the bulk of the crab's weight while it is hulking along river bottoms, the crab must have had great difficulty moving on land in the beginning. But it clearly developed a walking mode which was best adapted for its frame. Unlike other crabs, the Kuskokwim crab "jumps," a form of locomotion that is a combination of both scamper and low hop. These hops have been recorded as high as two feet with some of the larger crabs.† It has been alleged that this hop allowed the crab to make it over some of the lower branches of trees which otherwise might have blocked its passage on land. (There is little evidence to support this contention.)

Immediately after breakup in May, the crabs come out of hibernation. Since they have not eaten in months, they have one overriding desire: to eat. Should an animal be unfortunate enough to be in the water at this time, it could be stripped to the bone. Smelly meat, such as liver, will also create a feeding frenzy because the scent of meat will carry down the river. The miners quickly learned not to throw the offal of moose and caribou into the river or there would be consequences to suffer.

†Such jumps have been reported at the Bethel Crab Jump Contest.

On the land the crabs usually followed that which are known as "crab trails." These are not beaten paths, but broad areas where crabs gather to feed. Usually found in areas where there is food readily available, crab trails also aid the trapper in finding concentrations of the animal. The crabs, it must be noted, have developed very powerful leg and pincer muscles from foraging on land, and many a trapper has lost a finger in an attempt to beat off the frenzied attack of a Kuskokwim crab.

When the miners first came to the Kuskokwim area, they found the existence of the crabs hard to believe. Since they spent much of their time in and around the water, it did not take them long to discover the truth to the rumor that the Kuskokwim River did have large crabs. The miners solved their problems with the crabs by putting dams in areas around the river and screening the crabs out of the area. They were forced to sleep in hammocks to keep themselves off the ground while the crabs foraged at night. (Because the eyes of the crab are not able to adapt to bright light, the crabs are only out and around on land in twilight or darkness.)

The only known recorded incident of a crab attack took place in 1899 outside the village of Tanacross, when a miner was caught in a moose snare.* It was early spring, and the crabs were ashore in force. When the unfortunate man's friends were finally able to rescue him, he had to have his left leg amputated from the knee. It should be noted that although the crabs are at times vicious—particularly when they are in a feeding frenzy—they usually avoid human contact as much as possible. There are no recorded incidents of death from a crab attack.

But in recent years the Kuskokwim crab has become bolder and bolder. In its never-ending search for food, the crab has developed the ability to forage farther and farther from the river. At the turn of the century it was rare to find a crab farther away from the river than 100 or 200 yards. Today it is not uncommon to find crabs as far inland as a mile or two. And the longer the crabs remain on the land, the greater is their ability to forage. As a result, there has been an unmistakable though subtle

---

*Tanacross was named from a rather unusual development. In the days when there were few decks of cards in Alaska, bingo was the popular game. But in one particular collection of houses—a village whose name was never recorded—bingo became a great passion. Unfortunately the set became quite worn, and because of the unusual way they played it, the numbers were listed up and down as well as across. This increased the number of possibilities of winning—or losing—depending on how one wished to look at it. One particular piece of the set became so soiled that it was immediately recognizable. This was the "ten across" from which the village took its name. Gradually "tanacross" meant to deal oneself a winning chit intentionally.

change in their diet. Although they used to survive on water-related foods and supplemented their diet with carrion, berries and anything else they could find on land, it now appears that the crabs are merely hibernating during the winter and then seeking food exclusively on the land during the summer months.

This new manner of feeding has created a rather large headache for the citizenry along the river. Villages and communities along the Kuskokwim, which make their livings either ranching or farming, have had a substantial rise in crop damage in recent years. The crabs are, quite literally, devouring the truck gardens faster than they can be harvested.

Controlling the crabs is quite difficult. Dogs, understandably, are reluctant to tangle with a Kuskokwim crab, and farmers quickly learned that the thick carapace of the crab was sturdy enough to withstand the shock of a .22 caliber slug. As far as snares are concerned, if the crab is not trapped correctly it will "shed" a leg and escape. Thus the ranchers will find their snares full of legs but not crabs. And the crab has no qualms about shedding a leg. After all, it'll just grow another. The farmer, however, can only eat the leg and hope for better luck next time.*

But the people who have been having the greatest difficulty with the crabs are the ranchers. When they originally brought in penguins to stimulate the down economy, there was hope that the Bethel area would soon become world famous for down-filled parkas, pants and other arctic gear. It soon became apparent that this would not be the case, as the penguin feathers provided no insulation. (Penguin feathers simply keep the snow off the skin of the penguin; they do not insulate. As a result, penguin-down parkas are merely tourists novelties. The only worthwhile penguin-down products are the pillows, which sell for about $30 in local department stores.)

As the crabs grew bolder, the penguin population began to decrease. Even with retaining walls and fenced-in pools, the crabs seemed to be able to scramble into the pens and raise havoc with the herds. Snares and nets did little to reduce the attacks. As of the date of this article, June 1981, there is as yet no sure-fire method of reducing the crab population in the Bethel area. If a means is not devised soon, the penguin population might very well disappear from the area.

Currently, for the tourists, there are two events held yearly which will introduce the outsider to some of the more unusual aspects of Alaskan culture. There is a periodic "roundup" of crabs in the early

---

*In the springtime so many crabs elude the snares that Kuskokwim crab legs are exported around the world as well as sold in local establishments in Bethel.

spring, usually right after breakup. This event not only aids in reducing the crab population before the spring season, but it also provides a fantastic crab feed which draws tourists from around the world. It is usually held in late May or early June, depending on the locale.

Then, in the middle of summer in Bethel (July 15), there is the annual crab jumping contest. Villagers bring crabs taken from the river and have them compete against one another for prizes ranging as high as $20,000. This three-day festival is highlighted with a crab jumping contest, a crab scampering contest, as well as a who-can-drink-the-most-and-still-stand-up contest, an event for which training goes on year-round in Alaska. But until the biologists can find a way to reduce the population of crabs, ranching on the Kuskokwim may be on its deathbed.

How to Catch a Kuskokwim Crab

Perhaps one of the most asked questions in the Bethel area is "How do I capture a Kuskokwim crab?" To the locals it is not a matter of how to *capture* a crab, but rather how to keep the burly crustaceans *out* of the village. Whenever a villager has a yen for crab meat, it is simply a matter of putting a snare across a crab trail and waiting for one of the beasts to stumble into the loops of wire.

But a tourist doesn't have time to set a snare and wait a day or two to catch a crab. He or she has probably taken the morning flight to Bethel and hopes to leave that fair vicinity at three in the afternoon. Time, therefore, is of the essence.

The surest method of finding a Kuskokwim crab is to gather four or five tourists together and surround a bushy area on the banks of the river. Then, using sticks, they should beat the ground and make a great commotion. Any crabs hiding in the bushes will immediately rush out into the open. Once the crab is in the open it is fair game. However, do not try to beat the crab with sticks. Its claws are powerful enough to snap a fairly good-sized stick in two. The best method is to use a sturdy net to tangle in its legs. Once the crab is on its back it is virtually helpless. But the hunters should also play it safe and have one person carefully seize the crab's claws while another grips the hind legs firmly. This will prevent the crab from gaining any leverage to right itself.

If no crabs are to be found in bushy areas, then check along the crab trails and in areas one or two hundred yards back from the river. If you still have no luck, try crushing some berries and tossing them into the river in a back eddy. Or, better yet, try tossing a piece of meat into the eddy. Liver works more effectively than just a strip of steak. This last method is very risky, however, because if there is more than one crab in the area you may well start a feeding frenzy. If the two crabs seize upon the same piece of meat they will tear each other apart as they hack at the liver. If there is a collection of Kuskokwim crabs, the water will boil with activity. This feeding frenzy rarely takes place out of the water. Being near the water can be dangerous. Take those snapshots and slides from on the bank. Don't wade into the water for a "good shot of the action."

The Invasion of Nome

Though one may search the history books at length, one will not find a single reference to the Japanese invasion of Nome in 1906. Yet, it happened. Though many of the principals are now dead, there are still papers in the National Archives that deal with this incident. And, as recently as September 3, 1978, the United States War Department has insinuated that the release of this story could result in a full-scale investigation of my real estate holdings in the Nome and Anchorage areas. Here, however, courtesy of the *Barnsnaggle Gazette,* is the true story as it was related to me by my father, Christopher von Kringle, former maritime captain in the Dutch navy stationed in Rotterdam.

It occurred in Nome during the winter of 1906. War was in the air. At that time my father ran a rather lucrative business in reindeer hides out of Kruzgamepa. (Today that village is known as Pilgrim Hot Springs, which is odd, as there are neither pilgrims nor hot springs in the area.) He was a doer of odd jobs during the winter, and when the summer sun rose he fished for halibut, cod and salmon. My mother died when I was three. I never knew her.

The winter of 1905 was an exceptionally good one. My father was making extra money in Nome by sponsoring a sleigh ride with some of the reindoor from his ranch. To this day I can still recall him driving his sleigh and eight reindeer down the snow-covered streets, his white beard blowing in the wind. But the wind from the Norton Sound blew in more than winter storms that year. It blew the Japanese fleet to Nome.

The Russo-Japanese war had broken out, and the repercussions of that conflict were being felt profoundly in Nome. Put simply, the Japanese wanted the Nome coal fields. With control of this valuable mineral resource, it would be possible for the Japanese fleet to steam from Tokyo to Nome and then to Vladivostok, without having to bring sluggish coal barges along with the fleet. Thus, on November 5, 1906, the

Gold miners in Nome using candles as headlights. (Courtesy University of Alaska, Fairbanks: The Seppala Collection, ACC #68-41-60N, in the Archives of the Alaska and Polar Regions Department.)

garrison on Attu sighted the Japanese fleet. By the time word reached the United States Naval Garrison at Nome, the city had less than four days to prepare for a full-scale invasion by the Japanese.

Colonel William Lathrop Jennet III—whose memories have been squelched by the United States War Department—did not actually believe that the Japanese would be foolish enough to land. But he was a good enough soldier to think of preparing for the invasion. And all his preparations had to be completed within four days.

The moment the next tide went out Col. Jennet went to work with a passion. He quickly mobilized the community and ordered a maze of timber spikes and stone barriers in the harbor to thwart the fleet of junks and sampans from landing. It is perhaps fortunate that the Japanese elected to leave their most modern ships to spearhead the invasion; the history of Alaska might have been substantially changed.

Between the highwater mark and the city of Nome, Colonel Jennet ordered that a seawall be built, a structure that is still in existence today. Then he ordered that the area between the highwater mark and the seawall be filled in with snow. The logic behind this move was that enough snow would stop the Japanese from a full-scale charge up the beach. The Japanese, with their short legs, would have difficulty moving through deep snow. Though this may have been a racial attitude, it should be remembered that Nome was at war, and the niceties of political correctness had to be left to a future generation.

The filling of the beach required the longest bucket brigade in Alaskan history. Every able-bodied man, woman, and child pitched in to move snow from the city streets to the beach. When the brigade ran out of snow from the city, Jennet ordered wagons and dogsleds into the countryside to gather whatever snow was to be found. He also made sure that there was a substantial pile of snow left in the town square to facilitate drinking water. (The wells in Nome would freeze during the winter. Today they are kept liquid throughout the year by having the waste heat from City Hall passed through pipes beneath the surface of the water.)

Being a seasoned soldier, Jennet also prepared for the eventuality that the Japanese might actually make it up as far as the seawall. When the snowfill had been completed, he sent all the children in town along the seawall with reindeer bones. Into every crack and crevice they stuck a reindeer bone. Not only would this fill any holes that could be used for a hand or foot but it would make it impossible for a man with a pack to climb up the wall.

Then Jennet called my father aside. If there were going to be an invasion, a siege could be expected. Thus there were three things he had to have at his disposal: men, water and food. The first two he had; the food he wanted my father to gather.

This was a tricky business. Nome could fight for its existence, but the other smaller villages could have cared less. In fact, they might have applauded if Nome had been taken, as there was no love lost between them and Nome. It was my father's job to "impound" whatever reindeer he could find, drive them to Nome and slaughter them as the need arose. Since Nome was under martial law, my father was given an automatic commission as an officer.

Gathering the reindeer was not a difficult business. It was the branding season so most of the herds had been rounded up. (Once a year the Eskimos round up the reindeer and brand them in much the same way cattle are branded in Texas. Winter is the usual time for the roundup since the heavy winter coat of the animals protects them from any significant burn damage to their hides.) The mood of the Natives, however, was less than friendly. My father returned to Nome just before the first wave of Japanese hit the beaches.

It was an odd confrontation. On one hand there were the Japanese. They had expected an easy victory, so they had sent a fleet of flimsy junks and sampans filled with young, green troops. Many of the Japanese soldiers had never been to sea before, few had ridden horses and none had any weapons. Apparently the Japanese emperor expected them to ride to victory howling with no samurai swords flashing over their heads. There have been few military blunders as incredible as this one.

On the other side were the Eskimos. Rifles were few and far between. As a result, the seawall bristled with harpoons. Knives were used freely to wave in the air but would only be good for close hand-to-hand combat. But the Eskimos held the advantage in that they were on their own ground. And, Colonel Jennet had a surprise for the Japanese.

The first waves of invaders struck the timber pilings and took water. Most of them were able to return to the fleet before they sank, but until the tide went out the Japanese were picking their soldiers out of the brine. Then, when the timbers became visible above the waterline, the Japanese hit the beaches.

As the landing craft crunched to a stop on the golden sand, mounted Japanese moved across the sand and toward the seawall. They were sluggish in the sand and slowed to a crawl in the snow. Some of the Japanese had apparently never seen snow before. Several of the soldiers leaned over on their horses and tried a mouthful of the substance. Then, in the confusion, the Eskimos charged.

With a roar, 60 Eskimos on dogsleds charged into the ranks of the Japanese. For a moment there was a hesitation in the ranks of the Japanese. Some of the Japanese had never seen dogsleds. Some of the Japanese had never seen Eskimos. And it is an assured fact that no Japanese had ever seen a contingent of Eskimo cavalry led by a tall white man dressed in red overalls and a white trim jacket beating a team of eight reindeer.

The Japanese's horses shied and then bolted for the sea, leaving their cargo of military personnel bouncing on the sand. Pellmell the soldiers dashed for the sea, panicked. In an instant the Japanese were moving back toward the landing crafts. Without a single shot being fired, the first Japanese invasion of Alaska had been stopped. For the Japanese it had been a total defeat. And, as the ultimate insult, they had to exchange a case of saki for each prisoner repatriated from the Eskimos.

But here the story takes an odd twist. One would have expected that United States War Department would have been grateful for the successful repelling of an invasion. On the contrary, it immediately went to great lengths to hush up the entire matter. Just as the Japanese had been about to attack, President Roosevelt had gathered the Russian and Japanese envoys to discuss a peace treaty. The president had been successful and, as a result, had won a Nobel Prize for his efforts. At the moment that he had been informed that he had been nominated for the honor, he received word of the thwarted Japanese invasion.

This was indeed a ticklish situation. The president could have acknowledged the invasion and demanded an apology. But that was unthinkable. After all, a Nobel Prize was at stake. So, rather than risk the prize, the president hushed up any hint of the incident.

Colonel Jennet was called to Washington, where he was threatened with a court martial and loss of rank and pension if he discussed the matter with anyone—and particularly with a newspaper reporter. The charges were ludicrous: attacking a neutral on the open seas (Japanese), unauthorized confiscation of private property (reindeer) and the illegal authorization of a foreign national to a position of authority within the U.S. military establishment (my father). Jennet was transferred to Ellis Island, where he finished his career checking refugees into the United States, ironically, under the watchful eye of Lady Liberty.

This then is the tragic story of the Japanese invasion of Nome. A comprehensive research of this facet of Alaskan history has yet to be done and may never be done if the recalcitrance of the U.S. War Department continues. It is truly sad that such a dramatic incident should be pigeonholed for the sake of a president who has been dead for over 60 years.

23

STRANGE BUT TRUE TWO

In October of 1990, Stolt's Electric in Anchorage sponsored a half-hour program of *Alaska's Funniest Home Videos*. The second place winner was a clip of two men on snow machines who found a beaver on the top of a frozen lake. As the beaver tried to dive into its air hole in the ice, one of the men grabbed the beaver by the tail and held it up so that his buddy could video the animal.

The day after *Alaska's Funniest Home Videos* aired, animal rights activitists demanded that the man holding the beaver by the tail be prosecuted for harassing a wild animal. Alaska Fish and Game officials complied, and a subpoena was issued for the video tape as evidence of the crime.

The irony, as it turned out, was that both men had trapping licenses. Had they killed the beaver, they could not have been prosecuted. But because they let it live, they were liable for criminal action.

The late Claire Oakpeha of Barrow, the last person to see Wiley Post and Will Rogers alive, reported that when the pair landed on the lagoon where he was standing, Will Rogers' head popped out of the plane and he asked, "Anyone here from Paducah?" Five minutes later, Rogers and Post were dead.

In 1970, Vern Clark ran for City Council in Wrangell on the ticket, "IF ELECTED HE PROMISES TO CLEAN UP WRANGELL BY PUTTING DIAPERS ON THE SEA GULLS" (Art Clark's book *Wrangellitis*, Box 93, Wrangell, 99929).

In the mid– to late–70s, Spenard was an urban boomtown. Oil dollars from pipeline construction flooded into the area and strip joints, massage parlors and escort services proliferated. The best known strip joint was PJ's, a topless-bottomless bar right on Spenard Road.

In addition to the urban legends of what went on inside the establishment, there were many cases of the strippers, "dressed for work," dashing across Spenard Road to buy a pack of cigarettes before they had to go on stage.

———

Up until the production of oil on the North Slope, Eskimos had a functional use for the oil seeps which dotted the land. During the winter, Eskimos would cut the frozen petroleum into chunks and burn it for fuel. Inland, the Eskimo settlement at Anaktuvuk Pass burned oil shale rock for heat.

———

In 1940, Jens Forshaug was responsible for taking the census from Barrow east to Canada. He left by dogsled in March, and in April he came upon an unusual circumstance. On the banks of the Sagavanirktok River, near the present site of Prudhoe Bay, he came across John Seiguard.

Unfortunately Seiguard was no longer among the living. He was in his tent, under a sheet of ice. He had either died, and then been covered by the rising waters of the river, or had drowned in his tent when the river rose. In either case, the waters had frozen solid, entombing the man until the next spring.

Forshaug found a calendar in the tent which showed that Seiguard had been alive at least through November. This made him eligible for inclusion as a living resident of the Territory of Alaska for the 1940 census.

———

Alaska's most famous frontier prostitute, Big Dolly of Ketchikan, ran Dolly's, now an historical landmark. Dolly was once quoted as saying that her clientele, mostly fishermen, only talked about fishing when they were in her house and, when they were on their boats, only talked about her house on Creek Street.

———

In the 1940s, Paul Wilson and his wife were elementary school teachers in Point Lay, a village of 125 people north of Kotzebue. They were using the same books as those used in the Lower 48. Mrs. Wilson recalled that the students laughed when they received their first *Dick and Jane* book because "Dick was wearing short pants."

Mr. Wilson also recalled that the Eskimos had never seen such commonplace items as "trees, trains and cows. I remember a pilot brought me a banana one day," Mr. Wilson recalled, "and all the children pointed at it and said it was 'monkey food.'"

In late 1990, a defendant in the Bethel area was sent a letter by the State of Alaska Department of Law which stated, in the words of the newspaper, "to beat feet *toute de suite*" to an alcoholic rehabilitation program or a bench warrant would be issued for his arrest. The individual in question took a plane to Bethel where he entered a six-week detox program. However, his attitude in the program was so unruly that he was ordered to serve an additional two weeks. Only then was it discovered that the letter had been sent to the wrong person. When reported, a local lawyer had been retained to sue the state for "wrongful cure."

On August 8, 1900, the *Nome News* reported that the "Mit and a Half Kid," also known as Tommy Levins, had been arrested for "Shoving the Queer." As the newspaper reported, "Levins attempted to pay for a square meal at the North Star restaurant, offering his poke of brass filings to the cashier."

In October of 1990, Ray Sadler of Petersburg saved two deer who slid off an ice cake into the chilly waters of Southeast Alaska. Sadler was hunting for moose when he spotted two deer on an ice flow fighting each other. The iceberg tipped and both fell into the water. When he approached the swimming deer, Sadler was able to haul both of them, alive, into his 16-foot skiff. The deer, wet and cold, lay in the bottom of his skiff while he headed for Petersburg. A friend videoed the two animals in the skiff, and then the two men carried the weak and wet animals off to a grassy spot and set the animals free.

In November of 1990, the sea gulls of Dutch Harbor went crazy. Actually, they got drunk. Earlier in the fall, the Bering Sea fishery closed because too many halibut were being caught. This closing meant that the processing plants were closed. That, in turn, meant that no fish waste was being pumped into harbors, which—in the words of Joel Gray of the *Anchorage Daily News*—were "like Safeway to the sea gull."

Looking for an alternate food source, the sea gulls began eating anything they could find, which included fermented, frost-nipped berries. Inebriated, the tipsy birds began dive-bombing pedestrians and doing other un–sea gull–like activity, like flying so low that they were a traffic hazard. Particularly hard hit by the gulls, so to speak, were the taxi cab drivers, who were forced to keep a sharp eye out for low-flying, drunk birds.

"My wife has been zoomed a couple of times," said Unalaska city manager Herv Hensley. "She got out of her car at work the other day and one came out of no where, zinging right at her. It's sorta Alfred Hitchcock-ish."

In June of 1970, Darrell Allen of Wrangell had a whale tangle in his net near Snow Pass. But it was more than just a whale; it was a *blue* whale. The behemoth came to the surface gently lifting Allen's troller clear of the water.

Then the whale began slowly waving his flippers back and forth. "Each time he flopped that old big fin," Allen said of the incident, "it sent cascades of water over the deck and darned near drowned me."

Finally the whale tore free of the line and swam leisurely away. "It sounds funny now," Allen recalled, "but at the time it had very little humor in it for me."

Four years later, another Wrangell resident, Freddie "Boo-Boo" Lewis, had an encounter with a humpback known in the area as "Ma Baker." Among her many activities, Ma Baker was known for her propensity to remove the barnacles from her side by scraping herself on the bottom of trollers.

One day while she was scraping herself, Lewis stepped off his boat and onto the whale's back. Rather than submerge, Ma Baker gave Lewis a ride around the harbor. Only after Lewis was 50 yards away from his troller did it occur to him that he could not swim. He was only saved from his ticklish predicament by Ma Baker's willingness to stay on the surface until a rowboat came to Lewis' rescue.

In 1975, Hugh Sorenson of Wrangell ran afoul of a 30-foot Orca near Duncan Canal. He was backing up his troller in deep water when he unexpectedly struck the animal. As Sorenson watched helplessly, the Orca "came on like a runaway freight train and looked twice as big." Just before it collided with the troller, the Orca dove under the vessel. Three more times the whale charged the boat and dove under its keel. On its last charge it sprayed the deck with its foul breath, almost asphyxiating Sorenson and his deck hand. Then the whale left the area.

Later asked about the experience, Sorenson stated that what "the killer whale really needed was about 50 gallons of mouthwash to cure a king-sized case of bad breath!" (Art Clark's book *Wrangellitis*, Box 93, Wrangell, 99929).

In 1971, Lester Bjorge of Wrangell came upon a family of five otters jerking a struggling, 35-pound halibut out of the water. Lester frightened the otters away and took the halibut for himself. For years he said that he had certainly left "one mad bunch of otters" on the shoreline (Art Clark's book *Wrangellitis*, Box 93, Wrangell, 99929).

In the 1970s, the phone number in Wrangell for the United States Forest Service was 874-2323. Residents note that this is a "doggone good number" because after "874" it was "a dash to tree to tree" (Art Clark's book *Wrangellitis*, Box 93, Wrangell, 99929).

After the cold snap in 1990, a new bumper sticker appeared in Anchorage: "ALASKANS: GOD'S CHOSEN FROZEN."

While sleeping in the back seat of her car, Alaskan wildlife photographer Alissa Crandall was awakened to the sound of someone rapping on her windshield. Groggily she put on her glasses and looked over the top of the front seat to see who it was. But the rapper was not human; it was a raven, sitting on her wiper blade and knocking off the dead bugs that had peppered her windshield driving into the area (confirmed by Alissa Crandall).

Anchorage artist Gary Kremen began his career by painting in public for the tourists in his downtown gallery. While he painted he was asked all kinds of questions about Alaska by the tourists. The strangest, he recalled, was a woman who asked, "How much does Mt. McKinley weigh?"

Without wasting a moment to think about it, Kremen replied, "In the summer or winter? It's heavier in the winter because of the snow and ice."

In the early 1970s, two cars were barged into the community of Eek. Within a matter of days, there had been a head-on collision which destroyed both vehicles (apocryphal).

In April of 1989, Skagway's lawns and driveways received a facelift after local officials expressed fears about accumulations of lead left on the ground from decades of shipping ore through town.

Concerned that the lead might be hazardous to residents' health, the State of Alaska Department of Environmental Conservation vacuumed soil from lawns and driveways throughout the city. Large vacuum trucks criss-crossed the city, sucking up the soil several inches deep. The soil then was screened into a holding pond. The heavy lead fell to the bottom where it was recovered for shipment out of Alaska, back to the mine in Canada where it originated. There the lead would be separated from the overburden and resold.

In August of 1913, Nome grocer A. Polet set a record. He ordered bananas for his store. According to the *Nome Nugget,* this established a record for the longest direct haul of bananas. Polet's shipment left Boca Del Toro in Panama and arrived in Nome via New Orleans and Seattle, a journey of 7,134 miles.

An early editor of the Fairbanks *Daily News Miner,* W.F. Thompson (1909–1926), is largely remembered for his April 15, 1921, headline above a story on a local execution: JERKED TO JESUS. Widely believed, it later developed that no such headline had ever been written. An examination of the paper reveals the headline of that day to be THE WAGES OF SIN ARE NEVER REDUCED.

––––––––––

Some fishermen just never get it right. In October of 1970, a PBY landed in Wrangell with a 16 pound salmon "flopping from a leader tangled in the landing gear" (Art Clark's book *Wrangellitis,* Box 93, Wrangell, 99929).

––––––––––

George Hinton Henry was undoubtedly the most "sued-for-libel" editor in Alaska history. Between 1906 and 1914 he published six short-lived newspapers in six towns. All papers expired, some within a few months, with the editor in jail. One time, while in jail awaiting trial, Henry hired a printer to put out his paper.

His editorial comments on the magistrate who was to try his case, however, were so caustic that the magistrate had the printing press incarcerated in the cell next to Henry. There it remained, long after Henry had been released, until it was dumped into a pile of kitchen refuse, where it lay for years. Judge Wickersham retrieved it in 1923 and sent it to what is now the University of Alaska, Fairbanks where it remains to this day.

––––––––––

"Well, I'm pleased to meet you, Bishop. Of course I won't rob you; take your poke off the heap in the road, Bishop, and take that poke with the shoestring in it, too. Why, damn it all, Bishop, I'm a member of your church"—Blue Parka Bandit of Fairbanks (1906) refusing to rob a man of the cloth.

Once the Blue Parka Bandit robbed a man who only had $10. The Bandit returned the man's $10 and gave him enough for a drink.

––––––––––

"The difference between salvage and piracy is how fast the ship is sinking"—Alaskan salvage skin diver who threatened the author if his name was revealed.

———————

Speaking of the entangling federal bureaucratic lines of command with regard to Alaska, Franklin Delano Roosevelt once asked Senator Gruening of Alaska, "If a bear belonging to the Department of Commerce mates with a bear belonging to the Department of Agriculture, to whom does the offspring belong?"

When Gruening admitted he did not know, FDR replied laughing, "To Congress."

———————

If you want to know what a tedious job is, just ask Janelle Matz, Assistant Curator at the Anchorage Museum of History and Art. Using distilled water and Q-tips, Matz cleaned a 150-year-old, Aleutian seal-gut, floor-length cape.

"On sections that were broken," Matz said, "we used fish skin. We bought it in a music store, and it's usually used for storing reeds. We use it on the gut because it's as close to the original material as we can buy."

Noting that there was a difference in the texture of the fish skin she held and that which was used to repair the parka, Matz indicated that "when the parka was originally repaired, the State Museum [in Juneau] didn't have any fish skin. So they used the next best thing: natural skin condoms. I can just see the look on some administrator's face when he or she had to write out a State purchase order for two dozen condoms to repair a gut parka."

———————

In an interview with an Alaska Commercial Company executive, he stated that the most unusual item he had ever seen sold in rural Alaska was plastic flowers. Many villagers use them for funerals in the middle of the winter.

———————

In January of 1991, Sergeant Marie Quarterman had been in Alaska for about a month. She had just bought a new car. Driving down the

Richardson Highway outside of Fairbanks, she saw her first moose. The animal stepped out in front of her car and was immediately hit. The moose flew over the car's hood, smashed through the windshield rear first and ended up seated in the passenger seat.

When the episode was over, Quarterman stated that her next car would be "a tank."

Corkscrew Nellie of Unga Island was so named because she had a stiffened knee which caused her to list to the side. She was an obese Russian-Aleut woman who maintained a love/hate relationship with her husband Mac, a fact that was discussed up and down the Aleutian chain.

When she died one winter, Mac had a terrible time disposing of the body. The ground was frozen solid, so he decided to take the body to town where it could be buried by a priest. He laid the body on a storeroom door and then built an enormous coffin over the body. Fastening the coffin to the front of his fishing boat, he left for town.

But before he arrived, the weather turned ugly and the coffin was washed overboard. Mac managed to get a rope around the huge container and dragged it to a protected area where he ran into some friends. They gave him consolation in the form of a "drink" which became "drinks." The next morning he woke up to find the Marshal looking for him. Corkscrew Nellie's coffin had broken up, and she had washed up on a beach (Alaska Nicknames).

In the early 1950s, Joe Sadlier served as both the manager for the Bank of Sitka and the agent for Alaska Coastal Airlines in Pelican. One summer day he was handed a bag of fifty, one thousand dollar bills by the pilot of an Alaska Coastal Airlines Grumman Goose. Just as he was receiving the bag, an elderly woman needed some help getting out of the plane. Sadlier put the bag with the bills on the wing of the Goose and graciously assisted the lady out of the plane.

But he forgot about the bag. He only remembered it as the Goose started to take off. Then Sadlier saw the bag fly off the wing of the plane and settle in the water. In a flash, he was in a skiff racing to retrieve the bag before it sank.

"Later in the day," *The Alaska Southeaster Magazine* (February 1991) reported, "bank customers saw temporary clotheslines strung about the bank with fifty, one thousand dollar bills clothes-pinned to the line to dry."

In 1892, Bishop Issac O. Stringer, known as "Bish" to his friends, was caught with a friend during freeze-up on the Yukon River. They abandoned their canoe, made snowshoes of willow and then proceeded on their way. Unfortunately, they became lost and ran out of food. In order to stay alive, the two boiled their shoes, an incident that was later copied by Charlie Chaplin in his classic film *The Gold Rush.*

The two men survived, and thereafter Bishop Stringer was known as the "Bishop Who Ate His Shoes" (*Alaska Nicknames*).

In late January 1991, Commissioner of the Department of Natural Resources Harold Heinze discussed plans for using convict labor to cut down Alaska's bark beetle-infested spruce trees. He referred to these men as Alaska's "chainsaw gang."

During the Klondike Gold Rush, reindeer were seriously considered for the job of carrying the mail. Over 500 reindeer and 90 Lapplanders were imported to Alaska to fulfill the contract.

During the winter of 1898, a number of whaling ships, including the *Belvedere*, were stuck in the ice off Barrow. The mate of the *Belvedere* was Jimmy the Jib, a whaler with an unusually long nose. It was 56° below when the men trying to stay warm at the Refuge Station spotted Jimmy dragging a 150 pound box through the snow. (He subsequently lost ¼ inch of his nose to frostbite.)

Someone had apparently told Jimmy that whatever was in the box would be worth his while when he got to the Refuge Station. The whalers all gathered round as the crate was opened. It was full of Bibles (*Alaska Nicknames*).

On June 5, 1945, Porter Apple of Petersburg moored his fishing boat to an iceberg. While he was on the berg chopping, the cake of ice turned turtle and pulled his craft "high and dry." For three hours he balanced on the iceberg until the agitation of a bush pilot's plane caused the cake to gently roll back into its original position.

Few Alaskans believed the story until the bush pilot in question, Tony Schwamm of Petersburg, produced a picture to prove it. The photo appeared in the Friday, July 13, 1945, issue of the *Anchorage Daily Times*.

In the Ukraine there is a custom known as *Selaviq* or "Starring." For several days around Christmas by the Julian Calendar — 13 days later than Christmas in the West — processions go from house to house with a huge star. While the practice is dying out in the Ukraine, in many parts of Alaska, most notably the Yukon-Kuskokwim Delta, Prince William Sound and the Aleutians, the custom is alive and well.

In 1988, Kathy Hunter, of Palmer, published a collection of historical Alaskan nicknames which included:

> Accordian Hans of Kenai, who fashioned a boat propeller out of a moose shoulder blade.
> Airboat Turbo of Fairbanks, who ran his airboat out of the Chena River and rode down the Airport Highway to the Lonely Lady, a topless-bottomless club.
> Charles "Alabam" Laboyteaux of Livengood was a territorial legislator who was famous for saying of Livengood, "Anything goes here, except we sort of frown on murder."
> Arctic Leper, a Cessna in Nome so named because whenever the plane took off, shreds of its red paint would flutter to the ground.
> Black Mary of Petersburg ran a brothel known as the Star. One day a house was on fire but the firemen could not fight the blaze because the nearby stream was too low. Black Mary stripped off her clothing and "sat in the creek, damming the water with her ample black body."
> Captain W.P. ran a mail boat between Valdez and Ellamer. His nickname came from a phrase he used often, "Weather Permitting."
> Timothy "Chicken" Randolph was marooned on an island in the Gulf of Alaska with 25 chickens. When he was found five years later, there were thousands of chickens on the island. Randolph and a partner opened T&T Chicken Ranch and sold the meat to Seward, Valdez and Cordova. When cats unexpectedly appeared on the island and began eating the chickens, Randolph butchered the cats and sold them as

rabbit. When disease finally killed the chickens, and in the turn the cats which fed upon the chickens, Randolph retired to Cordova.

Evil Alice of Anchorage was so named because she was a sanitation officer, and whenever the prostitutes on C Street saw her coming they would yell, "Clear the Deck! Here comes Evil Alice!" [Evil Alice also used to handcuff drunks to street lights. People so constrained were said to be in "Evil Alice's Jail."]

Deepwater Mary, a prostitute in Ketchikan, was so named because every time she became depressed, she threw herself into a creek.

The Drifting Finn of Dillingham was a trapper who lived inland. Over several days one fall, the residents of Dillingham noticed that his boat was floating downriver as the tide fell and upriver as the tide returned. When they went to investigate, they discovered that the Finn was lying dead drunk on his boat. He had consumed his entire winter's supply of liquor.

———————

Kid Marion, a Yukon steamboat pilot, once hammered two stakes into the side of a bank beneath a cemetery. Then he stuck boots on the stakes. Each time he passed the cemetery on his route he told his passengers that "Old Sam" had been buried with his boots on and was slowly sliding down the bank into the river (*Alaska Nicknames*).

———————

In the mines of Nome, miners would wear candles on their hats for light.

———————

Paul Gliva of Anchorage and his wife Priscilla were fishing in Prince William Sound in 1985 when Paul hooked a large salmon. It had to be a large fish, he speculated, because of the way it was fighting the line. Only after he got the fish onboard did he realize that what was on his line was more than just a salmon. It was a seal, too. All the seal had left him was the skeleton of the fish with "a few pieces of meat here and there," his wife recalled.

———————

In 1900, almost every saloon in Alaska referred to itself as "First Class." Thus Dick Dawson and Charlie Suter opened "The Only Second Class Saloon in Alaska" in Nome.

———————

A double exposure showing the steamship *Senator* supposedly being loaded by an airplane in Nome in the early 1900s. (Courtesy Carey McLain Museum Archives, Nome.)

Augie Hiebert, owner of Northern Television in Anchorage, began his career as an engineer in Fairbanks' first radio station. Part of his assignment was to cover news events, and in the late 1950s, he went with the military on an airborne emergency evacuation. He flew on a C-54 out of Fairbanks dragging a glider on a cable behind the plane. When the rescue crew spotted the stranded man, the glider was released. After it landed, the ground crew set up a frame of cable so the glider could be snatched off the ground by the circling C-54.

"It was a perfect snatch," Hiebert recalled. "A few weeks later I was told that the military had abandoned that rescue practice. When I asked why, I was told, 'because we lose too many C-54s doing it that way.'"

In 1990, when the Anchorage Museum of History and Art was putting together its Russian exhibit, it accepted a traditional sea kayak from the Natives of Akhiok on Kodiak Island. Unfortunately, it took longer to make the kayak than expected. First, sea lion skins could not be used since the animal is an endangered species. Then, after the Natives had gathered deer-skins, it was discovered that the elders who were to do the sewing had arthritis so debilitating that artisans from St. Lawrence Island had to be flown in to do the work.

"They developed what we called a 'Museum Stitch,'" noted Barbara Smith, Special Curator of the Exhibit. "It looks authentic on the outside but leaks like a sieve on the inside."

When the kayak was finally finished, it was so long that it could not fit into the hold of any of the cargo planes which landed in Akhiok. Then, with less than a week to go before the exhibit opened, MarkAir strapped the 14-foot, deer-skin covered kayak to the belly of one of its planes and flew it into Anchorage.

In April of 1991, the Alaska Chapter of the American Diabetes Association held an unusual fund raiser called "Moose Marble Madness." Two thousand moose "nuggets" were numbered and dropped from a helicopter 150 feet in the air. The owner of the nugget that came closest to the bull's eye won $10,000.

As a young man in 1941, Paul Wilson of Anchorage was responsible for the census count in all of the villages between Kotzebue and Barrow. At that time, quite a few of the older Eskimos did not know the year in which they had been born, much less the day. Wilson solved the year problem by guesstimating. As far as the day was concerned, "I made almost everybody's birthday April 1. For many of the Natives, I wrote their name and birthday in their Bibles. Some day an enterprising anthropologist is going to discover that across the western half of the Arctic, all of the old people seemed to have been born on April 1st."

In Tatitlek Narrows, within sight of where the Exxon *Valdez* went aground in 1989, you could have made $50,000 in 20 minutes—if you happened to be a herring fisherman.

During the April 1990 harvest, the herring were so plentiful that during the 20-minute season, boats averaged a catch of 68 tons apiece. Herring sold for about $800 a ton. Fish and Game management estimated that the total catch should be 6,900 tons from Prince William Sound and the total tonnage would be caught in 20 minutes.

With a 20-minute season, every second counted. An illegal, 30-second head start had so much financial potential that all the fishermen have to keep an eye on each other. To ensure no one jumped the starting gun, no one was told when the 20 minutes would actually begin. The time was chosen at random.

But when the announcement was made over the citizen band radio, it was as close to a free-for-all as a run on the stock market. Launches roared across the water, dropping seine nets along the way. Then boats begin pulling the lines in, tightening the noose. The panicking herring bolted toward the net. Some of the nets filled to overflowing and tons of fish escaped in seconds.

Herring fishing is actually a very risky business. With a season of only 20 minutes, any mistake could be bankrupting. Bad weather or choppy seas has put many a fisherman out of business. A net catching on rocks on the bottom can tear a hole large enough to allow all of the fish to escape.

"It's just like a crapshoot in Vegas," noted Bob Hughes of the *Norma Jo*. "That's herring fishing for you."

Among many other attributes, the northland is famous for its "Alaskan birds." In 1988, lawyer Stephen Routh in Anchorage was dealing with two high-priced investment bankers from a large, prestigious investment firm in New York. They were seated in Routh's office and spending the hot summer afternoon haggling over the wording of a complex contract.

After several hours of formalities, the work was completed. As they were relaxing, Routh asked the New Yorkers if they were planning on staying in Anchorage for a few days to see more of Alaska. No, the bankers replied succinctly and coldly, leaving the clear message that they thought that anything Alaska had to offer was definitely *déclassé*.

At that moment, Routh happened to glance outside. "You might consider bird watching," Routh said. "Why, one of Alaska's most famous birds is right outside my window right now." He indicated his office window.

"It was obvious this guy could have given a s--- about birds," Routh remembered. "But he was being polite so he went over to the window and bent back my levolor blinds."

There, across the street, was one of PJ's "birds," standing outside smoking a cigarette dressed for work, topless and bottomless.

"I've still got creases in my levolors from where this guy bent handfuls of the blinds up and down so he could do some Alaskan bird watching."

Routh believes the men spent the next two days in Alaska, "probably at PJ's."

According to the January 1, 1991, edition of *The International Save the Pun Foundation* newsletter, in November of 1989 a group of traveling musicians encountered an unusual problem on their way to Anchorage. "Since the Alaska Airlines computer [was] programmed to reject any seat holder without a name, researchers will someday discover that in November [of 1990] a Ms. Harp C. Chord flew to Anchorage." Alaska Airlines was contacted for confirmation but declined to reply.

In 1990, the Talkeetna Moose Dropping Festival received an outraged call from an animal rights group in the Lower 48 demanding to know how high the moose was when it was dropped. "About 300 feet," replied an absurding Alaskan at Festival headquarters, "but we drop them on cement."

24

CORRUPTION IN PARADISE: THE SOCIALIST PARTY IN ALASKA

If there was ever a time and place ripe for the Socialist movement, it was Alaska in the first two decades of the twentieth century. In those days, the northland was as open to exploitation as had been the American West just before barbed wire was stretched across the frontier. The primary source of income for the white population was mining, a labor-intensive industry, which necessarily meant large numbers of laborers working in a confined area far from the laws and oversight of the United States government.

For union organizers, this was an ideal setting. There were enough workers to form a union and too many miles to the Pacific Northwest to make the importation of strikebreakers economic. On the flip side of the coin, from management's point of view, a strike would be so expensive that it would be more economic to negotiate wage increases than risk a shutdown. Finally, to the advantage of the union organizers, there was the attitude of the federal government.

As far as the American authorities were concerned, Alaska was politically insignificant and geographically remote. Federal authority followed a policy of neglect. Restrictions were weakened by this distance, and large corporations were left free to follow a policy of rape-and-run, leaving the northland with the corresponding boom-and-bust economy. Though the days of the Robber Barons were over in the Lower 47 — Arizona becoming the 48th state in 1912 — in Alaska, corporate exploitation was the name of the game.

Radical labor groups, reaching the apogee of their power before the Great Red Scare scattered their members around the world, saw a golden opportunity to establish a foothold in Alaska. This attitude was particularly true of the Socialists. Formed in 1911, the Socialist Party of Alaska expanded, and within two years it had established 28 locals with a recorded—i.e., paid—membership of 315. Fairbanks and Nome had the largest locals; Anchorage, Alaska's largest city today, was only scrub brush and wetlands then. Considering that Alaska had a working population of just 38,350 men and 1,723 women in 1910, a contingent of 315 members was statistically significant.

Even though the "nightmare of capitalism" was creeping into Alaska, as the Socialist Party of Alaska stated in its Preamble and Platform for 1914, Alaska was still a workingman's paradise. Wages were reasonable and thus strikes were few. The extraction industry appeared to have unlimited horizons, thereby assuring long-term jobs, and there was every reason to believe that the mineral industry would survive into the next century—maybe even beyond. From the point of view of labor, it was almost too good to be true.

But even in this paradise, the Socialists noted flaws in the system. In April of 1913, for instance, the Party began a letter-writing protest against Ward T. Bower, Fish Commissioner for Alaska. The Party claimed that Bower was a "pliant tool of those whose greed [was] fast making the salmon an extinct species." Bower had been the "guest of the cannery officials on . . . pleasure trips" and, as a public official, had proved to be "entirely subservient to the wishes of those who desire[d] to make fortunes in a few years at the expense of a great industry which would, under proper management, last forever." Further, Bower was currently working on the passage of the Jones Bill, which would legalize the fish trap in Alaska, a bill to which every "honest fiend [sic] of the Alaska industries [was] opposed." The Socialists wanted Bower removed and replaced with someone who had an "honest interest in the preservation of the fishing industry."

In the same month, on April 17, the Party involved itself in a national dispute. After a mass meeting—which was not covered in the Juneau newspaper—the Party sent an outraged letter to the Governor of West Virginia declaring that "we, the working men of Juneau, Alaska, in mass meeting assembled, bitterly protest against the brutal treatment of our fellow workers in West Virginia and against the high-handed outrages of the capitalist class." Further, the Party stated that it would "stand by [our] brothers . . . by refusing to burn, haul or handle coal mined in West Virginia in any shape or form, [and] by refusing to work in any factory, mill or any industry where West Virginia coal is used." How much West Virginia coal was actually being consumed in Alaska at that time is not known, but a good guess is none.

After the mass meeting, yet another letter was sent, this one to the Governor of New York protesting "against the foul manner in which the capitalist class has ... railroad[ed] innocent men ... on trumped up charges ... by a packed grand jury." There was no mention of any name in the letter of protest, nor any threat to boycott the products or services of New York state.

On the local level, it is important to note that, above all else, Socialists took pride in their own honesty. If there was any one aspect of the Socialist Party which marked its members different from other political groups, it was their sense of fair play for the individuals involved and respect for the integrity of the spirit of working as a team. Socialists stood tall for their colleagues across the United States and stated their willingness to participate in a nationwide strike to support even one worker who had been treated unfairly by management.

Even when it came to dealing with what other political groups would call clear-cut matters of policy, the Socialists gave its members the greatest degree of flexibility. As an example, in 1912, when W.D. "Big Bill" Haywood publicly advocated "direct action and sabotage" rather than ballot box power, individual ballots were mailed to Socialists across America as part of a national Socialist referendum to determine if Haywood was "unworthy to remain any longer a member of the National Executive Committee."

When it came to the individual representing the Party, the Socialists maintained their own integrity. To those interested in public office, the Party circulated blank resignation sheets which, undated, were to be signed by Party members seeking public office. Then, in the case of sudden unpleasantries, the resignation would be dated appropriately and accepted instantaneously. This practice was, according to the form, "used to protect the integrity of the party."

When corruption did come to the Socialist Party of Alaska, it came silently. On October 13, 1913, the Party decided that it should seek some means of reducing its overhead. One way, it was suggested, was to "take up vacant tide flats" below the court building in Juneau and there, "holding title by possession," establish a meeting hall. No justification, economic or political, for the Party to take public land for private use at no cost was mentioned in any of the minutes or letters in existence today.

Once it was decided that a hall would be built, one member, "Comrade Dorwaldt," offered to construct the foundation. It was moved, seconded and passed accepting Dorwaldt's offer. Shortly thereafter, $70 was appropriated toward building supplies.

Dorwaldt, an Industrial Workers of the World (IWW) member as well as a member of the Socialist Party of Alaska, then suggested that the local chapter of the IWW supply the labor to construct the building. As the IWW was then looking for a meeting hall, it seemed reasonable to assume that the IWW would be willing to construct the hall and exchange the wages earned as free rent when it wished to hold its meetings in the new building. This was also moved, seconded and passed.

A month later, on November 11, Dorwaldt reported back to the Socialist Party that the IWW had already worked 32 hours on the building and he had given them credit on the books for that work at the rate of $.50 per hour. Sufficient work had been done, he further claimed, to "hold the ground," but he would need $1.50 a day as a "personal expense account." This was moved, seconded and passed.

Dorwaldt was back the next week. He reported that the IWW had worked a total of 4 additional hours on the building and he had personally "worked four days." Apparently some of the IWW members had been working for free under the impression that the IWW was to receive "a half interest in the hall in consideration of the labor donated." Members of the IWW who were present at the meeting wanted to make certain that their work was going to be acknowledged in some manner, even if it was in the form of a free lease for "one or two nights a week for six or seven years." Other options were offered, but the bottom line, the IWW members made clear, was that they expected some reasonable form of compensation and "requested that the amount the hall was to cost them be determined at once." On motion, the matter was turned over to the Hall Committee of the Socialist Party.

The next week, on November 25, the Hall Committee determined that it would be possible to borrow money from a member to complete the hall, and it was recommended that all labor costs be henceforth paid in cash. Since there was no way of determining the rental cost of the hall as yet, none was established. On motion, the report was adopted.

However, it was soon discovered that Dorwaldt "intended to keep the property himself," and had, as an agent of the Socialist Party, acquired a quit-claim deed for the property by using the money borrowed by the Socialist Party. Dorwaldt's name, it was reported, rather than that of the Socialist Party of Alaska, had been placed on the deed as the legal owner. At the next meeting, Dorwaldt was confronted with the deed and told to sign it over to the Socialist Party. Dorwaldt refused. When asked for an explanation of his actions, Dorwaldt refused to respond. Having no choice, the Socialist Party expelled Dorwaldt for breach of trust on November 25th.

While this tidbit of history is hardly shattering, the importance of this episode is that history is simply the story of people. It is the story of people being people, of people trying to do the right thing, and of people succumbing to baser instincts. History is what happens each day, and sometimes, as in the case of Comrade Dorwaldt, our chicanery is on record forever. According to the Assessor's Office, City/Borough of Juneau, "R. Dorwaldt" appears in the 1913, 1914, and 1915 tax rolls. The land was sold on January 12, 1916.

25

THE CORDOVA COAL PARTY

One of the most persistent struggles in Alaskan history has been between the forces demanding the conservation of natural resources and those who favor full development of Alaskan potential. On one side are the developers, who often view Alaska as a gigantic milk cow bellowing to be drained. On the other are the forces of environmentalism, who favor pristine wilderness over the rape-and-run tactics of unscrupulous companies that care only for profit, not posterity.

Historically, the epitome of this struggle was the intertwined history of copper and coal. For Alaskans, coal was more than a black rock in the ground. It was the makings of a railroad. With an inexpensive source of transportation, particularly in the Cordova area, it would be possible to begin mining the copper, which was then just lying fallow.

There was a viable market for copper in the United States, but the cost of getting the mineral out of Alaska's vast interior was prohibitive. Yet there was a glimmer of hope. With extensive coal fields located close to the copper deposits in Cordova, the development of a railroad was a real possibility. The coal meant that a railroad was possible; with a railroad, a copper industry was possible; and with a copper industry, Alaskans would find employment.

Everything was going business's way until the unexpected happened: the United States government turned conservationist.

Historically, this sudden conservationism was an odd shift of gears. Few in Washington, D.C., had seemed particularly concerned when the fur seals had been hunted almost to extinction. While thousands of miners had raped the land in search of the elusive yellow metal, there had hardly been an outcry. Whaling did not have strong environmental opposition, nor did the inland fur industry have its potent adversaries. Yet, suddenly, when it came to coal, the federal government had what appeared to be an environmental position.

The logic behind this shift in policy was actually not environmental but defensive. Twenty years earlier, the United States Navy had been driven by wind. Now there was the Great White Fleet, a flotilla of steel ships that were powered by coal and oil. What had once been a resource for the world market was suddenly a fuel for national expansion. Coal thus became an instrument of national security.

Further, with Theodore Roosevelt in the presidency, the age of American imperialism prevailed. America was reaching commercially and militarily out into the Pacific. Hawaii had fallen into American hands, and the building of a United States–owned Panama Canal was underway. Hungrily, the businesses of America were eyeing a coaling station network across the central Pacific, including Midway, Wake Island, Guam and the Philippines.

Naval control of the North Pacific was generally assured by Alaska's strategic position on the globe and particularly by the Aleutian Islands, which reached well into the Eastern hemisphere. The United States had the coaling stations to sustain its global ambitions; all it needed now was a virtually inexhaustible source of coal and oil. Seward's Ice Box was to be a large part of that source.

There was yet another reason Alaska's coal fields were in jeopardy. Through Gifford Pinchot, Theodore Roosevelt was introducing the concept of conservationism to America. To save those lands which they considered pristine, Pinchot and Teddy Roosevelt earmarked millions of acres of public land for withdrawal from the public domain. Expanding the scope of presidential power, Roosevelt invented the mechanism for making parks, game reserves, monuments and restricted estuaries at the stroke of a presidential pen. From his prolific pen sprang national parks across the United States, quite literally, overnight. Alaska, America's great northern wilderness, was about to go under the pen.

The Alaskan coal fields were doomed. National security required coal be placed in reserve for the United States Navy. The conservationist impulse in the contiguous states was demanding that staggering acreages in Alaska be preserved for posterity. Thus, with this unfortunate combination, the coal fields of Alaska were destined for withdrawal from the public domain.

The impact on Alaska was chilling. As America entered the twentieth century as a growing economic power, Alaska was left with the dogsled as the symbol of its past, present and future.

There were other administrative twists in the federal government's policy toward the coal fields as well. Prior to 1900 there had been little effort to survey the coal fields because there was no law by which coal land could be acquired. Then, in 1900, when it became legal to mine in surveyed lands, Alaskans suffered the indignity of being told that they could not mine because the fields had not been surveyed, and the fields could not have been surveyed because it had not been legal to acquire coal lands in the first place.

This Catch-22 situation created such an uproar that the law was rewritten in 1904 to allow claims of up to 160 acres apiece. But the law did not allow for a joint venture of more than 640 acres, or one square mile.

On paper this law appeared to be a workable compromise. It gave the impression that the law favored the smaller enterprises, primarily Alaskan, at the expense of the larger, Outside businesses. It also appeared to give Alaskans the incentive to survey and mine the field before any newcomers rushed north for coal.

In practice the bill was unworkable. Coal mining was a complex process, and the allotted acreage was far too small to develop adequately any type of a profitable mining operation. Without being allowed to form mining cooperatives, miners were forced to operate piecemeal or resort to under-the-table, joint-venture arrangements to maintain profitable enterprises.

For about twelve months there was fevered surveying, the bulk of the work being done in the Bering River Coal Field. Then, on November 12, 1906, Theodore Roosevelt—by Executive Order—stated:

> It is not wise that the nation should alienate its remaining coal lands. I have temporarily withdrawn from settlement all lands which the Geological Survey had indicated as containing, or in all probability containing, coal. The question, however, can be properly settled by legislation.

This was a provocative statement. First, as this was an Executive Order, it raised the twin questions of its constitutionality in terms of the balance-of-power and its obligation on future presidents. Second, Roosevelt had given no indication as to how long "temporarily" would be.

Third, it was unclear as to exactly what was being restricted. The President had stated that he had withdrawn from "settlement" certain lands. Many wondered whether this word was a verb or a noun. Did this apply to previous settlements or just to those established after November 12? Was the president talking about all unsurveyed land in known coal fields or was he talking about all unsurveyed land on any public lands?

While lawyers pondered the implications of TR's Executive Order, the statement brought coal production in Alaska to a halt. The financial impact was devastating. In 1906, Alaska had only imported 5,541 tons of coal, as there were five producers in the Alaska. Within a year this number had dropped to four; by 1910 there were none.

Alaskans, locked out of their own fields, were now forced to buy coal from Seattle and British Columbian merchants. There was also an increase in price. Alaskans had once paid $2.50 a ton for a high quality ore. Now they were paying between $11 and $20 for a poor quality substitute. Most insulting, some of the people paying that outrageous price could look out their window and see the coal fields which were now restricted from mining.

With each passing year, the disdain for the federal government grew. But 1911 was to be a year of change. Six years had passed since the institution of the Presidential Order, and still the "temporary" conditions remained in force. With no termination of the Order in sight, Alaskans felt themselves the victims of government neglect, inaction and unreasonable red tape. By 1911 it was clear to many Alaskans that some form of protest was needed. Their economy was dying. Alaskans were growing more irate by the day.

The hot spot of the controversy was Cordova, the largest city in Alaska at the time. A new city council had recently been elected, and it did not wait long to represent clearly its constituents' feelings. On April 25, 1911, they hosted a mass meeting to "discuss the coal situation." Any Cordovan who had the "interest of the city at heart" was urged to attend. The message was unmistakable and was so stated by the *Cordova Daily Alaskan:*

> That Alaska is made the football for the big political game being played in the states there is no longer any doubt, and it is now up to the people to assert their rights and demand that justice be done the pioneers who made locations.

The meeting was a wild affair. "Aroused to a pitch of indignation," Cordovans "freely expressed themselves on the injustice" of the coal lands delay, the *Daily Alaskan* reported.

The next day the paper was pregnant with vituperation. Complaining of the "criminal treatment" accorded Alaska by the "pumpkin-head politicians back east," the *Daily Alaskan* blamed the "coal barons of Pennsylvania, Ohio, West Virginia and Indiana" who "toast[ed] their skinny shins before an open grate in a palatial Eastern residence that burns anthracite coal costing them three dollars a ton, while in Cordova we pay fifteen dollars a ton."

Another mass meeting was held on April 29th. By this time the temper of Cordovans had reached a fevered pitch. Within the few days between the two meetings the effect of the first gathering was clear. It was as though all the sentiment in the mining towns up and down the coast had been galvanized. Everyone was waiting for something to happen and for some city to take the lead. Reports from Valdez, Katella and Juneau showed that support for some sort of protest was overwhelming and building.

But by April 29, the day of the second mass meeting, the situation was so far out of control that any letters or telegrams to Washington, D.C., would have been just token efforts. Something stronger was needed. The second meeting simply added fuel to a raging fire. No one made any public suggestions at the second mass meeting but plans were already being laid for a protest that would be heard from one coast of the United States to the other. The community of Cordova became quiet as the plot thickened.

On May 3, 1911, Deputy Marshal Sam Brightwell received a call for assistance from Orca, three miles from Cordova. As there was no indication of any kind of trouble brewing in Cordova, he left for Orca. George Dooley, the Chief of Police for Cordova, was also out of town. He was on a "fishing trip." Coincidentally, a barge carrying more than 300 tons of coal from Seattle had arrived the day before and was moored to the dock.

Richard J. Barry, the agent for the railroad and steamship company, was sitting at his desk on what should have been a quiet morning. Then, in the distance, he could hear what sounded like a mob approaching the dock. Looking out the window, he saw a large body of men and women converging on the wharf.

Chanting "Give us Alaska coal! Give us Alaska coal!" the mob flooded around the steamship office and out onto the dock. From there it swarmed onto the moored barge. Helplessly, Barry watched as the landing lines were severed and the loaded coal barge was pushed away from the wharf pilings. Then scores of men began shoveling the coal into the harbor.

This was hardly a spontaneous affair. Included in the mob were some of the most respected citizens of Cordova: A.J. Adams, the President of the Chamber of Commerce, former Mayor W.H. Chase and Councilman James Flynn. When Barry demanded that they stop dumping the coal, someone in the mob yelled in reply, "We want none but Alaskan coal! Shovel away, boys!" Barry got a gun but was restrained by a clerk.

By this time the mob had grown to over 300 men and women. To the cheers of the crowd on the bank and dock, the mob shoveled ton after ton after ton of coal into the harbor. A touch of comedy was added when one man discarded a regular shovel in favor of one that was used for snow. The mob roared in delight.

Back in his office Barry placed a call to Mayor Lathrop. The mayor listened to Barry politely and then replied casually that he had no power to act in the circumstances since the alleged "illegal activity" was not within his jurisdiction." But he told Barry to contact the United States Commissioner. While Barry was making that call, Mayor Lathrop sent a wire to Governor Clark in Washington: "Big demonstration at ocean dock. Crowds armed with shovels dumping foreign coal into bay. Agent steamship company was telephoned for assistance. Deputy Marshal out of town on case. Have appealed to U.S. Commissioner. Situation desperate."

The United States Commissioner lost no time in deputizing both Lathrop and Dooley, the latter having returned from his "fishing trip." Lathrop and Dooley then walked down to the docks and demanded that the shovelers cease and desist. For a moment there was some hesitation on the part of the mob, but when reinforcements arrived, the mob relented and began dispersing. Thus ended the Cordova Coal Party.

In terms of press coverage and public relations, the Cordova Coal Party was a smashing success from coast to coast. The *Cordova Daily Alaskan,* of course, carried the exclusive story. Strategically placed above an article entitled "PINCHOT IS BURNED IN EFFIGY," the *Daily Alaskan* recounted the event. As Cordovans had "lost patience at the dilatory tactics" of the federal government, a large mob of Alaskans had marched to the docks and "proceeded to shovel the pile of foreign coal stored there into the bay." Just as the Boston Tea Party had been interested only in tea, "it must be said to the credit of the coal brigade that there was no disposition to destroy any property."

Reaction across the nation was strongly in favor of the "coal brigade." Front page headlines carried the story of the party as far away as New York, Kansas City, Philadelphia, Nashville, Detroit and Pittsburgh. A mass meeting in Seattle on May 9 was held in support of the Coal Party, and the *Alaska-Yukon Magazine,* a journal dedicated to the lifestyle of the north country, published an open petition by the Seattle Chamber of Commerce demanding that the coal fields be opened to legitimate claimants. In an editorial poem, the magazine stated, among other telling stanzas:

'Tis the spirit of our fathers,
　　When they dumped the English tea,
That is flashing through Alaska
　　From Cordova by the sea.

For Cordova, its rise to celebrity ended with the investigation by District Attorney Walker and United States Marshal Sullivan. On May 8th, five days after the coal party, Walker stated that he had made a thorough investigation, and as there had been no "loss of private or public property," the case was closed. No mention was made of more than 300 tons of coal that had disappeared into Cordova Bay.

Note: There have been a number of articles on the Cordova Coal Party over the years. The best sources for the incident are Lone E. Janson's Copper Spike *and Ernest Gruening's* The State of Alaska. *The* Cordova Daily Alaskan *is the best source and is available on microfilm.*

26
WHEN EAST IS WEST
AND WEST IS EAST

If Rudyard Kipling were alive today, he would probably be forced to rethink his immortal lines of East meeting West. The "twain" have met.

With the disintegration of the Soviet Union, for instance, the concept of "east" and "west" has become confusing. East Germany and West Germany for example, are now Germany, and the term Eastern Europe doesn't mean much any more. Even the term "West" is misleading. It could mean Europe, the Western hemisphere, Ohio, the Pacific Coast or where young men are supposed to go—according to Horace Greeley, that is.

If all this seems confusing, it should. What is "east" and "west" ranks right up there in importance with questions like "Do mice have shoulders?" or "Do chickens have lips?" Just like the childhood mind-bender "What can go up the chimney down but not down the chimney up?" the answer takes some explaining—particularly when it comes to Alaska.

According to the *World Almanac and Book of Facts,* which quotes the U.S. Department of the Interior Geologic Survey, the easternmost point in the United States is "West Quoddy Head, Maine," while the westernmost point is "Cape Wrangell" on Attu Island. The westernmost town is listed as "Adak," while the easternmost town is "Lubec, Maine." (There are also "easternmost" and "westernmost" cities, but why confuse things?)

As many Alaskans know, however, these facts can't possibly be true, since the Aleutian Islands cross into the Eastern Hemisphere at the 180th Meridian. That, as every school child knows, is where "west" becomes "east." Logic and any map of Alaska will show that Attu, which lies some six degrees into the Eastern Hemisphere, can't possibly be the most westerly chunk of American real estate since there are several islands that separate it from the 180th meridian—which lies to Attu's east.

In the interest of accuracy, the Geological Survey was contacted in 1990. In response, Lowell E. Starr, Chief of the National Mapping Division at the head office in Reston, Virginia, stated the *Almanac* was correct, since the terms easternmost and westernmost were "used to indicate a directional relationship when the United States [was] considered as an entity."

This is, of course, verbal tommyrot. What Starr is saying is that since Tucson is east of Los Angeles, that makes Tucson an eastern city.

Seeking a more knowledgeable source, the United States Geologic Survey in Anchorage was contacted. Being much more helpful, Tom Taylor noted that the 180th meridian "passed through Amchitka Pass and separated the Rat from the Andreanof Island groups in the Aleutian Islands."

Then his letter got complicated. According to Mr. Taylor, though the Andreanof Islands lie *east* of the meridian, they are actually labeled "West Longitude." Further muddying the waters, though the Rat Islands lie to the west, they are labeled "East Longitude."

If that wasn't bad enough, the curvature of the earth had to be taken into account as well. Since the further north one goes, the shorter the distance between the longitudinal lines, in the Aleutians a few miles makes quite a bit of difference. Thus there are two geographic points which are "closest" when discussing east and west. One is closest by miles, the other by degrees.

Thus, contrary to the *World Almanac and Fact Book*, the eastern and westernmost points of the United States, are:

> West: westernmost shore of Amatignak Island, Lat.—51 degrees 16.55 minutes North, Long.—170 degrees 8.7 minutes West.
> East: Pochnoi Point on the extreme east shore of Semisopochnoi Island in the Rat Island group, Lat.—51 degrees 57.6 minutes North, Long.—170 degrees 46.5 minutes East.
> [Note: *This will also change the easternmost "town" to Shemya, Alaska; not Lubec, Maine.*]

In actual fact, there is a solid link between east and west in Alaska, it just isn't above the surface of the water. About 1200 feet down on the 180 degree meridian there is land, and it probably has crab stalking about in the darkness. Crab are a good creature to mention in a chapter like this, because they move forward by walking sideways.

Further, since this author will be sending a copy of this chapter to the Geological Survey, and the fact sheet will have to be changed anyway, it should be pointed out that there is another geographic error as well. San Bernadino County in California, with its 20,102 square miles, is not the largest "county" in the United States; the North Slope Borough is — with 90,955 square miles.

What has been learned from this chapter? Well, we have officially established that the eastern and western most points *above water* lie on the Aleutian Islands about 65.72 miles from each other. We also know that Mr. Starr will be getting a letter from the author with a copy of this chapter urging him to revise a page in the next *World Almanac and Book of Facts.*

For the readers who were wondering about the questions raised at the beginning of this article: Yes, mice do have shoulders — but they are very small. Chickens do not have lips, as we know them. What can go up a chimney down but cannot come down the chimney up? An umbrella, of course.

27

THE WORLD ACCORDING TO ORTH or WHAT'S IN A NAME?

Every hard-core Alaskan has a copy of Orth's *Dictionary of Alaska Place Names*. It is the key source for settling arguments as to how Paradise got its name or who was the William for whom Prince William Sound was named. It is also a treasure trove for the unique manner in which many names of Alaska's geographic marvels came to be titled.

Airplane Flats on west coast of Umiak Island. Name published in 1943 on an AMS map. So named by U.S. Army during World War II "because planes landed there on the beach."

Amakomanak Creek in Brooks Range. Eskimo name meaning "wolf dung."

Antler Creek stream that flows into Nenana River. Named in 1965 by Alaska Department of Highways because "moose antlers are found in the area."

Atlasta Creek flows south to Lost Cabin Lake, near Glennallen. Name derived from a roadhouse which was named from a chance remark of the owner's wife on the completion of the first building: "At last a house."

Babel River flows to North Fork Swift River. So named in 1956 by Orth "because of the 'confusion of tongues' by authorities with respect to the name of this stream."

Beelzebub, Mount mountain near Eklutna Lake. Named by a party of climbers from the Mountaineering Club of Alaska in 1965. This "name for the devil was considered appropriate."

Benign Peak south of Eklutna Lake. So named in 1965 by the Mountaineering Club of Alaska because "nearby Bellicose Peak was a much harder climb, while this one's nature was quite benign."

Bering River heads at Bering Glacier terminus. Local name reported in 1903. Named "Rio de Lagartos" in 1779 by Don Ignacio Arteaga. "Arteaga, however, did not reach the river, so the name must have had some other source than any knowledge he had that there were lagartos, 'lizards,' in it."

Black Dog Creek   stream, heads in Sadlerochit Mountains. So named by USGS geologists in 1948 "because a black wolf came so close to a working geologist, he thought it was going to attack." Since "wolf" is a common name in Alaska, "dog" was used instead.

Black Titt   peak northwest of Crescent Mountain. Name appears on a 1906 map of Fourth Glacier.

Bona, Mount   mountain at head of Hawkins Glacier. Named by his Royal Highness, Prince Luigi Amedeo di Savoia, Duke of the Abruzzi, for the *Bona*, his racing yacht.

Boyan, Mount   mountain south of Kuzitrin Lake. So named because "from the north the contours of the mountain suggest a reclining nude figure. 'Boyan' is a Swedish feminine given name and was selected by members of the Geol. Survey Field party in 1948 for its euphoniousness and femininity."

Coldbar Mountain   between the Charley River and Middle Fork Fortymile River drainages. Prospectors' punning name reported in 1898. "Named for a dead bear found near top."

Deadlock Mountain   north of Sivukat Mountains, Brooks Range. So named in 1965 by geologists of the B.P. Exploration Co. because they "became deadlocked in attempt to interpret the local geology."

Deadwood Creek   flows to Crooked Creek, near Circle. Local name reported in 1896 by USGS as "Hogem" or "Deadwood Creek." "Hog 'em Gulch received its name from the fact that the discoverer tried to hold a large part of the richest diggings, taking up separate claims for the whole of his numerous family, and, it is said by some, for fictitious personages. When other miners came to the gulch and a meeting was held, among other things the question of naming the diggings came up, and one miner suggest that "Hog 'em" would be appropriate. This suggestion was not officially adopted, and the name Deadwood was given the gulch as being more dignified, but the original nickname has persisted and among most of the miners is used almost exclusively."

Extra Dry Creek   flows to Nome Creek, Seward Peninsula. Prospectors' name reported in 1899. Named relative to Dry Creek which is in the same area.

Fake Creek   west of Alapah Mountain. Named by Marshall in 1938. About it he wrote, "we pushed on across a high ridge to the place where all of us except Jesse Allen thought the main Anaktuvuk lay. He was right—the creek proved to be nothing but a false alarm—so we called it Fake Creek, and climbed over another ridge."

Flapjack Island   in Glacier Bay. Descriptive name given by USC&GS in 1942. So named because the island is in shallow water and at low tide "spreads out" like thin batter on a griddle.

Flower Mountain   southwest of Skagway. Name reported in 1952 to have been given by "an unknown botanist between 1932–42, who found a luxuriant growth of a great variety of flowers on the mountain."

Girls Mountain   northwest of terminus of Worthington Glacier, near Valdez. Named about 1962, suggested by the International Geophysical Year Bench Mark "Station Girls, 1957" located at the mountain's summit.

Goober Lake   northeast of confluence of East and South Forks Matanuska River. Named in 1956 by USGS "because of its resemblance to a peanut."

Goodhope Bay   on north coast of Seward Peninsula. So named by Lt. Otto von Kotzebue while exploring the region in August 1816 because he had "good hope" of making important geographic discoveries.

Goon Dip Mountain   north of Chichagof, on Chichagof Island. Named locally in 1939 "for Goon Dip, who died about 1936. He was Chinese consul at Seattle, Wash., for more than 25 years."

Goshelpme Creek   southwest of Survey Pass, Brooks Range. Name found on a prospector's map drawn in the 1920s and is evidently the combining of the words "gosh-help-me."

Grayling Creek   flows to Colville River, Arctic Slope. Named in 1925 by USGS because it was in this creek the "party caught the first grayling of the season."

Hardscrabble Creek   flows to Lake Grosvenor, on Alaska Peninsula. So named in 1923 by R.H. Sargent's USGS party, "on account of difficult traveling."

Hatbox Mesa   mountain, between Ayiyak and Chandler Rivers, Arctic Slope. So named by a USGS geology party in 1945 "because of the mesa's peculiar manner of weathering into boxlike blocks that from a distance resemble hatboxes."

Hatchet Lake   southeast of Healy. Named in 1954 by USGS because "a member of a survey party was hospitalized as a result of cutting his knee with a hatchet while setting up camp beside the lake."

Iceworm Gulch   near Nenana River, Alaska Range. Named in 1965 by

Alaska Department of Highways because "iceworms are the only indigenous wildlife whose name begins with an 'I'." The naming of
some features in this area was done ecologically and alphabetically.

Jabbertown   site of a whaling station, on Chukchi Sea coast. Name
shown on an 1898 manuscript map; so called because of the multiple
languages of the whalers and their families.

Lost Jim Cone   hill, northwest of Sandy Lake, Seward Peninsula. Reported in 1950 by D.M. Hopkins, USGS, so named because while
"mapping the [lava] flow in 1947, a member of the Geological Survey
field party was separated from the remainder of the group and lost
for nearly a day."

Lost Temper Creek   heads on Monument Ridge, Arctic Slope. Named
in 1950, USGS, because of a camp incident.

Lynx Creek   flows to Nenana River, McKinley Park. Named in 1965 by
the Alaska Department of Highways for the "many lynx which live
in the area."

Mallard Lake   on Kenai Peninsula northeast of Kenai. Named about
1963 by officials of Kenai National Moose Range for the Mallard,
"the one duck most important to the human race."

Maria Antonia, Punta   point of land, on south side of San Juan Bautista
Island, Alex. Arch. Named by the 1779 Don Ignacio Arteaga expedition. "One of the children of Fernando IV, King of Naples, bore this
name."

Marmion Island   southeast of Douglas Island in Gastineau Channel.
Named in 1883. The name was taken from the title of a narrative
poem by Sir Walter Scott.

Marshmallow Mountain   northeast of Anaktuvuk Pass, Brooks Range.
So named in 1930 "because the appearance of its summit looked like
a marshmallow."

Mechanic Creek   in DeLong Mountains. Named in 1953 by USGS "for
mechanical work on vehicles."

Memory Lake   in Matanuska Valley, near Palmer. Named by C.C.
Shrock, of Wasilla, in 1957 because "Swamp Lake," the former name,
"was not appropriate for the feature" and because a school was about
to be established on the lake front, and Mr. Shrock wished the students to leave the school with "happy memories."

Midnight Dome   mountain, south of Smith Creek Dome, Brooks
Range. Local name reported in 1932 by Robert Marshall "because it
is a spot to which the inhabitants climb on June 22, to see the midnight sun."

Midnight Mountain   south of Mount Dooneak, Brooks Range. Named in 1939 by Marshall, "we spent more than an hour, equally distributed around midnight, on the summit, and called our peak Midnight Mountain."

Mirror Lake   22 miles north of Anchorage. Named in 1958 by Mrs. Margaret Almdale because "the former name, 'Mud Lake,' implies that the water is muddy, while it is clear and has a sandy, rocky bottom. 'Mirror Lake' would be more appropriate since the lake itself is small in size and reflects the trees surrounding the lake along the water's edge."

Mishap Creek   on southwest coast of Unimak Island, Aleutians. The USC&GS reports that the former name "Big Loss Creek," was derived "from an incident. A lightkeeper attempting to swim the creek, when finding the foot bridge washed out, tried to throw his clothes ahead across the creek. Misjudging the distance, his bundle of clothes fell short of the far bank and were washed down stream."

Moose Pass   village, mile 29.3 on The Alaska RR on Seward Highway. Name of a station on The Alaska Railroad reported in 1912 by A.H. Brooks, USGS. It is reported that the village originally got the name Moose Pass because "in 1903, a mail carrier driving a team of dogs had considerable trouble gaining the right-of-way from a giant moose."

Nipper Cove   on northwest coast of Unimak Island, Aleutians. Named by USC&GS for "Nipper, a horse used by the 1939 field party on the island. The horse was accidentally killed during the season."

Nun Mountain   northwest of Juneau, St. Elias Mountains. So named because of the fancied resemblance to a nun.

Old Dummy Lake   southeast of junction of Kanuti Kilolitna and Kanuti Rivers. Local name published in 1951 by USGS; the lake is said to have been named for a deaf-mute Indian.

Pandora Peak   southeast of Flandreau Mountain, Chugach Mountains. Named about 1959 for Pandora of Greek mythology; a woman given a box by Zeus from which all human ills escaped when she opened it.

Pippin Lake   north of Tonsina, Chugach Mountains. Local name reported in 1932 "for a local teamster named Joe Pippen who fell into the lake about 1924."

Pirate Creek   in Mt. McKinley National Park. So named in 1923 by USGS, because "the drainage of this creek is a good illustration of stream piracy."

Powder Point   on northwest coast of Latouche Island, Chugach Mountains. Local name so called "because blasting powder for mining purposes was once stored here."

The Puppets two mountains at southwest end of Dall Ridge, on Gravina Island, Alex. Arch. Named in 1883. Punch and Judy Hills are nearby; "Punch" and "Judy" are the traditional names of characters in a puppet show in which the husband quarrels with his wife and does outrageous things in a ludicrous way.

Quail Creek flows southeast to Troublesome Creek, southeast of Rampart. Named by prospectors in 1898. Originally named "Ptarmigan Creek," but as "no one in the part could spell ptarmigan it was named 'Quail,' the spelling of which was easier."

Ram Point on southwest coast of Unalaska, Aleutian Islands. Descriptive name given by USC&GS "because the sole inhabitants of the locality are sheep ranchers."

Ready Bullion Beach on northeast coast of Douglas Island, southeast of Juneau. Named by Frank Berry, Antone Marks, William Meehan, John Prior, and James Rosewall, prospectors, in 1880. In their search for gold, they camped at the mouth of Ready Bullion Creek, where William Meehan, finding gold, is reported to have shouted "Look at this! Why it is almost ready bullion."

Seduction Point on south tip of Chilkat Peninsula, Coast Mountains. So named by Capt. Vancouver, 1798, RN, because of the designing nature of the Indians whom Joseph Whidby encountered here. In 1867, George Davidson, USC&GS, called the point "Seduction Tongue."

Sherman Glacier east of Cordova, Chugach Mountains. Named in 1910 by Lawrence Martin, USGS, for Civil War Gen. William Sherman of the Union Army. Martin's notes read "he [Sherman] said 'war is hell'; so I put him on ice, near the Sheridan Glacier."

Spooky Valley in Ray Mountains across headwaters of Kobuk Creek. Local name because of the weird rock formations there.

Strident Creek flows northeast to Jubilee Creek, Arctic Slope. Named in 1951 by USGS "for a camping incident," which may have been a noisy argument.

Sumdum Glacier heads on south slope of Mt. Sumdum, Coast Mountains. Tlingit Indian name reportedly representing the booming sound of the icebergs as they break off from the glacier.

Surprise Creek flows to Tupikchak Creek, Arctic Slope. Name proposed by geologists of the B.P. Exploration Co. because of their surprise at finding an unexpected rock sequence along the stream.

Torment Creek heads in Ry Mountains. Local name reported in 1956; so named because of the "tormenting course of the creek and the mosquitoes."

Torok Creek   flows northeast to Chandler River, Arctic Slope. Eskimo name given in 1948 by USGS party for the camp dog.

Tractor Creek   flows south to Nizina River, Wrangell Mountains. Local name for the stream in which "Sam Snyder got his Caterpillar tractor stuck."

Travelair Creek   flows northwest to Oolamnagavik River, Brooks Range. So named about 1950 by USGS geologists during exploration of the Naval Petroleum Reserve No. 4 because a "Travelair [plane] crashed and burned near the creek."

Turnaround Creek   heads in De Long Mountains, Brooks Range. Named in 1950 by USGS, "for a game of chance played while resting on this stream."

Walkaround Creek   flows south to Hunt Fork, Brooks Range. Named in 1931 by Marshall as a result of his party's lighthearted approach to a difficulties they encountered in trying to cross this storm-flooded stream. His companion remarked, "'There's one safe rule in traveling this north country in summer. If you can't get across them, you can always walk around them.' So as we headed upstream once more, we christened this stream Walkaround Creek."

Ward Creek   flows west to Chatham Strait on west end of Admiralty Island, Alex. Arch. Named in 1920 by USFS, with no known significance.

Waterboot Creek   flows northwest to Atsaksovlik Creek, Kilbuch-Kuskokwim Mountains. Local name refers to "an incident in connection with prospectors boating on this stream."

Watermelon Lake   northeast of head of Ikpikpuk River Arctic Plain. So named by geologists in the 1940s "because a supply airplane which landed here brought a rare treat — a watermelon."

Whiteface Mountain   southwest of Harvey Mountain, Brooks Range. So named "because of its resemblance to a peak of the same name in the Adirondacks."

Whiteout Peak   southwest of Upper Lake George, Chugach Mountains. Descriptive name given in 1963 by members of the Mountaineering Club of Alaska pertaining to the "usual weather conditions experienced by climbers in this area." A whiteout is an "opaque diffusion of sky and snow."

Wilbur, Mount   in Fairweather Range, Glacier Bay National Monument. Name honors Wilbur Wright, who with his brother Orville designed the first succesful airplane. When published, this name was misapplied to a mountain 4.5 miles to the southeast.

28
STRANGE BUT TRUE AS WELL

One of the services the National Weather Service currently offers in Alaska is a daily report on the thickness of ice on the rivers. This is particularly important to Bush residents, who use the frozen rivers as dog-sled trails, and in the spring, dog sledders or snow mobilers do not want to travel on dangerously thin ice.

Because a geo-stationary satellite cannot "see" the thickness of the ice, the weather service has local spotters who report the thickness in their locale. This information is then aired each day along with the regular weather forecast.

In the spring of 1992, the weather service in Anchorage called their spotter in Ruby and asked how thick the ice was on the Yukon River.

"Strong enough to hold a moose," the spotter replied.

"Are you sure?"

"Better be," replied the spotter. "I'm watching a moose cross the river right now."

On November 20, 1939, the *Nome Nugget* published a letter to the Chamber of Commerce from the Milk Industry Foundation inquiring about milk delivery in Nome. Reportedly, the Nome milkman didn't worry about spillage because the reindeer milk came "frozen into a block." Further, a piece of string "frozen to the block serves as a handle," and when "wrapped in oil paper," the milk looked like ice cream.

"We were wondering if this was a fact," wrote the Milk Industry Foundation. "We try to collect interesting and unique items about milk and milk distribution from all parts of the world."

On April 3, 1917, the *Juneau Daily Empire* ran a headline featuring territorial senator Charles Kingsley Snow of Ruby. The headline read, "INSANE MAN KNEW SNOW AT ONE TIME THEN WENT DAFFY."

In May of 1950, a funeral service in Palmer had to be delayed because a moose had blundered into the open grave pit. Fish and Wildlife personnel had to use a tow truck to lift the moose out of the hole ("Stumbling Moose Spared," *Bits and Pieces of Alaskan History*, Alaska Northwest Publishing Company, I, page 99).

During a cold snap in the winter of 1991, radio news personality Cary Anderson had his passenger-side windshield wiper break. In an effort to save his Jeep's windshield from becoming scratched, he put an old, fluorescent orange glove on the windshield spindle shaft. The glove did keep the windshield from being scratched and everywhere he drove, people waved at him, mistaking the moving glove for Cary's hand.

In 1918, Casey Moran, an old timer, was reported dead, and his obituary ran in many Alaskan newspapers. Casey, who was at Fort Dix, New Jersey, wired the *Juneau Empire* and noted: "Am greatly interested and highly appreciative of my obituaries. It almost makes me wish it were all true, but unfortunately I am still alive and have to pay rent and board."

A storyteller *par excellence*, "the world [did] not have paper enough to copy all the stories that Paul [Davidovics of Kotzebue] told," reported Father Llorente, the Catholic priest in Kotzebue, in his memoirs. One of the few that has been recorded, and is probably true, was of a night in the 1930s when Davidovics was lost in a driving storm. More dead than alive, he stumbled upon an abandoned shack, where he immediately sought shelter. He fed his dogs in the dark and then crawled inside his sleeping bag and went to sleep, using a log on the floor of the cabin for a pillow. When he awoke the next morning, he discovered that the 'log' was not a log at all; it was a frozen, dead man."

In September of 1960, Northern Consolidated airlifted 43 reindeer out of Nunivak Island on the first leg of their journey to becoming "assistants" to Santa Clauses across the United States. These reindeer deplaned in Anchorage and were soon heading for California in a "deluxe van." (Courtesy Anchorage Museum of History and Art.)

Llorente also told reporters for the *Nome Nugget*, August 7, 1937, that Eskimos "visualized Hell as a fine place to live" because they would have to "haul no wood."

———

Sometimes Mother Nature had a hand in the fate of a pilot. Jack Jefford was flying between Golovin and Elim when he was caught in a powerful down draft and felt "an awful jar on the airplane." Not sure what had happened, he began easing back on the throttle.

Nothing happened so he eased back another increment.

Again, he felt no difference in his flying.

He kept easing back on the throttle and feeling no effect until he realized that he could not possibly be flying. So he turned his engine off.

When the weather cleared, he found himself perched on a mountain top. There he stayed for seven days until he was rescued.

There were quite a few stories of how some of the old timers supposedly developed substitutes for aviation instruments. There is an old Alaskan Bush tale, possibly true because the older pilots do not laugh, of the sourdough who bought a plane that was so old it didn't have any instruments. Rather than fork out the money for an altimeter, artificial horizon and directional gyro, he just got a compass, cat and duck.

The compass told him which way to fly. As he flew through clouds, he kept his eye on the cat that was on the seat beside him. Since a cat will always sit with its head level, if the cat dipped its head to the right, the sourdough pulled the right wing tip up until the cat's head was level.

For the altimeter, he used the duck. If he could not see the landing strip clearly, as he came down he kept a sharp eye on the duck. As soon as the plane was about to reach ground level, the duck would suddenly become active and start flapping its wings to cushion its own landing. Then the sourdough knew that *terra firma* was imminent.

While this story is a shade beyond the edge of believability, when it was told to a grizzled Bush pilot, his reaction was "Why didn't he use a spark plug?" When asked to explain, the old-timer stated that the pilot in question could have dispensed with the cat by simply suspending a spark plug from the top of the windshield. By keeping an eye on how the spark plug hung, the pilot could fly level. "Saves on mice, too," he remarked.

After decades of not being allowed to dance by the religious community in Kotzebue, the Bureau of Indian Affairs (BIA) finally gave the Eskimos written permission to dance in BIA schools. But after so many years of *not* dancing, the Eskimo faced yet another problem. They did not have a drum. It was too late in the year to find a walrus stomach to use in the construction of the instrument, so they made their instrument with the vulcanized rubber from weather balloons provided courtesy of the CAA station in Kotzebue. Only then did Eskimo dancing return to Kotzebue (story from Willy Hensley, Kotzebue).

In 1917, Barrow, with "the largest voting precinct in the world," had only five eligible voters—"including the illiterate wife of a trader"—of which none voted. According to the United States Commissioner, who did not vote, Barrow "didn't want the honor of casting the smallest vote." According to the *Iditarod Pioneer,* February 10, 1917, the residents didn't feel they knew a thing about the candidates and thus did not see any sense in "putting the government to the expense of a vote being taken."

On April 7, 1992, *Weekly World News,* a supermarket tabloid reported that drilling at Umiat punctured a hole in Hell and Satan himself was loosed. Allegedly, 13 oil riggers in a community with a population of three were consumed in the resulting conflagration. "Stung by having missed the cosmic event, *[Anchorage] Daily News* investigators jumped on the story" on April 13, 1992. To the *Daily News'* dismay, state officials were "unable to confirm the explosion" or the appearance of the "terrifying Satanic face" that was prominently illustrated on the front cover of *Weekly World News.*

Asked to comment, a geologist at the University of Alaska, Fairbanks noted, "I guess Hell is where you find it. Some places you have to go deeper than others. For instance, right now in Fairbanks . . . I'd say you don't have to drill at all."

In the 1930s, air passenger David Strandberg was on his way through Merrill Pass in the Alaska Range when the plane went down. Both Strandberg and the pilot were uninjured and waved to the first plane that flew overhead. The plane slowly circled as the pilot eye-balled the men on the ground. Then the plane flew away. Three days later the two men were picked up. During the intervening time, the pilot who had initially spotted them had stolen every one of the grounded pilot's passengers (story from Doug Strandberg, David's grandson).

The law in the Territory of Alaska has not always been lenient. In June of 1917, George Hinton Henry, the editor of the *Free Press of Fairbanks,* was sentenced by Fairbanks District Court Judge Charles E. Bunnell to five months for "criminal libel." What was Henry's crime? He had

Copper River Salmon [postcard]. (Courtesy University of Alaska, Fairbanks: Alywin H. Humphries Collection, ACC #83-148-184, in the Archives of the Alaska and Polar Regions Department.)

published the alleged fact that a Fairbanks resident, H.R. King, "had stolen copies of the newspaper from the doorsteps of subscribers" (*Alaska Labor News,* June 9, 1917).

———————

In the spring of 1992, Judge Larry Weeks of Juneau, was petitioned by the Democratic Party of Alaska to examine Independent Governor Walter Hickel's reapportionment plan. On May 11, 1992, Weeks ruled that Hickel's plan was too partisan.

In a section entitled "Improper Motives," Judge Weeks noted that two members of the Reapportionment Board as well as the husband of a board member and the executive director found themselves in districts with no incumbents. Further, the man who was distributing copies of the reapportionment plans in Anchorage "for a fee" and who was owed $800 by the executive director for his last campaign *also* ended up in a district with no incumbent. *And,* the state senator against whom the executive director had run and lost would, under the new plan, now be "representing a substantially different district than he ha[d] represented in the past, and [was] paired against another incumbent who is now in this odd-looking district."

Tongue-in-check with a straight judicial face, Judge Weeks wrote: "It is possible, of course, that all of these things are coincidence."

––––––––––

In the winter of 1916, the *Fairbanks Citizen* published a story stating that a Native woman in Fairbanks who had been jailed for vagrancy had been the common-law wife of Rex Beach, the famous Alaskan writer of *The Iron Trail, Spoilers,* and *Silver Horde,* to mention but a few of his classics. Beach, in February of 1917, wrote to the *Fairbanks Citizen* and commented

> I am lost in admiration of the *[Fairbanks Citizen]*'s enterprise, its accuracy and its nose for news; it represents journalism in its highest form. And I congratulate [the paper] upon its staff of fiction writers. Undoubtedly there is something in the Alaskan climate which stimulates the imagination.

Beach confirmed that he probably knew the woman and, if it was the same individual, she was known as "Short and Dirty" around Ramparts. He confessed "that the same roof sheltered both of us for a time," though the roof "likewise sheltered five other white men," one to whom "Annie belonged." They, meaning the six men and Annie, were "not a happy family," Beach related, because Annie

> insisted upon boiling frozen fish heads in a tomato can and eating the eyes while we college boys were at our meals. It was not appetizing to try to eat while those fish craniums were being vacuumed clean. Nor were Annie's other habits those to which we were accustomed in our homes.

(The complete letter appeared in the *Chitina Leader,* February 13, 1917.)

––––––––––

The headline on a story in the May 7, 1992, *Anchorage Times* was cute but not eye-catching: "SCHOOL-RUN HATCHERIES TEACH SALMON ABC'S." But the first two sentences were: "Ray Vergin's school of 1992 will graduate in a few weeks. Most of them will die soon after." The story was about 47,700 pink salmon fry that would be released near Sand Point. Only "a lucky 5,000 or so fish" were expected to survive long enough to spawn.

––––––––––

The Alaskan sheepsled. (Courtesy University of Alaska, Fairbanks: Arnie Wahte Collection, ACC #64-34-19N, in the Archives of the Alaska and Polar Regions Department.)

In Sitka, on February 6, 1901, nine men—Kah-too-quish, Too-quan, Koo-nock-ish, Katl-doo-ta-ish, Koo-hotch, Too-yek, Skoo-yek, Gus-nah-shoo-hoi and Thlah-kee-thlek—

> did unlawfully, wilfully, violently and knowingly, without authority of law, with diverse other evil disposed persons ... assembl[e] and [meet] together, to the great disturbance and terror ofthe *[sic]* citizens and inhabitants of said town of Sitka, and those living near by, by tumultuous and offensive carriage, and by threatening to assault and destroy certain property, to wit, a totem pole.

The Tlingits were sentenced to 30 months in jail.

In the late 1980s, Libyan leader Moammar Gadhafi had a solution for the conflict in the Mid-East. The Jews should be removed from what once was Palestine, he noted, and resettled between France and Germany. If the United States *really* had sympathy for the Jews, he then suggested, "why doesn't [the United States] give them Alaska?"

According to the *Nome Nugget*, August 20, 1902, the story that Noah's Ark had been discovered in the Alaskan interior were false. Supposedly, Noah's vessel had been located 300 miles from Coldfoot. The vessel was half a mile long and apparently in good condition, as there was the insinuation that a Dr. Cleveland was considering opening "a roadhouse in the mythical vessel."

Four years later, on May 9, 1906, the *Dawson Daily News* reported that the elusive Noah's Ark had again been found, this time "on a high hill overlooking a string of lakes, 30 or 40 miles from the head of the Chandlar river." This craft was one story high, "reaching 12 to 14 feet to the eaves," was 100 yards long, "made with copper nails, bolts and washers," and displayed Russian words on the structure. An eyewitness supposed that it could have been a floating Russian fort that had become beached when the river water receded.

During the maritime rush to Skagway, the Pacific Coast Steamship Company's ship *Corona* was momentarily stranded on some rocks. When the ship was drydocked for repair, according to McCurdy's history, it was discovered that:

> a large blackfish had been drawn into the gaping hole in her hull by the inrush of water, probably preventing [the *Corona*] from sinking immediately with possible heavy loss of life. So firmly was the mammal [sic] wedged that it was necessary for shipyard workers to cut it apart with axes.

(In all fairness, other sources list "blackfish" as whales, and therefore the term mammal may be appropriate.)

Not only are Alaskan bears and mosquitoes world-class, so too, reported the *Nome Nugget* on October 31, 1935, are the grasshoppers. According to "prominent big Game hunters" Mr. and Mrs. Peterson of Nashua, New Hampshire, they landed with their guide, Lee Waddell, in a "nameless valley locked by glaciers in the remote area between Knik Glacier and Prince William Sound" to hunt for game. There they discovered grasshoppers "massed on the ground in a veritable carpet." The insects flew in clouds and were so ravenous that they ate "large holes in [the Peterson's] tent and bedding and destroyed much of their food supply," as well as "gnawed axe handles and gun stocks."

Interested in Liz Walker's recipe for pickled walrus flippers as presented in the May 19, 1967, *Tundra Times?* Here it is:

1. Cut walrus flippers at the joints and cook about four pounds of walrus flippers in salted water until tender.
2. For about five minutes, boil together two cups of vinegar, one and a half cups of water, one tablespoon of sugar, and two tablespoons of pickling spices. Allow to cool.
3. Put a layer of drained flippers in a crock or deep dish. Then add a layer of onions and a little bay leaf.
4. Repeat.
5. Pour the cooled vinegar mix over the flippers until the meat is covered.
6. If you add two tablespoons of salad or seal oil, and keep the crock or deep dish where it is cool and dry, "this pickled meat will keep several months."

In December of 1906, there was a rash of dog thievery in Fairbanks. To stop this crime wave, law enforcement officials proposed to "forever put the fear of God and justice in that most despicable class of criminal, the dog thief." City officials were hot on the trail of a "half dozen clues" while Marshal Driebeibis was "flying over ice and snow in hot pursuit of a dog thief now en route to Eagle."

Apparently the crackdown on dognapping worked. "Two dogs have reappeared in their right owner's kennels," a sure sign of success. Further, alleged the paper, once the dog thieves were made aware of the fact that being found guilty would sentence them to a "year each on the federal saw buck," the crime wave ended.

Though many Alaskans found it hard to believe, on April 9, 1992, the *Anchorage Daily News* reported that a company was considering transporting Alaskan water to California by barge. Sun Belt Water Inc., of California, proposed using a tug to haul fresh water in bags 60 feet deep, 250 feet wide and 1000 feet long. The 72 million gallons of fresh water in the bag would weigh 300,000 tons.

In its May 5, 1937, edition, the *Nome Nugget* reported that Albert Murray and Charles Harper of Cache Creek had invented horse snow shoes so their animal could "navigate" deep snow.

Territorial Representative William Egan—later to be Alaska's first governor—introduced a bill in 1949 calling for a $50 tax on single women, reported the *Nome Nugget*, March 16, 1949, to "further the happy state of marriage—and relieve the housing shortage." After he got letters of protest from as far as Seattle, Detroit and New York, he said he "was joking."

Occasionally Alaska parka-maker Deborah Ives of Posh House receives a strange request. "In August of 1990, George Chamberlain wanted a stuffed, four-foot long, salmon mounted on the back of his parka. He was in a Fox Production *Pure Insanity* contest, and he wanted to slip down a water slide on his belly with this stuffed salmon visible above the spray. When he hit the pool at the bottom of slide, he would release red, gelatin-filled, balloons to make it look like he was spawning. I was his last hope because no one else in town could make a water-resistant, padded salmon on the back of a parka. I thought it was a kick and made the outfit. He barely missed first place."

In 1917, Robert "Bobbie" Beggs of Eagle was one of a host of Alaskans appointed by the Territorial Governor to the Alaska Council of Defense. The function of this organization was to keep an eye out for suspicious activity such as sedition, anti-war sentiment, pro–German activities, sabotage, labor unrest and the like. While Beggs may have been a sterling member of the business community during World War I, by the end of the 1920s, he had fallen on hard times. In 1992, an Eagle Historical Society member remembered Beggs:

... an old, dirty man who owned a smelly goat. When the goat died, he kept the hide as a rug, and his small cabin always smelled like the goat. He purchased the Riverside Hotel in 1929, but he was so dirty no one but the Canadian mail carrier, Percy DeWolfe, would stay with him.

In 1898, L. Mooser of New York City proposed to "introduce camels as beasts of burden in Alaska." The story ran in the *Seattle Post-Intelligencer*, February 24, 1898. Mooser claimed that "camels can carry from 400 to 500 pounds from Dyea to Dawson in from six to eight days, and that the cost for feeding and caring for them will be practically little or nothing, as they are peculiarly adapted to foraging as they travel."

On July 25, 1900, according to the *Nome Daily News*, the steamship *Robert Dollar* sighted what the crew and passengers thought was a "wrecked vessel." Upon closer examination, however, they claimed that it was the "skeleton of a mastodon measuring 80 feet in length. The skull itself was ten feet long and the great ribs 36 inches in diameter."

While the Alaska Education Association, the state chapter of the NEA, has always supported binding arbitration as a form of contract dispute finality, for years they did not extend this contractual privilege to their employees.

On September 6, 1960, a cargo load of 43 reindeer were flown from Nunivak Island in a Northern Consolidated airliner to Anchorage, where they were loaded onto trucks for the Lower 48. The buyer was John W. Carrothers, owner of Reindeer Enterprises, Inc., who trained reindeer for department store Santa Clauses. Two herders were onboard, so flight attendant Jan Shulz had to be on duty because of FAA regulations. The flight was uneventful except for a torn curtain that became entangled on a reindeer's horn. Pilot Don Johnson and copilot Fred Richards did not report "who had to clean the cabin after the flight."

29
THE ALASKAN PASSPORT

Though Alaska has been a state in the United States for more than three decades, there are still a lot of Alaskans who believe that statehood was a mistake. Actually, that's not quite correct. They believe that statehood was a *real* mistake. Just think how much better off we would be, they say, pointing at Alaska's dependence on the federal government. Alaskans pay the highest per capita income tax, have the highest cost of living and have the highest rate of IRS audits in the country. Alaska's cost of living is so high that federal workers are given a tax-free Cost of Living Allowance (COLA) for working in the Northland — but Alaskans aren't given a similar break on their taxes.

The indignities grow the more Alaskans think about them. On most maps of the United States, Alaska and Hawaii are squashed down in a corner. This gives young people the impression that Alaska and Hawaii are about the same size and, in comparison to the contiguous states, could both fit in Arizona easily. And, because everyone knows that Hawaii is an island, and because both states appear in the same place on most maps, some Americans believe that Alaska is also an island. Just as bad, national television networks do not even bother to put Alaska or Hawaii on their weather maps, even though their satellite pictures include Central America all the way to Costa Rica.

Though Alaska is 1/5 the size of the contiguous states, almost 90 percent of the land is owned by the federal government, and virtually all of the state is subject to rules and regulations that are conceived in Washington, D.C., on the basis of Lower 48 standards. From mining regulations to the size of rest rooms and the frequency of curb cuts, the sins of the federal bureaucracy pile up, one on top of another. Abuses stack on complaints which rest on outrages that are piled on grievances.

No indignation is so great, however, that an Alaskan cannot find a strain of humor therein. Thus, on April 1, 1986, three enterprising

234

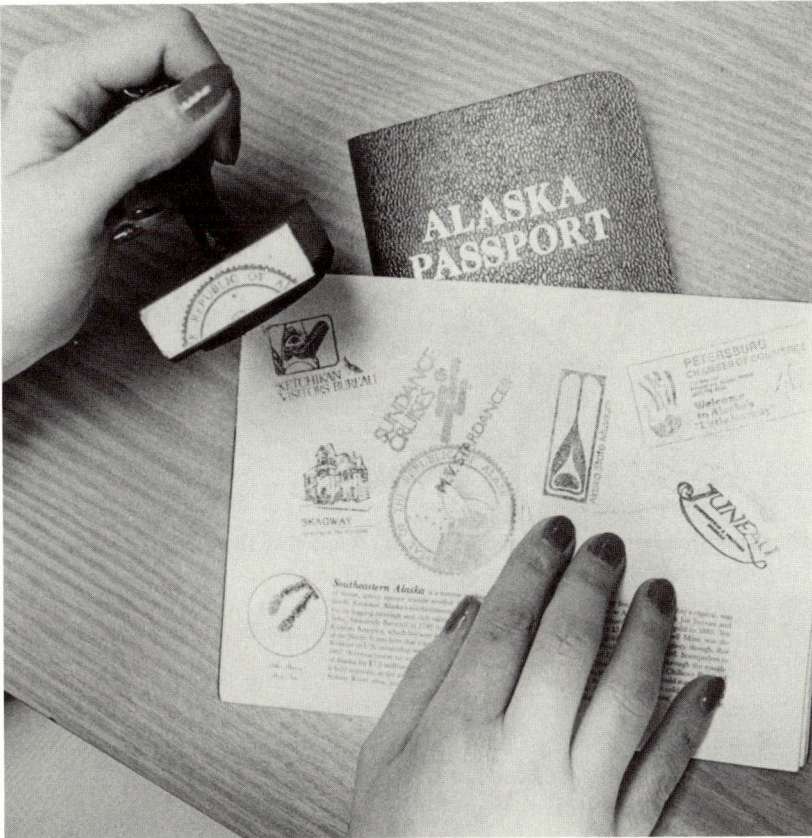

The Alaska passport. (Courtesy of the Republic of Alaska.)

Alaskans announced the formation of the Republic of Alaska and began issuing passports.

The Alaska passports look exactly like American passports, with the exception that the blue cover stock is a shade different than the authentic item and there are no numbers drilled from cover to cover. The words "Alaska Passport" are prominently displayed on the cover and embossed on the back is an eagle flying over an Alaskan flag. Inside there is the Great Seal of the Republic of Alaska which is, of course, a great seal (animal), seated at the crest of a mountain with the Big Dipper and North Star in the background.

Inside, there is the usual for-bearer signature and vital statistics such as birth date, blood type and who to contact in case of emergency, as well as an entire page for the bearer's "favorite Alaska photo." The balance of

The Great Seal of the Republic of Alaska. (Courtesy the Republic of Alaska.)

the pages, which look remarkably like passport pages—as they were intended—have a faint outline of the state at the center. There are five sections of the passport, each corresponding to a different geographic region and each preceded by short descriptive paragraphs discussing the flora and fauna of the region, illustrated with drawings of the state mineral, sport, mammal, fish, bird, tree, flower and gem.

Of interest to tourists from Outside—and Alaskans with a sense of humor—is a list of "Republic of Alaska Consulates." At each of these locations, the bearer of the passport could get an official stamp. The consulates included all the convention and visitor bureaus across Alaska, the ferry system, the Alaska Railroad and other attractions.

The idea of the passport came about, naturally, during a card game—pinochle, embarrassingly, not poker. On New Year's Eve in 1985, Don Neet, of Alaska Underwater Construction, Inc., mentioned the passport idea to his friend Ted Smith, who was in the forestry business. Neet thought they should create a country and issue passports for a price. Smith said it sounded great and immediately demanded to be President. Neet had no objection and declared himself Prime Minister. They joined with Sally J. Suddock and officially established the Republic of Alaska. "Suddock was given the title of Secretary General because she's the woman," stated the official correspondence of the Republic states. Other honorary ambassadors of the Republic of Alaska soon included Ariel Jones, "Princess and First Kid," "First Lady" Joyce Smith, Ayse Gilbert, the "Artist Laureate" who designed the passport, and Police Captain Warren Suddock (retired) as "Le General, to preserve the public order and guard the money."

Thus united with an inner circle, the trio raised the money to produce 50,000 passports for distribution across the state. The passport was an instant hit. They started selling as soon as they hit the distribution racks, and visitor centers across the state were besieged with tourists wanting stamps for their passports. Both the State Division of Tourism and the Alaska Visitor's Association "enthused" over the idea. Even Alaskans were impressed. After all, every one of their relatives living in the Lower 48 was sure that Alaskan travel required *at least* a visa; the Alaska passport merely confirmed that fantasy.

Oddly, quite a few oil field workers bought passports, but for a different reason. When one of the founding trio saw a slope worker buying a handful of passports, he asked why so many? Because, the worker replied, the Alaska passport looks so much like a real passport that it just might pass as one. "If I ever got hijacked in the Middle East, I figured I'd better not show my American passport."

Contacted at the Main Embassy complex in downtown Anchorage, Secretary General and (lately elevated to) Minister of History, Information and Propaganda, Sally J. Suddock had grave words for those who considered the Republic of Alaska crass commercialism held up for amusement in a book of Alaskan humor. "We may be a bunch of funny guys chasing tourists," she said. "Go ahead and laugh. The Republic has the world's lowest tax rate (none), no balance of trade deficit, no oil spill, no meddlesome citizens as legislators to foul up our ruling class, no unemployment, and no dissidents—we ship them to Attu."

When this chapter was shown to officials of the Republic for their approval, the author was informed that it was "unauthorized and revisionist," and if printed, the author and publisher may very well find themselves in the "Gulag of the east," picking up caribou nuggets.

30

MISCELLANEOUS ALASKANA

7 AAC 15.315 Classes of Shippers

This was an actual section of the Alaska Administration Code. See if you can read it aloud without laughing.

There are four classes of shippers, as follows:
1. reshippers are shippers who transship shucked stock in original containers or shell-stock from certified shellfish shippers to other dealers or to final consumers; reshippers may not shuck or repack shellfish.
2. repackers are shippers other than the original shucker who pack shucked shellfish into containers for delivery to the consumer; shippers classified as repackers may shuck shellfish if they have the necessary facilities; a repacker may also act as a shell-stock shipper if he has the necessary facilities;
3. shell-stock shippers are shippers who grow, harvest, and buy or sell shell-stock; they are not authorized to shuck shellfish or to repack shucked shellfish.
4. shucker-packers are shippers who shuck and pack shellfish; a shucker-packer may act as a shell-stock dealer; shucker-packers are classified as repackers if shucked shellfish are regularly repacked. (In effect before 7/28/59; am 1/10/75, Reg. 53)

Authority AS 17.20.180
AS 18.05.040

Naming Alascattalo Plateau

BE A PART OF ALASKA'S HISTORY: DEMAND ALASCATTALO PLATEAU BE LISTED ON THE MAP OF ALASKA. (Copy this letter *and* the next one and SEND IT!)

[Today's Date]

National Mapping Division
USGS
4230 University Avenue
Anchorage, Alaska
99504

Staff:

It has come to my attention that there is not a single geographic feature in Alaska named for Alaska's most illustrious mammal, the *alascattalo*. This is rank discrimination.

To end this detestable circumstance, I am urging that a plateau in the Chugach be named in honor of this beast. Specifically, I recommend the *Alascattalo Plateau* be listed on all future maps to describe the plateau found in Sections 16 and 17, Township 12 North, Range 2 West, in the Anchorage A-8 Quadrangle.

Thank you for your prompt attention to this matter.

Sincerely,

[Your name and address]

BE A PART OF ALASKA'S HISTORY: DEMAND ALASCATTALO PLATEAU BE LISTED ON THE MAP OF ALASKA. (Copy this letter *and* the previous one and SEND IT!)

[Today's Date]

Alaska Geographic Names Board
Office of History and Archeology
P.O. Box 107001
Anchorage, Alaska
99510-7001

Staff:

It has come to my attention that there is not a single geographic feature in Alaska named for Alaska's most illustrious mammal, the *alascattalo*. This is rank discrimination.

To end this detestable circumstance, I am urging that a plateau in the Chugach be named in honor of this beast. Specifically, I recommend the *Alascattalo Plateau* be listed on all future maps to describe the plateau found in Sections 16 and 17, Township 12 North, Range 2 West, in the Anchorage A-8 Quadrangle.

Thank you for your prompt attention to this matter.

Sincerely,

[Your name and address]

Impersonating a Police Dog

On June 3, 1983, Senator Ziegler offered the following amendment to CS *for House Bill No. 312 (JUD)* (Harming a Police Dog).

Sec.3. 11.56.840 IMPERSONATING A POLICE DOG

a. A person or other animal commits the crime of impersonating a police dog if that person or animal pretends to be a police dog and does any act in that capacity.

b. The act prohibited in (a) of this section includes but is not limited to:

1. the use of police facilities
2. riding in a police vehicle
3. consuming of police dog food
4. unauthorized biting of criminals
5. attempting to travel in the first class or tourist section of an aircraft
6. searching for controlled substances
7. impersonating a police dog to avoid the dogcatcher
8. soliciting dog biscuits while on patrol
9. unlawful entrance into state property
10. defacing public and private property
11. loitering in the vicinity of fire hydrants
12. harboring fleaing criminals

c. Impersonating a Police Dog is a Class A misdemeanor.

The Amendment was adopted, and then Senator Bennet offered an amendment to the amendment to "insert before the period, ', unless there are under attack' in sentences 13 and 20."

Senator Bennet was the only vote in favor of the amended Amendment. (*Senate Journal,* June 3, 1983, 1199-1201.)

"So You Want to Come to Alaska?"

In the late 1970s, William "Wild Bill" McConkey was working for the State of Alaska Department of Commerce. So many people wanted to come to Alaska for all the "big bucks" that the Department of Commerce was being deluged with letters for information on Alaska. McConkey decided that something extra should be sent with the generic information. The following was actually sent with the State of Alaska information packet.

SO YOU WANT TO COME TO ALASKA

Each year, thousands of people from the Lower 48 write for information on moving to Alaska. Although Alaska welcomes newcomers, prospective immigrants should be aware of the following facts:

1. Alaska is 4th in the nation in incidence of reported rape. Alaska's rate is three (3) times the nation's average.

2. Child abuse incidents per capita are more than twice as high as similar populations in the Lower 48.

3. Alaska is 3rd in the nation for automobile thefts and 9th in automobile-related fatalities. For a nine-month survey on motor vehicle deaths by the National Safety Council, Anchorage ranked highest out of 62 reporting cities in the population range of 100,000 to 200,000 people.

4. With regard to the crime rate, Alaska is 13th in murder, 14th in aggravated assault and 10th in larceny. Alaska's arson rate is 10.5 per 100,000 people while the national average is 8.7.

5. The rate of suicide for Alaska is one of the highest in the nation. While only 1.4 percent of all deaths in the United States are because of suicide, 5.5 percent of all deaths in Alaska are because of suicide.

6. The rate of alcoholism-related death ranks Alaska number one in the nation. Death related to cirrhosis of the liver rank Alaska third, and deaths due to alcoholism rate Alaska as number one. Overall, Alaska leads the nation in alcohol-related deaths.

7. Temperatures in Alaska are severe. In some places it is not unusual to hit 100 degrees below zero. The average family spend about $400 per year on winter clothing as winter weather lasts approximately six (6) months a year.

8. Alaska also has a high incidence of destructive earthquakes and tidal waves.

9. Using a national base of 100, Anchorage is a "high-cost city" with a price index of 159, a housing index of 221, and a food index of 124.

10. Average income in Alaska is reported at 159 — 59 points above the United States average — but income tax payments for Alaskans is 221 — 121 points above the national average.

11. Unemployment in Alaska for 1978 was almost twice as high as the nation's average.

A Legislative Conversation

Since Juneau, the capital of Alaska, is so far from Anchorage and Fairbanks, mail is often delayed, sometimes for days. Since newspapers come on the same plane as the mail, they are delivered late as well. It is a rare occasion when a legislator or aide can read the evening Anchorage paper on the day it was printed.

Below is an actual conversation between a legislative aide and an Anchorage newspaper legislative reporter in Juneau talking about the delivery of the evening paper.

"Did you see my article in the paper yet?"

"Which one was that?"

"On HB . . . ."

"No. When was it printed?"

"I wrote it yesterday so it should be in today's paper."

"I read today's paper but I didn't see it."

"It was in yesterday's second edition so you won't see it until tomorrow."

"You mean the article you wrote yesterday won't be in today's paper but will be in tomorrow's?"

"Yeah. And if the planes don't come in it won't be here until the day after tomorrow."

"You mean that yesterday's article will be in tomorrow's paper?"

"No. It's in today's paper but you won't get it 'til tomorrow."

"Wait a minute. You're telling me that yesterday's story in today's paper won't be in until tomorrow and it's still today's paper?"

"No. The article I wrote yesterday appeared in today's paper and you'll get that tomorrow."

"Why am I reading yesterday's news tomorrow? Why can't I read today's news today?"

"Because it won't be in until tomorrow."

An Alaskan Bear Story

No book on Alaskan humor would be complete without a bear story. Here is one which appeared in *Alaska Outdoors*.

BEAR INSURANCE

"Bear Insurance — a very large gun, usually a .357 magnum" — Alaskan phrase.

The only person who has lower credibility than a politician talking tax break three days before an election is an Alaskan with a bear story. That's not to say that Alaskans tell tall tales. They don't. They just lie. Alaskans don't tell bare-faced lies because many of them have beards, but most Alaskans feel little guilt in s-t-r-e-t-c-h-i-n-g the truth until it hurts.

Now some stories are true. Take, for instance, the story of the joggers in Anchorage who heard the pitter-patter of four feet, er, paws, behind them. They turned around and nearly jumped out of their Nikes. There, a handful of feet behind them, was a grizzly. It wasn't a large grizzly, but when there's only a few yards between it and you, *every* grizzly is a large one.

At first the joggers tried to outrun the animal. This was not a good idea. As the joggers ran faster, so did the bear. The animal only stopped chasing them when they came across another jogger. This one happened to be wearing a .357. The bear left. (Now who but an Alaskan would be jogging with a .357?)

Other bear stories are a bit harder to swallow. There was a case, allegedly, in Skagway, where an Anchorage banker and a foreign visitor were fishing for salmon. The visitor was a Czechoslovakian who should have known something about bears. After all he came from a country that was used to dealing with the Russian bear. (That's a joke.) The two men caught some fish, cleaned them right down by the riverbank and left the fillets in a cooler in the water nearby. (That was not smart.) When the two went back later to retrieve the fish, a boar and a sow brown bear exploded out of the bushes. The banker barely got away with his life, but the Czechoslovakian, well, let's not go into that.

The bear has always been a part of the folklore of Alaska. The Natives gave the bear a lot of respect — with good reason — but didn't give the animal a lot of credit for brains. At one time the bear had a long tail, Eskimo legend goes, but he lost it in a battle of wits with Fox. Bear was out hunting one day when he came across Fox near a seal breathing-hole on a wide expanse of ice. Fox was afraid of being eaten by bear and, stalling for time, began talking to Bear. Bear, who was in no hurry to eat Fox, sat down for conversation but foolishly allowed his long tail to slide into the seal's breathing hole. Fox talked and talked and talked, until the breathing hole froze solid capturing Bear's tail in the ice. Then Fox sauntered away. Bear raged for a while and finally pulled himself loose, at the expense of his magnificent tail. Thus, the legend concludes, bears have short tails today.

Bears haven't gotten a lot smarter since those early days. But they don't have to be smart. When you're the biggest, baddest guy in the forest, there's no reason to be smart. Cagey they can be, but not all that brainy. As an example, in one of the national parks there was a "problem" bear that became quite fond of tourist lunches. The bear had learned that tour buses meant tourists and, at the noon hour, this also meant packaged meals. Like clockwork, the animal would wait until unsuspecting travelers sat down on park benches for a leisurely noonday repast. Then the bear would saunter out of the forest and make for a table.

The sight of a full grown, brown bear pushing about 1,000 pounds was usually enough for the tourists to beat a quick retreat — leaving their lunches intact, it should be added. As the tourists scattered, the bear dined. Upon occasion, however, just advancing on a table was not adequate to move the tourists to flight. In such cases, the bear had a Plan B.

He charged.

He didn't need a Plan C.

Sometimes it almost seems that bears have a sense of humor; twisted though it may be, it is a sense nonetheless. Perhaps the most famous bear in Alaska in the early 1950s was Archie Ferguson's polar bear cub. (The story of Archie's exploits in getting the bear to Kotzebue are included in this book in the chapter "Alaska's Clown Prince.")

For years the polar bear cub, which grew rather large, was a fixture in Kotzebue. During the winter it would crawl under a building, but throughout the tourist season, the bear would lounge around in the sun and attract the attention of tourists. This bear was also adept at frightening tourists. Often it would lie on its belly hiding its chain with its body. Whenever a tourist the bear didn't like approached, the animal would explode off the ground and charge to the end of the chain. The shocked tourist would stumble backwards, often ending up seated in a three-inch muddy pool of water. If the bear could have laughed, it probably would have.

Over the years, Alaskans in the bush have come to understand bears. In most cases, as long as the bears are left alone, they will leave people alone. Unfortunately this is not always possible. Bears like food, and if they suspect that there is food in a cabin, they will enter the structure, making it a bit difficult for people who happen to be *in* the cabin at the time. In most cases, however, the bear waits until the cabin is empty before entering.

The worst bear with which Alaskans living in the bush must deal is known as the "carpenter bear." A carpenter bear is one who makes his own door into or out of a cabin. Carpenter bears are a problem to bush dwellers because they are usually the ones that have learned that cabins have food, even if they can't smell it. These bears will enter cabins and bite all of the cans until they taste food. Then they clean the place out. The residents have to clean the place out as well, because after the bear is through there is not that much salvageable on the inside of the cabin — except for walls.

There is a cure, incidentally, for carpenter bears. One method of discouraging bears is to fill a balloon with ammonia and then coat the plastic with bacon grease. The bear, smelling the bacon grease, will take a bite of what he believes is a tasty meal. When he comes away with a mouthful of ammonia, he is guaranteed to leave the area immediately. Of course, he may take a wall or two with him when he goes.

Overall, bears are fairly easy animals to deal with. Just leave them alone. If you don't bother them, they won't bother you. Keep a clean campsite, gut your fish away from where you are going to sleep and don't fight the bears for your garbage. If the animal wants your coffee grounds, let him have them.

As a final note, take a tip from the plight of the banker, who escaped from the attack of the two bears near Skagway that was reported earlier. The banker reported the incident to Alaska Fish and Game wardens, who immediately went back to where the devouring had occurred. They found the two bears and tranquilized them. Not wishing to destroy both animals, the wardens asked the banker which bear had eaten his friend, the sow or the boar. The banker thought it was the male, the boar, so the wardens killed the bear and cut the animal open. There wasn't anything in the stomach. Now they would have to kill the other animal as well.

With bear blood to his elbows, one warden looked at the other and said disgustedly, "Trust a banker to tell you the Czech's in the male."

BIBLIOGRAPHY

Alaskan Almanac. Bothell, WA: Alaska Northwest Publishing Company, 1989.

Alaskans. Time/Life Series: "The Old West." Alexandria, VA: Time-Life Books, 1977.

Anderson, Thayne I. *Alaska Hooch, The History of Alcohol in Early Alaska.* Hoo-Chee-Noo, Box 80384, Fairbanks, Alaska, 99708, 1988.

Berton, Pierre. *The Klondike Fever.* New York: Carrol & Graf, 1958.

Bits and Pieces of Alaskan History. Bothell, WA: Alaska Northwest Publishing Company, 1982.

The Bush Pilots. Time/Life Series: "The Epic of Flight." Alexandria, VA: Time-Life Books, 1983.

Carlson, Phyllis, Mike Kennedy and Cliff Cernick. *Anchorage: The Way It Was.* Anchorage: Anchorage Historic Landmark Preservation Committee, 1981.

Clark, Art. *A Touch of Wrangellitis.* Art Clark, Box 93, Wrangell, Alaska, 99929.

Clark, M. *Roadhouse Tales.* Girard, Kansas: Appeal Publishing Company, 1902.

Clifford, Howard. *The Skagway Story.* Bothell, WA: Alaska Northwest Publishing Company, 1975.

Cohen, Stan. *Flying Beats Work.* Missoula, MT: Pictorial Histories, 1988.

_____. *The Forgotten War.* Missoula, MT: Pictorial Histories, 1988.

_____. *The Great Alaska Pipeline.* Missoula, MT: Pictorial Histories, 1988.

_____. *The Old Rush Gateway, Skagway and Dyea.* Missoula, MT: Pictorial Histories, 1986.

_____. *The White Pass & Yukon Route.* Missoula, MT: Pictorial Histories, 1980.

Cole, Terrence. *E.T. Barnette.* Bothell, WA: Alaska Northwest Publishing Company, 1981.

_____. *Nome: City of Golden Beaches.* Anchorage: Alaska Geographic, 1984.

Day, Beth. *Glacier Pilot.* New York: Holt, 1957.

Eberhart, George M., compiler. *A Geo-Bibliography of Anomalies.* Westport, CT: Greenwood Press, 1980.

Garfield, Brian. *The Thousand Mile War: World War II and Alaska in the Aleutians.* New York: Doubleday, 1969.

Geeting, Doug, and Steve Woerner. *Mountain Flying.* Blue Ridge Summit, PA: TAB, 1988.

Gregory, Albro B. *Tall (But True) Tales of Alaska Sourdoughs.* Self-published, no date, contact the Nome *Nugget* for details.

Greiner, James. *Wager with the Wind.* Skokie, IL: Rand McNally, 1974.

Gruening, Ernest. *The State of Alaska.* New York: Random House, 1954.

Guide to Alaska's Newspapers. Compiled by Phyllis Davis for the Alaska Division of State Libraries and Museums with Some Vignetters in Alaskan Journalism by Evangeline Atwood. Gastineau Channel Centennial Association and Alaska Division of State Libraries and Museums, 1976.

Harkey, Ira B. *Pioneer Bush Pilot*. Seattle: University of Washington Press, 1974.

Harrison, E.S. *Nome and Seward Peninsula, History, Description, Biographies and Stories*. E.S. Harrison, 1905.

Helmericks, Harmon. *The Last of the Bush Pilots*. New York: Alfred A. Knopf, 1970.

Hertz, Henriette. *Gods from the Far East*. New York: Ballentine, 1975.

House, Boyce. *Friendly Feudin', Alaska versus Texas*. San Antonio, TX: Naylor Press, 1959.

Hunt, William. *Arctic Passage; The Turbulent History of the Land and Its People*. New York: Charles Scribner's Sons, 1975.

————. *Distant Justice*. Norman, OK: University of Oklahoma Press, 1987.

————. *North of 53*. New York: Macmillan, 1974.

Hunter, Kathy. *Alaska Nicknames*. Palmer, AK: Lazy Mountain Press, 1988.

Janson, Lone E. *The Copper Spike*. Bothell, WA: Alaska Northwest Publishing Company, 1975.

————. *Mudhole Smith*. Bothell, WA: Alaska Northwest Publishing Company, 1981.

Levi, Steven C. *The Alaska Traveler*. Lexington, MA: Mills & Sanderson, 1989.

Nashe, Clause-M., and Herman E. Slotnik. *Alaska, A History of the 49th State*. Grand Rapids, MI: William B. Eerdmans, 1979.

Noorbergen, Rene. *Secret of the Lost Races*. Indianapolis: Bobbs-Merrill Company, 1977.

O'Meara, Jim, and Steven C. Levi. *Bush Flying*. Blue Ridge Summit, PA: TAB Books, 1990.

Orth, Franklin G. *A Geographic Dictionary of Alaska Place Names*. Washington, D.C.: Government Printing Office, 1960.

Potter, Jean. *Flying Frontiersmen*. New York: Macmillan, 1956.

————. *The Flying North*. New York: Bantam Books, 1945.

Sitka, Warren. *Sourdough Journalist*. Anchorage: Parsnackle Press, 1981.

Solka, Jr., Paul, and Art Bremer. *Adventures in Alaska Journalism Since 1902*. Fairbanks: Commercial Printing Company, 1980.

Stevenson, Ivan, M.D. *Twenty Cases Suggestive of Reincarnation*. Charlottesville, VA: University Press of Virginia, 1966.

Stone, David, and Brenda Stone. *Hard Rock Gold*. Juneau Centennial Committee, 1980.

Wharton, David B. *The Alaska Gold Rush*. Bloomington, IN: Indiana University Press, 1972.

Wilson, William H. *Railroad in the Clouds, the Alaska Railroad in the Age of Steam, 1914–1945*. Boulder, CO: Pruett Publishing, 1977.

Wold, Jo Anne. *The Way It Was*. Bothell, WA: Alaska Northwest Publishing Company, 1988.

Primary Materials

Abercrombie, W.R. "Copper River Exploring Expedition 1898," in *A Compilation of Narratives and Explorations in Alaska*, United States Senate Document 1023, 56th Congress, First Session. Washington D.C.: Government Printing Office, 1900, pp. 758–59.

Alaska Administrative Code
Alaska Flying Magazine
Alaska Geographic
Alaska Host
Alaska Independent Shopper
Alaska Journal
Alaska Labor News
Alaska Magazine
Alaska Outdoors
The Alaska Southeaster Magazine
Alaska Sportsman
Alaska State Archives
Alaska-Yukon Magazine
Alaska Department of Commerce
Alaska State Library
Alaska Telephone Association files
American Journal of Psychology
American Legion Magazine
American Naturalist
Anchorage Daily News
Anchorage Magazine
Anchorage Museum of History and Art Archives
Anchorage Times
Anthropological Papers of the University of Alaska
Bristol Bay Times
Chugach Electric Association Outlet
Cordova Times
Cravez, Pamela. *Seizing the Frontier: Alaska's Territorial Lawyers,* manuscript
    funded by the Alaska Historical Commission, 1984, in the possession of the
    Z.J. Loussac Library.
Fairbanks Daily News Miner
Fate Magazine
Gleam
House Journal
Iditarod Pioneer
Illustrated London News
Jessen's Weekly
Journal of Geology
Juneau Daily Empire
Juneau What
Kodiak Daily Mirror
Life
Mukluk Telegraph
National Geographic Magazine
Natural History
Nature
New Alaska Outdoors
New York Times
Nome Daily News
Nome Nugget
Permafrost. Fairbanks: University of Alaska, 1981.

Reader's Digest
Ruby Record-Citizen
Senate Journal
Socialist Labor Party of Alaska Papers in the Alaska State Library in Juneau
Sports Afield
Sports Illustrated
Winter & Pond collection, Alaska State Library in Juneau

INDEX